Inter-Act

Using Interpersonal Communication Skills

Fifth Edition

RUDOLPH F. VERDERBER
University of Cincinnati

KATHLEEN S. VERDERBER
Northern Kentucky University

Wadsworth Publishing Company
Belmont, California
A Division of Wadsworth, Inc.

to Allison

Communication Editor: Kristine M. Clerkin
Editorial Assistant: Melissa Harris
Production Editor: Jane Townsend
Designer: Andrew H. Ogus
Print Buyer: Barbara Britton
Copy Editor: Thomas Briggs
Photo Researcher: Audrey Ross
Compositor: Graphic Typesetting Service
Cover Illustrator: Dick Cole

Acknowledgments are listed on page 406.

Printed in the United States of America   85

    4 5 6 7 8 9 10---93 92 91

Library of Congress Cataloging-in-Publication Data
Verderber, Rudolph F.
    Inter-act : using interpersonal communication skills / Rudolph F. Verder-
ber, Kathleen S. Verderber. — 5th ed.
        p.   cm.
    Includes bibliographies and index.
    ISBN 0-534-09684-0
    1. Interpersonal communcation.   2. Interpersonal relations.
I. Verderber, Kathleen S., 1949-   . II. Title.
BF637.C45V47 1988
158'.2—dc19   88-19052
                                                                  CIP

Contents

Preface

What kind of communicator are you? Do you consider yourself quite skilled? Perhaps you're like many people who find that they have trouble communicating effectively. Or perhaps you see yourself as a rather typical communicator—one with the usual number of communication successes and failures. Regardless of your current communication skill level, we believe this textbook has a great deal to offer you.

If you are already a good communicator, this book will help you identify what it is that makes you as effective as you are. By understanding the elements of effective communication, you will be able to create environments that will bring out the best in others. If your communication efforts bring you mixed success, this book will introduce you to several new skills and review many others that you may be able to use to greater advantage. Effective communication requires the competence and behavioral flexibility to be able to use a variety of skills well in different circumstances. You will learn how better to turn your ideas and feelings into words, how to listen more effectively and respond more appropriately to what others have said, and most important of all, how to maintain and develop good interpersonal relationships. This textbook also will acquaint you with significant communication theory and lead you to current research that verifies and validates our discussions.

Changes in the Fifth Edition

In this fifth edition of INTER-ACT we have tried to preserve and strengthen the material that made the fourth edition so useful. We have also added material to better meet your individual needs. In addition to including many new examples and illustrations and ensuring that every key point is stated as clearly as possible, this edition features several important changes:

Chapter 7, "Listening Skills," has been completely rewritten to cover attending, understanding, interpreting, evaluating, and remembering—five of the six aspects of listening. (The sixth aspect, responding, is covered in a separate chapter.) Each of the discussions includes both an explanation of that aspect and specific guidelines for helping you improve your own listening.

Chapter 1, "Interpersonal Communication: An Orientation," has been rewritten to include a more comprehensive explanation of the transactional process. It also includes a more detailed analysis of communication functions, a more comprehensive discussion of interpersonal communication principles, and a clearer analysis of the communication contract, along with a better explanation of taking your communication inventory.

Chapter 3, "Verbal Communication," has an expanded discussion of the nature and use of language in human communication, includes a new discussion of language domains, and has an increased emphasis on means of learning language skills and enacting them.

Chapter 4, "Nonverbal Communication," has expanded discussions of verbal/nonverbal contrasts and the functions of nonverbal communication, an expanded discussion of chronemics, and a newly organized discussion of space.

Chapter 5, "Communication in Relationships," has a completely revised discussion of communication in life cycles of relationships, and features a total chapter reorganization.

Part 3, Applying Skills to Communication Contexts, is now organized into eight short *Modules* instead of four chapters. From our survey of previous users we discovered that although nearly every professor assigned all the chapters in the first two parts of the book, few had time to cover all the context chapters in a single course. With eight short modules, each professor will have a better opportunity to elect those contexts that fit best with the teaching philosophy of the particular course. The advantages of this organization are several: each module is relatively short; each module focuses on key communication skills related to that context; and students can be introduced to recent sources that provide more detailed discussion of that specific subject matter.

Organization of the Book

Part One lays the groundwork of interpersonal communication. Chapter 1 discusses the transactional nature of interpersonal communication and how it works. It also defines the goal of the book—interpersonal communication competence—and suggests ways of achieving it. Chapter 2 explains how all people "see" from a personal perspective and outlines how what you see affects you and your relationships. Chapters 3 and 4 discuss the nature of verbal and nonverbal communication.

Part Two presents basic interpersonal communication skills in a five-chapter unit that addresses communication in relationships, communication of ideas and feelings, listening, response skills, interpersonal influence, and managing conflict.

Part Three presents eight modules that apply interpersonal communication skills to the eight contexts of real-life communication: family communication, male-female communication, cross-cultural communication, communicating in groups, leadership in groups, interviewing for information, job interviewing, and communicating in work relationships.

Particular features that you will appreciate in this book include the appendices. **Appendix A** is a glossary of the interpersonal skills that are presented elsewhere in the book. In an easy-to-use, quick-review format we have included the particular skill, its importance, the procedure for putting it into practice, an example of its use, and the pages in the text where the skill is discussed in detail. **Appendix B,** a glossary of the most common communication problems, lists each problem, its harmful effects, the kinds of skills that are most likely to solve it, and the pages in the text where it is discussed. **Appendix C** offers guidelines for analyzing interpersonal communication.

The text provides both a means of practicing the skills and an opportunity to learn them by experience in the **communication exercises** that follow major sections of each chapter. The exercises appear within rather than at the end of each chapter to encourage you to work with each concept or skill at the time you encounter it.

We hope you find, as a result of working with this textbook, that we have realized our goal of helping you learn the kinds of skills that will enable you to function more effectively in your day-to-day relationships.

Acknowledgments

We give our thanks to the many teachers and students who have offered suggestions while using the fourth edition. We also appreciate the challenging and thoughtful reviews of the manuscript by Charles Apple, University of Michigan, Flint; Dan B. Curtis, Central Missouri State University; Richard D. Halley, Weber State College; Virginia T. Katz, University of Minnesota, Duluth; Randall Koper, University of the Pacific; Diane C. Mader, Nassau Community College; Dan Robinette, Eastern Kentucky University; and Florence I. Wolff, University of Dayton.

One

Understanding Interpersonal Communication

This four-chapter unit lays the foundation for the study of interpersonal communication. Chapter 1 presents the basic definitions necessary for understanding interpersonal communication. Chapter 2 shows the important relationship between your perceptions and your ability to understand yourself and communicate with others. Chapters 3 and 4 explore the verbal and nonverbal bases of communication, the vehicles through which communication occurs.

Chapter 1

Interpersonal Communication: An Orientation

Objectives

After you have read this chapter, you should be able to define or explain:

Transactional nature of interpersonal communication

Interrelationships among context, participants, rules, message, channels, noise, and feedback

Psychological, social, and decision-making functions of interpersonal communication

Principles of interpersonal communication

Communication competence

"**J**ack, I was up until 12:30 and you still weren't home. What time did you get in?"

"A while after that."

"How much is 'a while'?"

"I said, a while!"

"Was it 1:00? 1:30? 2:00?"

"Dad, why are you always on my back about what time I get in? Don't you trust me?"

"It's not a matter of trust, it's just that . . ."

"Forget it. I don't want to talk about it."

"Well, if you can't tell me when you got in, I'll damn well tell you that you're not going to get the car again until you can!"

"We'll see about that," Jack mutters to himself as he stomps off to his room.

"Marcia, I wanted to talk with you about your work. I've been very concerned. Your last two reports have been late and both of them appear to have been hastily written. Is there anything wrong?"

"I know my work hasn't been good lately, Julie. I've really had a bad couple of weeks."

"Is it anything you'd like to talk about?"

"Well, my brother's engagement is off, and I've been spending a lot of time helping him through it. On top of that, I've been fighting some kind of an infection that has just kept my energy level at zero. But the medication the doctor gave me is finally having some effect and I think I'm getting back on track."

"I'm glad you're feeling better. As I said, I was just worried. Your work has always been top-notch—I felt there must have been something else happening."

"Thanks for your concern and for your patience. I probably should have come in to talk with you about it, but I really thought I'd be OK sooner. As I said, though, I think I'm about back in shape. I've already got a draft of the sales report done, and I should have time to rework it and get it in to you tomorrow."

These two transcripts are examples of typical conversations. Each represents interpersonal communication—the first one a conversational failure, the second one more successful. Why did the first encounter end unsuccessfully? What factors combined to make the second conversation more successful? These questions will be answered in this chapter as we

(1) *define* interpersonal communication, (2) discuss the *complexity* of interpersonal communication, (3) consider the *functions* of interpersonal communication, (4) look at *principles* of interpersonal communication, and (5) discuss *improvement goals* to give you an appreciation of your personal stake in the study of interpersonal communication. To this end we will outline a method for assessing your current communication skill level and writing an improvement contract.

Interpersonal Communication Defined

Interpersonal communication is the transactional process of creating meaning. A *transactional process* is a process in which those communicating are *mutually* responsible for what occurs. The prefix *trans* means "beyond; through; on the other side of." Thus, to understand the meaning of any message, you must look at what happens as a result of that action.

In a conversation, then, the symbols that you use in *relationship* to the symbols that the other person uses define the content and level of understanding achieved. For example, suppose Joe says to his brother, "Go upstairs and get the thing-am-a-jig off my whatch-am-a-call-it." The meaning that has been created, or the extent to which this message has been understood, depends on what happens next. If his brother says, "OK," runs upstairs, and returns with the object that Joe seeks, then one level of meaning will have been successfully created. If, however, Joe's brother responds, "Go get it yourself. I'm not your slave," a different meaning will have come about. Or if Joe's brother says, "I don't mind fetching for you, but I don't know what you want me to get," yet another level of meaning has been created. The key point here is that Joe's original statement has no meaning until his brother responds. And furthermore, his brother's response is given meaning through Joe's subsequent activity.

The purpose of studying interpersonal communication is to help you improve both the effectiveness and the appropriateness of your interpersonal communication transactions. Communication is *effective* when it achieves the goals of the participants. The first dialogue in the chapter was ineffective because neither Jack nor his father achieved their goals: Jack was unable to convince his father that he was mature enough to monitor his own curfew, and Jack's father did not find out when Jack came in or why he was late. Communication is *appropriate* when each participant believes that the other person has abided by the social rules of behavior that apply to the type of relationship and conversation they have.[1] The conversation between Jack and his father was a failure also because neither person perceived the process as appropriate. Jack was angry with what he may have believed to be his father's lack of trust, and his father was upset by Jack's unwillingness to provide a direct answer to a question from his parent.

In contrast, the second dialogue was both more effective and more appropriate. Julie was able to determine what had been affecting Marcia's work performance and was assured that it would improve; Marcia was able to share her recent problems with her boss. Julie's inquiry was perceived by Marcia to be appropriate because Julie is her boss and has a right to be concerned. Further, Marcia's explanation is acceptable in part because it is accompanied by an apology. Marcia acknowledges that she has not performed as well as she should have, nor did she inform Julie of her problems. Thus, their conversation appropriately follows the social expectations for boss-employee relationships.

Throughout this book we will focus on the skills that can improve your communication effectiveness and that can aid you in behaving appropriately. Although skills development is the focus of this book, you must understand many important concepts about communication and relationships if you are to use these skills successfully. The study of interpersonal communication theory and research lays a foundation for skills development, because it provides insight into and evidence about how to communicate effectively and appropriately. Thus, in this book we will present the theories, as well as the supporting research, that can help you to understand why certain skills are useful and when these skills are appropriate.

The Complex Process of Interpersonal Communication

Because you've been communicating for as long as you can remember, the process may seem to be almost second nature. But in reality, competent interpersonal communication is difficult to achieve because communication is a complex process. Whether ideas and feelings are indeed effectively and appropriately shared by those communicating depends on the interrelationship of many elements. For example, an observer of a communication episode between two other people may easily mark when the participants begin and end speaking. The observer can record the conversation, watch the gestures used, note the tones of voices, and so on; nevertheless, part of the communication that takes place between the two people is affected by factors that the observer may not detect. These factors include previous encounters they have had with each other and with other people, their personalities, and their intentions. For purposes of study we will isolate and discuss how seven primary factors—context, participants, rules, messages, channels, noise, and feedback—that are part of this dynamic communication process affect the success of the exchange.

Context

Interpersonal communication takes place in a context. By context we mean the physical, historical, and psychological setting within which a particular communication episode occurs. The context of interpersonal communication affects (1) the expectations of the participants, (2) the meaning these participants receive, and (3) their subsequent behavior.

Physical Setting. The first aspect of context is the *physical setting* in which the communication episode occurs. The physical context includes the location of the event, the time of day, the physical distance between communicators, and any seating arrangements. Each of these factors can affect the communication. Context helps to define what behaviors or messages will be seen as socially appropriate and thus indicates to the participant what type of conversation to expect. For example, a conversation in a crowded company cafeteria may differ in volume, topics covered, and intentions inferred from a conversation in an elegant restaurant. In Chapter 4, "Communicating Nonverbally," you will study how the physical setting may affect the expectations and meanings received by the participants.

History. A second aspect of context is the *history* of the participants. This aspect acknowledges that previous communication episodes between participants affect the meanings that are created during subsequent episodes. For instance, suppose one morning Phil tells Marcie that he will get the draft of their report that they had left for their boss to read. As Marcie enters the office that afternoon, she sees Phil and says, "Did you get it?" Another person listening to the conversation would have no idea what

What you say and how you say it depends partly on where you are—mentally and physically. *Context* in interpersonal communication includes the physical setting, previous exchanges between the participants, and how participants perceive themselves. When a basketball coach disputes a referee's call, is a calm exchange of views likely to be effective? Can shouting ever be the most appropriate way to communicate?

Marcie is talking about. Yet Phil may well reply, "It's on my desk." What is *it*? The report, of course. Marcie and Phil understood one another because the subject of their conversation was determined in an earlier exchange.

Psychological Set. A third aspect of context is the *psychological set* each person brings to an episode. Psychological set refers to how people perceive themselves as well as how they perceive those with whom they are communicating at the time of the communication event. This "set" affects the meaning that is shared. For instance, suppose Corinne has had a really rough day. The typist she hired to do her report couldn't get it done, so she now has to do it herself. In addition, she has to finish the outline for a speech she is to give to the crime task force the next day. If her husband bounds into the apartment and jokingly suggests that she take a speed-typing course, Corinne may lose her normally good sense of humor and become angry. Why? Because her feelings of stress are part of the psychological context for this interpersonal episode.

In many instances the physical, historical, and psychological aspects that form the context of a communication episode may detract from com-

munication effectiveness. If there is some problem with the physical setting (for example, the room in which the episode takes place is noisy),
with the historical setting (for example, something has occurred between
participants that makes them distrustful of each other), or with the psychological setting (for example, one or both participants are emotionally
upset by something that has happened), then the participants may communicate ineffectively or inappropriately and thus fail to reach their goals.

Participants

*The participants in a communication transaction engage in sending and
receiving messages.* These processes usually occur simultaneously. When
speaking, we form messages and attempt to communicate them to others
through symbols. When listening, we process the messages that are sent
to us and react to them.

People bring to any communication event their individual experiences, attitudes, and values. As a result, the messages they send to each
other and the meanings they receive from one another may differ. For
instance, when Art speaks of a good job, he may mean one that pays well.
To Glenna, the person to whom he is talking, a good job may be one that
is stimulating and that has good career potential, regardless of the pay.
So when Art tells Glenna he has found a good job, she may have a very
different understanding of his new job than he meant for her to have.
When people have different cultural, religious, economic, or educational
backgrounds, they are likely to experience difficulty sharing meaning
because they will have had different experiences and have developed different values and attitudes.

In many instances peoples' natures or their perceptions of each
others' natures will affect the quality of the communication and may
result in communication failure.

Rules

*Rules are the guidelines that we establish (or perceive as established) for
conducting transactions.* Rules exist at the beginning of a communication
episode and grow, change, or solidify as people get to know each other
better. Rules tell us what kinds of messages and behavior are proper in a
given context or with a particular person or group of people. For instance,
students who pepper their conversations with four-letter words when

talking with friends in a dorm are likely to use a much different vocabulary when talking with their professor about an assignment.

Sometimes we don't know the rules; we have to learn them through experience. People who are used to interrupting others to speak at an informal gathering may find it difficult to raise their hands to be recognized at a business meeting.

The rules for communication may be formal (such as parliamentary procedures for organizational meetings), may be accepted social guidelines (such as never discuss politics at the dinner table), or may simply develop within the context of a particular setting.

Messages

In interpersonal communication meaning is created through the sending and receiving of messages. These messages represent the meanings that people seek to communicate. Symbols are chosen to convey the meanings and are organized in order to express the meaning.

Meanings and Symbols. *Meanings* are the pure ideas and feelings that exist in the mind of a person. You may have ideas about how to study for your next exam, what your career goal is, and whether taxes should be raised or lowered; you also may have feelings such as jealousy, anger, and love. The meanings you have within you, however, cannot be transferred magically into another's mind. Rather, to share these ideas and feelings you must form messages that are comprised of both verbal and nonverbal elements. *Symbols* are words, sounds, and actions that represent meaning. As you speak, you choose words to convey your meaning. At the same time facial expressions, gestures, and tone of voice—all nonverbal cues—accompany your words and affect the meaning your listener receives. As you listen, you take both the verbal symbols and the nonverbal cues and assign meanings to them.

When meaning is complex, people need to communicate it in sections or in a certain order. In these situations the meaning must be *organized.* For instance, when Julia tells Connie about the apartment she looked at yesterday, her symbols take a certain form. If her description moves logically from room to room, meaning is likely to be clearer than if she attempts to describe in random order various aspects of the apartment.

Encoding and Decoding. The process of transforming ideas and feelings into symbols and organizing them is called *encoding* a message; the process of transforming messages back into ideas and feelings is called *decoding.*

After giving her account of an incident up the street, this woman may ask her friend, "Do you see what I mean?" Whether she answers yes or no, the listener may sense a meaning that differs from what the speaker intended. In the interaction of communication, both participants create meaning by sending and receiving messages through words and gestures.

You have been communicating for so long that you probably don't consciously think about either the encoding or the decoding processes. When your eyes grow bleary and you say, "I'm tired," you aren't thinking, "I wonder what symbols will best express the sensation I am now experiencing." Conversely, when you hear the words, "I'm tired" and see the bleary eyes of the other person, you are not likely to think, "*I* stands for the person doing the talking, *am* means that the *I* is linked to some idea, and *tired* means growing weary or feeling a need for sleep; therefore, the person is feeling a need for sleep and the bleary eyes confirm the accuracy of the statement." At the same time, you are not likely to consider whether you have the same mental picture of "tired" as the person using the word. Nevertheless, these encoding and decoding processes do occur. You are probably aware of the encoding process only when you must grope for words, especially when you sense that the right word is on the tip of your tongue. Likewise, at times you become aware of the decoding process when you must figure out the meaning of an unfamiliar word by the way it is used in a sentence.

Because meaning is created *between* the participants, the person receiving a message *may perceive* a meaning different from the one intended. Although competent communicators consciously encode verbal messages designed to share meaning, nonverbal behaviors that accompany the verbal message and that are less controllable often create unintended and conflicting meanings. *Unintended meanings* are created when the decoding person receives a meaning unrelated to that which the encoder thought was being shared. *Conflicting meanings* are created when the verbal symbols are contradicted by the nonverbal cues. For instance, if someone says, "Yes, I'm very interested in your story," the meaning you actually decode depends upon whether the person actually looks interested or whether the person's nonverbal cues say, "I'm bored stiff."

The processes of encoding and decoding messages are at the heart of interpersonal communication. Thus, many of the skills you will learn in this book relate directly to improving your message formation and accuracy of interpretation so that your effectiveness and appropriateness are enhanced.

Channels

A channel is both the route traveled by the message and the means of transportation. Messages are transmitted through sensory channels. Verbal messages are conveyed from one person to another through sound waves; nonverbal messages, including facial expressions, gestures, and movement, are conveyed through light waves. Although interpersonal communication has two basic channels—light and sound—people can and do communicate by any of the five sensory channels. A fragrant scent and a firm handshake may be as important as what is seen or heard. In general, the more channels used to carry a message, the more likely the communication is to succeed.

Noise

Noise is any stimulus, external or internal to the participants, that interferes with the sharing of meaning. Thus, interpersonal communication success can be impeded if the sensory channels are affected by noise. Much of your success as a communicator depends on how you cope with external, internal, and semantic noises, each of which can create blocks in the sensory channels that interfere with the decoding process.

External Noise. The sights, sounds, and other stimuli in the environment that draw people's attention away from intended meaning are known as *external noise*. For instance, while giving directions on how to work the new food processor, your attention may be drawn to the sound of the doorbell, an external noise. External noise does not have to be a sound, however. Perhaps, while giving the directions, your attention is drawn momentarily to an attractive man or woman. Such visual distraction also constitutes external noise.

Internal Noise. The thoughts and feelings within people that interfere with the communication process are known as *internal noise*. Have you ever found yourself daydreaming when a person was trying to tell you something? Perhaps your mind wanders to thoughts of a dance you attended last night or to the argument you had with someone this morning. If you have tuned out the words of the person with whom you are communicating and tuned in to a daydream or a past conversation, then you have experienced internal noise.

Semantic Noise. Those alternate meanings aroused by certain symbols that inhibit the accuracy of decoding are known as *semantic noise*. Suppose a friend describes a forty-year-old secretary as "the girl in the office." If you think of "girl" as a condescending term for a forty-year-old woman, you might not even hear the rest of what your friend has to say. Rather, you might focus on the chauvinistic message such symbol use has for you. Symbols that are derogatory to a person or group, such as ethnic slurs, often cause semantic noise; profanity can have the same effect. Because meaning depends on your own experience, other people may at times decode a word or phrase differently from the way you intended. This is semantic noise.

Feedback

Feedback is the response to a message. This response reflects what meaning has been created through the original message. Feedback indicates to the person sending a message whether and how that message was heard, seen, and understood. If the verbal or nonverbal response tells the sender that the intended meaning was not received, was received incorrectly, or was misinterpreted, the originator may reencode the meaning in order to alter the receiver's perception of the original message. This reencoded message also constitutes feedback because it represents a response to the receiver's response.

In this textbook we will emphasize the development of feedback skills, because ineffective feedback messages account for the second largest opportunity for communication failure.

A Model of the Communication Process

Let's look at a pictorial representation to see how these factors of interpersonal communication interrelate during a communication exchange. Figure 1.1 illustrates the interpersonal communication process. The left-hand circle represents the *sender*, the person who is initiating the communication exchange. In the center of that circle is a message—a thought or feeling that the person sends. The encoded message based on that thought or feeling is created, shaped, and affected by the sender's total field of experience—represented in the outer circle by such specific factors as values, culture, environment, experiences, occupation, sex, interests, knowledge, and attitudes. The bar between the two circles represents the channels used to convey messages.

The right-hand circle represents the *receiver*. The sender's message passes through the sending channel and is decoded by the receiver. The manner in which this message is decoded and the meaning that the receiver perceives is affected by the receiver's total field of experience—that is, by the receiver's values, culture, environment, experiences, occupation, sex, interests, knowledge, and attitudes. Based on the meaning assigned to the message, the receiver encodes reactions and conveys these as feedback to the sender through the sensory channels. The sender receives and decodes this feedback and assesses whether the message has been clearly received. At the same time this exchange is taking place, external, internal, and semantic noise—represented by the "lightning bolts"—may be occurring at various points in the communication process. These noises may affect the ability of originator and receiver to share meanings.

Let's review the process of an interpersonal transaction by looking at a specific example. At breakfast (physical context), Joel says to his wife, Gloria, "Hey, babe, what do you say we go out to dinner tonight?" Gloria (responding to the message she has received) frowns and says, "I don't know that I want a hamburger." Joel sees that Gloria has not decoded his message correctly and seeks to remedy this. Nonverbally he puts a lilt in his voice, and verbally he says, "I meant let's go to the Chalet!" Gloria

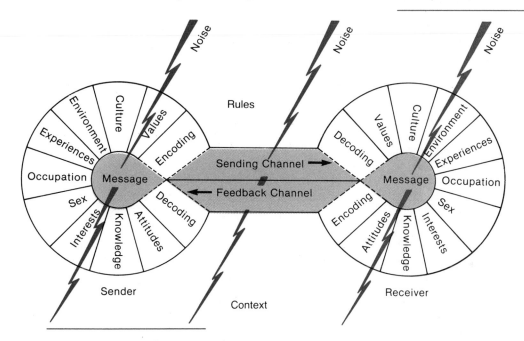

Figure 1.1 A model of communication between two individuals.

may now gasp and say, "the Chalet—wow—you have a deal!" Because the meaning has been shared, the communication is complete. The inaccurate meaning initially created may have resulted from Gloria's perception of the type of restaurant Joel usually is willing to pay for (prior history) or from annoyance with Joel's use of the word *babe*, which she considers degrading (semantic noise).

PRACTICE in Identifying Communication Factors

By Yourself

For the following episode identify the context, participants, channel, rules, message, noise, and feedback.

Rita and her mother are shopping. As they walk through an elegant dress shop, Rita, who is feeling particularly happy, sees a dress she wants. With a look of great anticipation and excitement Rita says, "That's a beautiful dress—can I have it? Please, Mom!" Her mother, who is worried about the cost, frowns, shrugs her shoulders, and says hesitantly, "Well—yes—I guess so." Rita, noticing her mother's hesitation, continues, "And it's only fifty dollars!" Her mother relaxes, smiles, and says, "Yes, it is a beautiful dress—try it on. If it fits let's buy it."

The Three Functions of Interpersonal Communication

So far, we have seen how the communication process works; now let's consider what it does for us. The study of communication is important because the communication process serves psychological, social, and decision-making functions that touch every aspect of our lives.

The Psychological Function

Interpersonal communication can serve two psychological purposes: (1) It is the process through which we seek contact with others and (2) it provides a mirror through which we can see ourselves.

    1. *We communicate to meet needs.* Psychologists tell us that people are by nature social animals; that is, people need other people just as they need food, water, shelter, and so on. Without at least some contact with others, most people hallucinate, lose their motor coordination, and become generally maladjusted.[2] Of course, we have all heard of hermits who choose to live and function alone, but they are the exception—most of us need to talk with others. Often, the topic of the conversation is unimportant. Two people may converse happily for hours about relatively inconsequential matters. When they part, they may have exchanged little real information, but they may carry away from the interaction the pleasant feeling of having met a need simply by talking with another human being.

    2. *We communicate to enhance and maintain our sense of self.* Through our communication we seek approval of who and what we are. How do you know what you are good at? Through communication—people tell you. Did you run a good meeting? Did you do the job as you were

expected? Do you have the right to be happy? angry? guilty? You learn the answer to such questions in part from what others say to you.

The Social Function

Interpersonal communication can serve at least two social purposes: (1) It can help us develop relationships and (2) it can fulfill social obligations.

1. *We communicate to develop relationships.* When you encounter people you do not know, you communicate with them to get to know them. Depending upon the results of that first conversation, you may be content to remain simply acquaintances or you may try to build a friendship. Few relationships stay the same. This is a fact of life—and an important part of the interpersonal communication process.

2. *We communicate to fulfill social obligations.* Why do you say, "How are you doing?" to a person you sat next to in class last quarter but haven't seen since? Why do you say such things as "What's happening" or simply "Hi" when you pass by people you know? People use such statements to meet social obligations. When you recognize people, you feel a need to let them know that you recognize them. By saying, "Hi, Skip, how's it going?" you conform to societal norms—you acknowledge a person you recognize with one of the many statements you have learned to use under these circumstances. Not speaking is perceived as a slight—the person may regard you as arrogant or insensitive. Recognition efforts thus serve to demonstrate your ties with people.

The Decision-Making Function

As well as being social animals, people are also decision makers. Starting with whether or not you wanted to get up this morning, through what you had for breakfast, to whether or not you decided to go to class, you have made countless decisions already today. Some of these decisions you made alone; others you made in consultation with one or more persons. Decision making involves the processing of information and consideration of outside influences.

1. *We communicate to exchange information.* Information is a key ingredient for effective decision making, because one cannot function in our society without information. Some information you get through observation, some through reading, some through television, and a great deal through interpersonal communication. For example, Jeff runs out to get the morning paper. As he hurries through the door, Tom asks, "What's it like out there this morning?" Jeff replies, "Wow, it's cold—it couldn't be more than twenty degrees." Tom says, "I was going to wear my jacket, but I guess I'd better break out the old winter coat." Such a conversation is typical of countless exchanges that send and receive information. Because decisions are generally better when they are based on information, anything that you can do to improve the accuracy of your information exchange will benefit your decision making.

   2. *We communicate to influence others.* Because the results of many of the decisions you make involve the agreement or cooperation of other people, a second goal of decision-making communication is to influence others' attitudes and behaviors. Examples include convincing your friends to go to a play rather than to a movie, campaigning door to door to gather voter support for a political candidate, persuading your parents to let you use the car this weekend, and (an old favorite) trying to convince an instructor to change your course grade. Some theorists even argue that the primary purpose of all communication efforts is to influence the behavior of others.

PRACTICE in Analyzing Communication Functions

By Yourself

Keep a log of each communication episode you have today. Tonight, categorize each episode according to the psychological, social, and decision-making functions it served. Note: Each episode may serve more than one function.

Principles of Interpersonal Communication

Based on our discussion of the interpersonal communication process and its functions, we can identify several underlying principles of interpersonal communication.

Underlying Purpose

Interpersonal communication has purpose. When people talk with each other, they have a purpose for doing so. Let's look at two examples. Beth goes to the library to do research for a paper. When she consults the card catalog, she discovers that an important source she needs is on microfilm. She knows neither where the microfilm room is nor how to use the equipment. Therefore, she plans to ask the librarian where the microfilm room is and when she finds the room, to ask the attendant how to use the equipment. Her communication will be effective if she is directed to the room and if someone there explains the use of the equipment to her. Beth's purpose here is to gain information.

Now let's consider communication in a different context. Beth wants to use her parents' new car this weekend to drive her friends to the beach. She knows her parents are reluctant to let her drive the new car, so she will need to offer some good reasons why she should be allowed to. Moreover, she is well aware that she must not lose her temper or in any way endanger the positive communication climate she hopes to establish. She will have achieved her goal if her parents consent to let her use the car. Her purpose in this case is to influence.

Speakers may not always be aware of their purpose. For instance, when Charley passes Al on the street and says, "Al—what's happening?" it is not likely that Charley consciously thinks, "I see Al coming. I haven't talked with Al for a while. I hope (1) that Al is aware that I recognize him, (2) that he realizes the lines of communication between us are still open, and (3) that he understands I don't have the time to talk with him right now, but that I may like to later. So I'll say, 'Al—what's happening.' " In this case the social obligation to recognize Al is met spontaneously with the first acceptable expression that comes to Charley's mind.

Continuity of Behavior

Interpersonal behavior is continuous. Because communication can be non-verbal as well as verbal, we are always sending behavioral "messages" from which others may draw inferences or meaning. The fact is that even if you are silent or absent, another person may infer meaning from your silence or absence. Why? Because your silence or absence represents a reaction to your environment and to the people around you. If you are cold, you may shiver; if you are hot or nervous, you may perspire; if you are bored, happy, or confused, your face may show it. Whether you like or dislike what you are hearing, your body will reflect it. As a communicator you need to be aware of the kinds of messages, overt or implicit, you are sending that may carry unintended meaning.

Variations in Encoding

Interpersonal communication messages vary in conscious encoding. As we discussed earlier in this chapter, the meaning you wish to share with another person must be encoded into verbal and nonverbal symbols that form the messages you send. This encoding process may occur spontaneously, may be based on a "script" that you have learned, or may be carefully contrived based on your understanding of the situation in which you find yourself.[3]

For each of us there are times when our interpersonal communication reflects a spontaneous expression of emotion. When this happens, our messages are encoded without conscious thought. For example, when you burn your finger, you may blurt out "ouch," or some such expression. When something goes right, you may break out in a broad smile. In this sense much of our communication is spontaneous, natural, and appropriate.

At other times, however, our communication is scripted. R. Abelson defines a script as a "highly stylized sequence of typical events in a well understood situation."[4] Thus, in some communication episodes we use conversational phrases that we have learned from past encounters to be appropriate to the present situation. In order to be used effectively, scripted reactions may be learned and practiced until they become automatic. These scripts often are learned in childhood. For example, when you want the sugar bowl but cannot reach it, you may say, "Please pass the sugar," followed by "Thank you" when someone complies. This conversation comes from your table manners script. Scripts enable us to use messages that are appropriate to the situation and are likely to increase our effectiveness of communication. One goal of this text is to acquaint you with new scripts (or skills) that you may find useful in your communication encounters, to provide you with opportunities to practice these scripts in a variety of contexts, and to suggest when the use of certain scripts may be appropriate.

Messages also may be carefully contrived to meet the particular situation. Contrived messages are those that you fashion at the moment because you believe they are necessary to help you communicate both effectively and appropriately.

Well-contrived responses are perhaps the ideal communication vehicle. When you find yourself, in a given situation, able to envision both what you want to say and how you want to say it, you are well on your way to being a truly effective communicator. Another goal of this text is to help you become so familiar with a variety of skills that you can use them to fashion effective and appropriate messages at any particular time.

In short, emotional situations breed spontaneous reaction, familiar encounters breed scripted behavior, and unfamiliar circumstances breed contrived behavior.

Complementary and Symmetrical Relationships

Interpersonal communication is relational. People communicate to define the nature of their relationships.[5] That is, through communication people in relationships continually define and redefine the distribution of power and affection that exists between them by what they say and how they say it. Thus, when Tom says to Sue, "I know you're concerned about the budget, but I'll see to it that we have money to cover everything," he is, through his words and the sound of his voice, saying that he is in charge of finances, that he is in control. Or when Sue says to Tom, "Of course the girls have enough money to cover both the movie and any other expenses," she is, through her words and the sound of her voice, saying that she is in charge of the girls. As a result of their communication people's relationships are likely to be perceived as complementary or symmetrical.

In a *complementary relationship* one of the individuals lets the other define who is to have greater power. Thus, the communication of the one person asserts dominance and the communication of the other person accepts the assertion. Most student-teacher relationships are complementary, with the teacher in the higher power/status position. The teacher assigns Joan a certain task to do and Joan does it. Or, in the example just cited, if Sue's response to Tom's attempt to control the budget is, "OK, Tom, I agree that you should handle our finances," the relationship would be complementary.

In a *symmetrical relationship* each person is constantly challenging the other's definition of who holds power. For example, Tom and Sue are having continual trouble living within their budget. Their communication may define their relationship as symmetrical in one of two ways. Each may say things and act in such ways that indicate each believes him- or herself to be in charge. To Tom's previous statement, "I know you're concerned about the budget, but I'll see to it that we have money to cover everything," Sue might respond, "I think I'd be better at doing that because I know how much we need for household expenses." Or both may say things and act in ways that indicate they perceive each other as having equal rights in making budgetary decisions. Tom may say, "What do you think we should do about these bills?" to which Sue may respond, "I'm not sure, what do you think?"

Although we cannot draw conclusions from a single exchange about whether a relationship is complementary or symmetrical, by observing message exchanges over time, we can draw valid conclusions about the relationship. The interaction of communication messages, as shown through both language and nonverbal behavior, defines and clarifies the complementary or symmetrical nature of people's relationships. Neither complementary nor symmetrical relationships, however, are necessarily to be preferred. In complementary relationships conflicts are less prevalent than in symmetrical ones, but in symmetrical relationships power is more evenly shared. The appropriateness of the type of relationship is determined by the feelings of the individuals involved.

Acquisition of Skills

Interpersonal communication is learned. Because interpersonal communication appears to be a natural, inborn skill, most people pay little attention to the skills that comprise their communication styles. Each of us tends to think, "I am what I am." Thus, we give little thought to what we do poorly and what we do well. Moreover, some people are unlikely to make any conscious effort to improve their skill levels, despite the fact that their interpersonal communication style is the product of a great number of skills that can be improved. In each person some of the skills are fully developed, some partially developed, and some totally undeveloped. As a result, none of us is as effective in our interpersonal relationships as we could be.

Becoming an Effective Communicator

Interpersonal Competence

Although the original notion of interpersonal effectiveness is credited to H. S. Sullivan,[6] N. N. Foote and L. S. Cottrell coined the term *interpersonal competence* in 1955.[7] During the last ten years much research has been

Whether you're designing an urban mall or asking for directions, communication is a complex process. Blueprints help architects share ideas and information. But such drawings are only a reference point for those who have learned how to interpret them. You can learn techniques to help you communicate more effectively and appropriately—in whatever career you pursue.

devoted to understanding competence in interpersonal communication, and the definition of interpersonal competence has developed over this period. In their article written in 1974, Arthur Bochner and Clifford Kelly defined interpersonal competence as a judgment of a person's ability to interact effectively with others.[8] In order to be competent, they asserted, a person's communication must reflect empathy, descriptiveness, owning of thoughts and feelings, self-disclosure, and behavioral flexibility. In 1977, J. M. Wiemann emphasized the ability to choose among communication behaviors in order to accomplish individual interpersonal goals—all while proceeding in a tactful manner with others within the constraints of a particular context.[9] In 1984, Brian Spitzberg and William Cupach defined relational competence as "the extent to which objectives functionally related to communication are fulfilled through cooperative interaction appropriate to the interpersonal context."[10] As you have seen in our discussion thus far, the effectiveness and appropriateness of interpersonal communication are of central concern in this book.

Although Spitzberg and Cupach assert that *competence* is an inference or judgment that one person makes about another,[11] they state that it is *through* the use of skills that a person creates the perception of competence. Thus, regardless of the specific definition of competence, the interpersonal communication skills you will be studying in this course are central to your success in communication. The skills repertoire you have, and the scripts built from these skills, enables you to initiate and manage your social interactions. Getting to know people, building and maintaining relationships, developing intimacy, dealing with your family, and learning to cope with people of different races, sexes, religions, and cultures—all are dependent on your use of key interpersonal communication skills.

In this text you will be introduced to more than thirty specific skills that, if mastered as scripts, you can choose from to help you achieve your communication purposes and become a competent communicator. You already use some of these skills, although you may not be conscious of them; others are not currently part of your repertoire. But no matter what the size of your current repertoire, your competence can be enhanced by careful study of and practice with these basic interpersonal skills.

To help you increase your competence, skills are presented in a unit that defines the skill, gives examples of its use, lists the steps necessary to learn it, and outlines ways that you can practice it. Note, however, that a few of the skills do not lend themselves to such a complete discussion.

The Communication Contract

In concluding this chapter we want to help you set a personal goal to improve some aspect of your own interpersonal communication during this course. To do this, we suggest you write a formal communication contract.

Why a written contract? A familiar saying goes, "The road to hell is paved with good intentions." Although right now you may be serious about changing some aspect of your communication, bringing about such a change is going to take time and effort. Because you are probably very busy, it is important for you to commit in writing to a specific goal. Otherwise, your good intentions to improve will easily get lost in the business of your life. By writing down a description of the change you wish to make, formulating a plan for completing it, and having another person witness your pledge, you are more likely to honor the commitment you have made than you would be simply by making a mental resolution. Research on goal setting suggests that people who set specific goals achieve more than do those who just try to "do their best."

Taking Your Communication Inventory. Before you can write such a contract, you must first analyze your current communication skills repertoire. We recommend that you do this by reviewing the skills categories that will be used as the framework for skills development in this book.

To help you understand how skills relate to one another, we have grouped the skills under five broad headings and previewed them for you here. This preview will provide you with an opportunity to take a first critical look at your own skills repertoire so that you have some basis for determining your current strengths and weaknesses.

1. NONVERBAL SKILLS: These skills relate to your intentional use of the nonverbal elements of message encoding and decoding.

> *Eye contact:* Do I look at people while I talk with them? (pp. 98–100)

> *Facial expression:* Do my facial expressions complement my ideas and/or feelings? (p. 100)

> *Gesture:* Are my hand and arm movements effective as supplements, complements, or substitutes for my verbal messages? (pp. 100–101)

> *Paralanguage:* Does the sound of my voice convey the meanings I intend? (pp. 105–109)

2. VERBAL SKILLS: These skills relate to your ability to accurately encode your meaning in word symbols.

> *Precision:* Do I select words that are recognized by others in our culture as symbolizing my thoughts and feelings? (pp. 79–81)

> *Being specific/concrete:* Do I use words that indicate a single item within a category or a single representation of an abstract concept or value? (p. 81)

> *Dating:* Do I include, where necessary, a specific time referent that indicates when a fact was true? (pp. 85–86)

> *Indexing:* Do I mentally or verbally account for individual differences? (pp. 86–88)

3. SELF-PRESENTATION SKILLS: These skills can help people better understand you, your ideas, and your feelings.

Self-disclosure: Do I share appropriately biographical data, personal ideas, and feelings that are unknown to other persons? (pp. 157–161)

Describing feelings: Am I able to put my emotional state into words? (pp. 163–170)

Assertiveness: Do I state ideas and feelings forcefully in interpersonally effective ways? (pp. 254–259)

Asking for criticism: Do I ask others for their reactions to me or to my behavior? (pp. 173–176)

4. LISTENING AND RESPONDING SKILLS: These skills relate to your ability to decode the intended meaning more accurately and form feedback messages.

Listening: Do I attend to and understand what people mean? (pp. 181–235)

Emphathizing: Am I able to detect and identify the immediate affective state of another? (pp. 192–195)

Supporting: Am I able to say something that soothes, reduces tension, or pacifies when necessary? (pp. 221–225)

Paraphrasing: Do I verbalize the meaning I get from another's statement before I respond? (pp. 216–221)

Perception checking: Do I make verbal statements to communicate my understanding of the meaning of another person's nonverbal cues? (pp. 58–61)

Questioning: Can I ask for additional information without creating defensiveness? (pp. 212–215)

Interpreting: Am I able to point out an alternative or hidden meaning to an event when appropriate? (pp. 225–227)

Describing behavior: Can I accurately recount specific observable actions of another without labeling the behavior as good or bad, right or wrong? (p. 229)

Praising: Do I give people positive feedback for their behavior? (pp. 227–228)

Criticizing: Can I give people negative feedback about their behavior in appropriate ways? (pp. 228–231)

5. INFLUENCING SKILLS: These skills relate to your ability to change another person's attitude or behavior.

Persuasion: Can I construct arguments that result in a person changing his or her attitude or behavior? (pp. 245–254)

Problem solving: Can I use problem solving to make more effective decisions? (pp. 318–323)

Negotiating: Can I manage conflict through trade-offs? (pp. 277–278)

6. CLIMATE SKILLS: These skills relate to your ability to create a positive climate in which effective communication can take place.

Descriptiveness: Do I put my observations into words objectively? (pp. 143–144)

Crediting others: Do I verbally identify the source of the ideas I use? (p. 171)

Owning feelings: Do I make "I" statements to identify when the idea or feeling is mine? (pp. 171–172)

Making provisional statements: Do I phrase ideas tentatively rather than dogmatically? (pp. 145–146)

In which of these areas are you weakest? When you communicate, do you get defensive reactions from others? If so, the skills in the climate section may be particularly helpful in improving your communication competence. Do people often misunderstand your meanings? Perhaps this stems from your use of language, in which case you may want to concentrate on verbal skills. Do people whom you know tell you that they feel distant from you? Do you have trouble standing up for yourself or letting others know how you feel? If so, then it may be worthwhile to work on the skills of self-presentation. Do you often misunderstand others' meaning? During conversations do you daydream or rehearse your next lines? If so, then the responding skills may be a place for you to focus your attention.

As you reflect on these skill categories, you may notice that some of these problems in your communication occur at all times whereas others occur only with one or two specific people and/or under certain circumstances. Thus, the contract you write should not only reflect the problem area but also specify a relationship or situation that you desire to improve.

Once you have isolated a problem situation, you are ready to write a contract and plan your improvement.

Writing the Contract. The contract we suggest has four parts:

1. *A statement of the goal:* After you have analyzed your communication and determined the area in which you wish to improve, write your goal specifically. For example: "Goal: To improve my work relationship with my boss; specifically, to describe my feelings about being assigned tasks that don't match my abilities"; or "Goal: To listen to my parents more efficiently—especially my mother."

2. *A description of the problem:* Here you describe, to the best of your ability, the specific nature of the communication problem including the relationship or situation, if appropriate. For example: "Problem: Currently, my boss tends to give me all the routine and/or less interesting jobs. When something really exciting comes along, he gives the job to Jones or Marshall. Consequently, I feel angry because I find myself thinking I'm being overlooked, but I don't say anything about it"; or "Problem: When my mother talks with me, I find myself daydreaming or rehearsing my replies. Consequently, I miss important points or misinterpret what she is telling me. Then she gets angry."

3. *A procedure for reaching the goal:* As your study in this course continues, you will learn which of the many skills presented can help you to achieve your goal. If you cannot determine those skills by the brief overview presented in this chapter or by skimming the text and the appendices, ask your instructor for help. Then write a procedural state-

---

1. Statement of the goal:

2. Description of the problem:

3. Procedure for reaching the goal:

4. Method of determining when the goal has been reached:

   Signed:

   Date:

   Witnessed by:

Figure 1.2 Communication contract.

ment that includes the skills you want to develop. For example: "Proce-dure: I will learn to describe feelings and be assertive"; or "Procedure: I will learn to withhold evaluation of my mom's ideas and paraphrase her meaning."

4. *A method of determining when the goal has been reached:* Here you need to write your minimum requirements for knowing you have achieved your goal. For example: "Test of Achieving Goal: This goal will be considered achieved when I think my boss understands my position and my feelings and I can express those feelings when his behavior excludes me"; or "Test of Achieving Goal: This goal will be considered achieved when I can listen calmly to what my parents have to say to me and can paraphrase their ideas easily without having to force myself to do it."

After completing the contract, sign it. We strongly suggest that you have another person in class act as a witness to the contract. Your witness can serve as a consultant, someone to talk with during the term about your progress. (Perhaps you can witness his or her contract in return.) If your goal relates to a particular relationship you have with another per-son, you may also want to consider telling that person about your goal. If that person knows you are trying to improve, he or she may be very willing to help. At the end of the term you and your witness/consultant can meet to assess your progress and further discuss your development in this area.

PRACTICE in Writing a Communication Contract

By Yourself

Write a communication improvement contract using the form in Figure 1.2.

Summary

We have defined interpersonal communication as the transactional process of creating meaning. Interpersonal communication is transactional because the meaning that is created occurs between the two participants based on both the original message and the response to it. The communication process consists of context, people, rules, channels, messages, noise, and feedback.

Interpersonal communication serves psychological, social, and decision-making functions. Psychologically, people communicate to meet needs and to maintain a sense of self; socially, people communicate to develop relationships and to fulfill social obligations. In terms of decision making people communicate to share information and to influence others.

Based on our discussion, we can draw several principles of interpersonal communication. First, interpersonal communication usually has purpose. At times a speaker may not always be aware of purpose; at other times a person may give careful thought to exactly what he or she wants to achieve. Second, interpersonal communication conveys implied messages. Third, interpersonal communication messages vary in degree of conscious encoding—messages may be spontaneous, scripted, or contrived. Fourth, interpersonal communication is relational, defining the power and affection between people. Relational communication can be either complementary or symmetrical. In complementary relationships one of the individuals defines who is to have greater power; in symmetrical relationships people compete with each other for power. Fifth, and most important, interpersonal communication is learned.

Effective interpersonal communication transactions depend on the communication competence of the individuals who are conversing. Because the communication situations you face are complex and diverse, the key to communication competence is behavioral flexibility, which is based on having a wide variety of interpersonal skills available for use.

Skills can be learned, developed, and improved, so you can help enhance your learning this term by writing a communication contract to improve some aspect of your skill repertoire.

Notes

1. Brian H. Spitzberg and William R. Cupach, *Interpersonal Communication Competence* (Beverly Hills, Calif.: Sage, 1984), p. 101.

2. John A. R. Wilson, Mildred C. Robick, and William B. Michael, *Psychological Foundations of Learning and Teaching*, 2nd ed. (New York: McGraw-Hill, 1974), p. 26.

3. Kathleen K. Reardon, *Interpersonal Communication: Where Minds Meet* (Belmont, Calif.: Wadsworth, 1987), pp. 11–12.

4. R. Abelson, "Script in Attitude Formation and Decision Making." In J. Carroll and T. Payne, eds., *Cognition and Social Behavior* (Hillsdale, N.J.: Erlbaum, 1976), p. 33.

5. Paul Watzlawick, Janet H. Beavin, and Don D. Jackson, *Pragmatics of Human Communication* (New York: W. W. Norton, 1967), p. 51.

6. H. S. Sullivan. "Tensions Interpersonal and International: A Psychiatrist's View," in H. Cantril, ed., *Tensions That Cause Wars* (Urbana, Ill.: University of Illinois Press, 1950).

7. N. N. Foote and L. S. Cottrell, Jr., *Identity and Interpersonal Competence* (Chicago: University of Chicago Press, 1955).

8. Arthur P. Bochner and Clifford W. Kelly, "Interpersonal Competence: Rationale, Philosophy, and Implementation of a Conceptual Framework," *Speech Teacher* 23 (November 1974): 288.

9. J. M. Wiemann, "Explication and Test of a Model of Communicative Competence," *Human Communication Research* 3 (1977): 198.

10. Brian H. Spitzberg and William R. Cupach, *Interpersonal Communication Competence* (Beverly Hills, Calif.: Sage, 1984), p. 100.

11. Ibid., p. 153.

Chapter 2

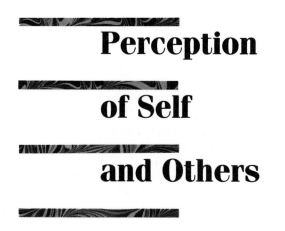

Perception

of Self

and Others

Objectives

After you have read this chapter, you should be able
to define and/or explain:

Perception

Processes of selection, organization, and interpretation

Factors that affect selection
and organization

Self-concept

Functions of self-concept

Monitoring self-concept

Factors affecting the accuracy
of perceptions of others

Methods of improving social
perception

As was traditional at Grafton, Inc., all new employees were invited to an orientation party in the Board of Directors' Room. This occasion was Pat's first chance to meet many of the new employees. As people were chatting before the formal orientation began, Pat's attention was drawn to a person on the opposite side of the room whose facial expression and sparkle in the eye impressed Pat tremendously. While pretending to make small talk with others, Pat slowly maneuvered across the room to talk with this person.

Stop right here and, without rereading the material, answer the following question: Is the person maneuvering across the room male or female? How do you know? Now reread the passage. Were you correct?

The questions in the preceding paragraph asked you to assess your *perceptions*. As a matter of fact, the passage does not identify the sex of the person. Still, you likely drew some conclusion about the sex of the person based on your own perception. Moreover, how you perceive that person would affect your thinking about and communication with that person.

Perception is the process of gathering sensory information and assigning meaning to it. Your sensory equipment—eyes, ears, nose, skin, and taste buds—gathers information; your brain selects from among the items of information gathered, organizes the information, and interprets and evaluates it. The result is perception. Perception does not necessarily give an accurate representation of the event being perceived, but rather a unique portrait on which a behavioral response can be made.

Understanding perception forms the foundation of understanding interpersonal communication in general and interpersonal relationships in particular. Why? Because *you* define yourself through your perception of yourself and of how others see you; likewise, *you* define others through your perception of them. In addition, your relationships with others are formed in part as a result of the interaction of these perceptions. We'll begin this chapter by looking briefly at the process of perception. Then we'll focus on how perception of self and of others affects our communication. Finally, we'll consider methods of improving both self-perception and perception of others.

The Perception Process

We can think of the process of perception as occurring in three stages: selection of stimuli, organization of stimuli, and interpretation of stimuli. Although the three stages of perception happen virtually simultaneously, here we'll consider each stage separately.

Selection of Stimuli

Because you are subject every second to a multitude of competing sensory stimuli, you have learned to cope by focusing your attention on relatively few of these stimuli. Right now you are reading this book, so your attention should be focused on making sense out of the visual information you are seeing on this page. Yet at the same time you could be focusing on many other sights, sounds, tastes, and smells. Perhaps a noise that you hadn't noticed before distracts you, making it difficult for you to concentrate on the book. As you refocus your attention on the book, the noise you heard recedes into the background. On what bases are these sensory selections made?

Limitations of the Senses. One factor in the selection process is the *physiological limitations of the senses*. If your eyes are weak, then you have trouble selecting visual stimuli that are far away—you just can't see them. Even when the senses are working properly, however, they have limitations. For example, human eyes perceive only certain rays—you do not see the infrared or ultraviolet ends of the color spectrum. Likewise, human ears cannot pick up many of the sounds that come to them—they are limited to a range between 20 and 20,000 cycles per second. This is why, for example, you cannot hear certain kinds of dog whistles.

Interest. A second factor affecting the selection process is *interest*. Consider the perceptions of different people visiting your campus for the first time. An architect may be primarily aware of the beauty (or ugliness) of the buildings; a person in a wheelchair may see the steps and curbs that have to be negotiated to get from building to building; a naturalist may see the trees and shrubs that grace the campus. Or you may have had the experience of buying a new car, then suddenly seeing that make and model of car wherever you look.

Figure 2.1 Rule of simplicity.

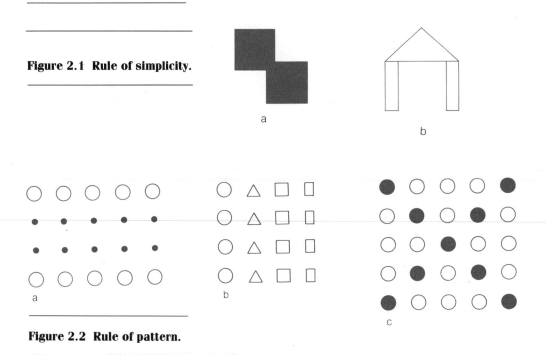

Figure 2.2 Rule of pattern.

Need. A third factor in the selection process is *need*. You tend to focus on objects and people related to your immediate needs or wants. When you drive from one place to another, you see those things that affect your driving: traffic lights; cars in front, behind, and next to you; people darting across streets; potholes in the road. Passengers in the car may be oblivious to all of these—they may be noticing a store they hadn't seen before or the condition of the neighborhood.

Due to sensory capability, interest, need, or any of a number of other potential factors, you do focus, consciously and unconsciously, only on certain of the stimuli around you.

Organization of Stimuli

Information is transmitted from the senses to the brain, which selects certain parts of that information and then organizes them. Four of the most important rules of information organization, according to psychologists, are the rules of simplicity, pattern, proximity, and good form.

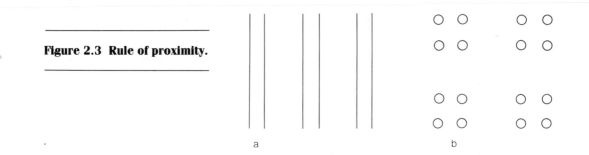

Figure 2.3 Rule of proximity.

a   b

Rule of Simplicity. Given a relatively complex perception, people are likely to simplify it into some recognizable form. For example, you probably perceive the shape in Figure 2.1a as overlapping squares rather than as an eight-sided figure and the shape in Figure 2.1b as a triangle on legs or as a covered bridge.

Rule of Pattern. When people look at sets of shapes, they tend to group them along common lines, or patterns. Thus, in viewing a crowd, for instance, instead of perceiving a number of individual human beings, you may see males and females, marrieds and singles, or young, middle-aged, and elderly. Some examples of usual patterning are shown in Figure 2.2.

Rule of Proximity. People also tend to group together those things that resemble one another physically. In a classroom, if you see a group of five students sitting apart from the rest of the class, you may decide they have something in common. The concept of visual proximity is illustrated in Figure 2.3.

Rule of Good Form. Even if a perception has a gap in it, a person is likely to see it as a closed figure. For example, three lines that almost join one another will tend to be perceived as a triangle even if there is a gap or if part of a line is missing. This rule explains why you may read a neon sign correctly although a portion is burned out, or why you may finish a sentence correctly even when the speaker leaves out a word. Some examples of the rule of good form are provided in Figure 2.4.

Factors Affecting Organization. How you organize perceptions is a result of many factors, including the degree of ambiguity the information contains and your emotional state. The more ambiguous or the more complicated the information, the more difficulty you will have in organizing it. Most people have been startled by something they saw from the corner of their

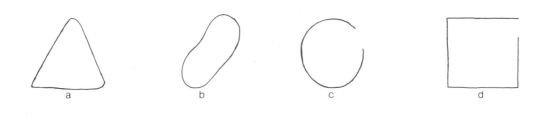

Figure 2.4 Rule of good form.

eye, only to discover that what they thought they saw was far different from what was actually there. Some examples of ambiguous visual stimuli are shown in Figure 2.5. Similarly, most people have mistakenly perceived a stranger as someone they knew because they saw what seemed to them a familiar coat or hair style or gesture. The more ambiguous the information, the more time it may take to go through the organizational process and the greater the chance for error.

How you organize sensory information may also be affected by how you feel. For instance, if you are tired, you may have difficulty identifying a complex object. Likewise, if you are nervous or on edge, you may jump to an erroneous conclusion.

Interpretation of Stimuli

As the brain selects and organizes the information it receives from the senses, it completes the perceptual process by *interpreting* the information. *Interpretation* is the process of explaining what has been selected and organized. Because two people are unlikely to select the same stimuli or organize stimuli in the same way, they are also not likely to arrive at the same interpretation of events or other people. Yet the unique portrait you derive from a situation directly affects your communication. Whereas in the processes of selection and organization you *identify*, in the process of interpretation you *evaluate*. For instance, two people driving down a highway crowded with neon signs may both identify an object as a logo for a fast food restaurant (McDonald's golden arches, perhaps). But only one person may then get excited about the sign; the other person, who might not be hungry or who might not care for hamburgers, may not.

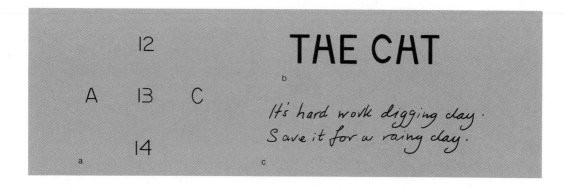

**Figure 2.5 Ambiguous stimuli. (a) The middle figure is seen as a *B* or as *13*
depending on its position in a row of letters or a column of numbers. (b) The
central letter is perceived as *H* or *A*. (c) The last word is perceived as *clay* or
day depending on the word you expect to find there.**
**(a, from *Introduction to Psychology*, 7th ed., by Ernest R. Hilgard et al., ©
1979 by Harcourt Brace Jovanovich, Inc. b, from O. G. Selfridge, "Pattern
Recognition and Modern Computers," *Proceedings of the Western Joint
Computer Conference*, © 1955 IEEE. Used by permission. c, after *Seeing;
Illusion, Brain and Mind* by John P. Frisby, Oxford University Press, 1980.
Reprinted by permission of Roxby Publications Limited.)**

Perception and Communication

In order to demonstrate the link between perception and communication,
we want you to examine Figure 2.6 very closely. Describe aloud what you
see: the age of the person, the person's features, how attractive the person
is, what the person is wearing, what you believe the person is thinking or
feeling, and so on.

What did you see? If you perceived a picture of a young woman,
your description was much different from what it would have been if you
had seen the picture of an old woman. In fact, the picture is an optical
illusion—there are actually two distinct images you might see. Your interpretation of this picture depends on how you select and organize the
stimuli.

Look at the picture again. Keep looking until you have seen both
women. "Ah," you say, "but this is just a trick. No real-life situation is as
ambiguous as this one." Perhaps not. But any police officer can attest to
the frustration of talking with three eyewitnesses to the same event. More
likely than not, each witness will describe very different situations. Which

Figure 2.6 Is this a drawing of a young woman or an old hag? Your interpretation depends on how you select and organize the stimuli.

is correct? The trained officer realizes that in some ways they all are and in some ways none of them is.

Although people believe strongly in the accuracy of their senses, their perceptions may well be inaccurate. While the degree of inaccuracy varies from insignificant to profound, communication based upon inaccurate perception results in communication that can be misleading, unsuccessful, and even dangerous.

Validating Perception

Because perceptions can be inaccurate and such inaccuracies in perception will lead to communication errors, we must have some means to validate the accuracy of our perceptions. Two methods that you can learn to use are multisensory cross-check and consensus.

Multisensory Cross-Check. Often, perceptions are based solely on data received through one sense—what you see or hear or taste. In some instances you can validate the accuracy of your perception by cross-checking the interpretation through another sense. For example, a ball of material may *look* coarse and hard; when you touch it, however, you can *feel* that it is really smooth and soft. A glass of liquid may *look* like a cola; it isn't until you *taste* it that you can confirm that it is a cola and not in fact root beer.

Consensus. A second way you can validate a perception is to compare your interpretation with that of other people. When you hear what sounds like an air raid warning siren, you may become alarmed and act inappropriately. Before you do, however, you may want to find out (1) whether others heard the same sound and (2) what conclusions they draw from that sound. In Cincinnati, for instance, at noon on the first Wednesday of each month, all civil defense agencies test their sirens to make sure they are working properly. A visitor to Cincinnati who is unfamiliar with this practice may be frightened by these sirens but be comforted to notice that other people are ignoring them.

To this point we have been discussing the process of perception—how we select, organize, and interpret stimuli. In the remainder of this chapter we will examine a special case of perception that is particularly important to communication. *Social perception*, or social cognition, consists of those processes by which people perceive themselves and others. In the study of social perception particular emphasis is placed on how people interpret their own and others' behavior, how people categorize themselves and others, and how people form impressions of themselves and others. In order to simplify our discussion of social perception, we will begin by talking about self-perception and then discuss perception of others.

PRACTICE in Analyzing Your Perceptions

By Yourself

1. Take a minute to look at everything that is around you. Now close your eyes and describe what you "saw." Open your eyes and look again; what did you miss? How can you explain why you selected the items you were able to describe? What caused you to notice these and not other aspects of the scene you were looking at?

2. On a day that there are cloud formations, take at least five minutes to examine the clouds. What forms are the clouds taking? Identify the organizational rules that affected your perceptions.

Perception of and Communication about Self

Now that we have examined the perceptual process, we need to understand how social perceptions affect communication. In this section we will study perception of and communication about self; in the next section we will study perception of and communication about others.

Why start with self? If, as we have been trying to demonstrate, your communication defines your relationships, how you define a relationship begins with how you see yourself. Furthermore, how you see yourself is revealed to others through your verbal and nonverbal communication.

Almost all your communication reveals something about yourself. The simple question "Isn't it a beautiful coat?" not only asks another to comment on the coat but also suggests what the speaker considers to be attractive in clothing. Even silence can be revealing. If people remain silent during a discussion, it may indicate their boredom with the subject or their shyness in speaking in a group. The collection of perceptions you have about yourself is called your *self-concept.* In order to understand the role of self-concept in communication, we must begin by understanding how a person's perceptions of self are formed.

Formation of the Self-Concept

As mentioned previously, your self-concept represents a collection of perceptions about every aspect of your being including your physical and mental capabilities, your vocational potential, and your communication abilities. Your self-concept is formed through self-appraisal and is based on a series of judgments you make about yourself as you behave in different contexts. These judgments are influenced by the reactions and responses of others to you. Through the process of making these self-appraisals, you develop an overall perception of yourself. Your self-concept is then presented to others through roles you play. In this sense, you may have more than one self-concept.

Self-Appraisal. Some of the information you use in forming your self-concept comes from your own perceptions. You form impressions about yourself based on what you see in yourself. For example, you look at yourself in the mirror and make judgments—about your weight and size, the clothes you wear, your smile—that affect how you feel about yourself. If you like what you see, you feel good about yourself; if you don't like what you see, you may try to change. You might go on a diet, buy some new clothes, get your hair styled differently, or begin jogging. If you don't like what you see and you cannot or are unwilling to change, you will probably begin to develop negative feelings about your physical appearance. Thus, "I'm fat" or "I have an ugly nose" becomes part of your self-concept.

Your impressions of yourself may also result from your reactions to your experiences. Through experience you learn what you are good at and what you like. If you earn high grades in several math classes, you are likely to see yourself as being "good at math." If you can strike up conversations with strangers and get them to talk with you, you will probably consider yourself friendly, engaging, or interesting to talk with. Keep in mind that a single satisfying experience may not give you a positive perception of your math ability or conversational skills (just as a single negative experience may not give you a negative perception), but if additional experiences produce similar results, then the initial perception will be strengthened. Interestingly, people are more likely to draw conclusions based on what they choose to do rather than on what they choose not to do. For instance, although people who sketch may see themselves as artistic, people who do not sketch do not necessarily think of themselves as nonartistic.[1]

In general, then, the greater the number of positive experiences you have—whether as a cook, lover, decision maker, student, worker, or parent—the more positive your self-concept becomes. Likewise, the greater the number of negative experiences you have, the more negative your self-concept may become.

Reactions and Responses of Others. In addition to your self-perceptions, your self-concept stems from how others react and respond to you. Suppose a person looks at you and says, "You have beautiful hair." Or suppose that after you've given your opinion on developing alternate means of marketing a product, one of your co-workers tells you, "You're a logical thinker and a convincing speaker." Comments like these are likely to positively affect your perception of self, especially if you respect the person making the comment. And, just as positive comments may have a great impact, so too may negative comments. You will tend to use other persons' comments to validate, reinforce, or alter your perception of who and what you are. The more positive comments you get about yourself, the more positive your total self-concept becomes.

A mirror can show you what you look like, but how you see yourself is largely
a reflection of how others respond and react to you. Nearly everything you
say or do expresses some aspect of your self-concept.

Presentation of Self

Although your self-concept is well formed by the time you are an adult,
you continue to present it publicly through various roles you play. Based
on how you appraise yourself and how others respond to you, you may
choose or be forced to play various roles. How those roles are received
further strengthens or changes your self-concept.

   A *role* is a pattern of behavior that characterizes a person's place
in a given context. Roles are products of the value systems of society, of
groups, and of the self. Society's value systems are easy to illustrate. Con-

sider, for example, some of the roles that society expects you to play. Over the past thirty years the sex-role expectations for women have changed; nevertheless, little girls are encouraged to play with dolls and homemaking toys to prepare them for the nurturing roles of wife and mother. Little boys are taught to hold back tears, to be aggressive in sports, and to play with mechanical toys in preparation for their roles as husband, father, and breadwinner. If these children are caught playing with "inappropriate" toys, the boy is called "sissy," the girl "tomboy." Both are derogatory terms that could injure self-concepts.

The value system of a specific group may also influence your role. Your family, your class, your athletic team, your theater club—every group you belong to approves or disapproves of what you are, do, and say and thus helps determine the kind of person you become. For instance, if you are the oldest child in a large family, your parents may cast you in the role of disciplinarian, brothers' and sisters' keeper, or housekeeper, depending on how they see family relationships. Or if your peers look upon you as a "joker," you may go along by playing your role, laughing and telling funny stories even though you really feel hurt or imposed upon.

Other roles are products of one's own value system. You may present yourself as "easygoing fellow," "with-it mom," or "serious student" to fit your perception of self based upon your own experience, to conform with the impressions of others, or to reflect a role you have chosen to play.

Everyone plays a number of roles. Some roles that you play in private may be either the same as or different from those you play in public. For instance, Samantha, who is perceived as a warm, quiet, sensitive person in private or with a close friend, may play the role of a boisterous party girl in a group. In each new encounter you may test a role you have been playing or you may decide to play a new role.

Accuracy of Self-Concept

A key question is, "How real or accurate is your self-concept?" The answer depends on the accuracy of your perceptions. Everyone experiences success and failures, hears praise and blame. In determining your self-concept, if you focus your awareness on successful experiences and positive responses, your perception of self will probably be high. If, however, you perceive and dwell on negative experiences and remember only the criticism you receive, your perception of self will be negative and your self-concept will be low. In neither case does that self-concept necessarily conform to reality. Yet in terms of behavior, your *perception* of self is likely to have far greater impact than is the reality of the situation, assuming that some objective reality can be determined. For example, you may really be a good leader, but if you don't perceive yourself as a good leader, you won't choose to lead.

Functions of Self-Concept

Now that we have seen what self-concept is and have analyzed briefly how it is formed, let's consider what part this self-concept plays in your communication. Your self-concept serves at least five basic communication functions: (1) It predicts behavior; (2) it filters messages received from others; (3) it influences word selection and tone of voice; (4) it moderates competing internal messages; and (5) it affects your perception of others.

Predictor of Behavior. An important communication function of your self-concept is to express predictions of behavior. The higher your self-concept is, the more likely you are to talk in ways that predict positive experiences. The lower your self-concept is, the more likely you are to talk in ways that predict negative experiences. Soon your self-concept begins to shape reality—you begin to profit or lose by what are called "self-fulfilling proph-

A self-fulfilling prophecy is a prediction that comes true because you predicted it. The woman on the right has asked her friend to teach her how to use sign language. Because she considers herself a fast learner, and because she expects to do well, it's most likely she'll soon be using her new language with ease.

ecies," predictions that come true *because* you predicted them. For example, Ed sees himself as a good test-taker; he says, "I'm going to do well on the economics test." Then, as a result of his positive self-concept, he remains relaxed, studies, takes the test confidently, and, just as he predicted, does well. In contrast, Jeff believes himself to be a poor test-taker; he says, "I just know I'll blow the economics test!" Then, because he fears tests, his study is interrupted by negative thoughts; he goes into the test tired, irritable, and worried; and, just as he predicted, he does poorly. Positive thoughts and positive language do, in fact, often produce positive results; similarly, negative thoughts and negative language may produce negative results.

Filter of Statements. Self-concept may also affect your communication by filtering what others say to you. Even though you may receive all messages adequately (that is, your ears receive the messages and your brain records them), you do not *listen* equally to all of them. Moreover, what you choose to listen to will likely be those messages that reinforce your self-concept. If someone says something that contradicts your perception, you are likely to act as if it had never been said. For example, you prepare lunch for your study group, and someone comments that you're a pretty good cook. Because this remark contradicts your self-concept, you may ignore it, not really hear it, or perhaps reply, "No, this was more like a lucky accident" or "Thanks for being kind to me, but it really wasn't that good." If you think you are a good cook, though, you will seek out those messages that reinforce this positive view and screen out those that don't.

Perhaps you have spotted what appears to be a contradiction in this analysis of self-concept. Earlier we stated that your self-concept is formed partly by listening to other people's statements. Now we are saying that it is the self-concept that determines whether you listen to those statements or screen them out. In fact, your self-concept is *both* a result and a filter of others' comments. Certain comments seem to help form a self-concept. Then the self-concept begins to work as a filter, screening out selected messages. At times, however, comments will get past the filter and change the self-concept, and then the newly changed self-concept begins to filter other comments. Thus, changes in self-concept do occur.

Influencer of Word Selection and Tone of Voice. There seems to be a definite link between self-concept and a person's word selection and tone of voice.[2] People's self-concepts are likely to be revealed by the kinds of statements they make about themselves. Continual self-criticism and self-doubt generally indicate low self-concept. Constant statements such as "I never was any good at—," "I don't know why I'm even trying, I know it won't work," and "I know you're disappointed with me, I just can't seem to get it right" reveal low self-concept. In contrast, a speech style characterized by confidence, honest effort, and anticipation of success is a sign of a positive self-concept. "I know it will be tough, but I look forward to trying," "You can count on me, I'll be giving it my best," or "I'll get the job done; you'll be pleased" are examples of the positive approach.

Signs of self-concept are especially prevalent in statements about competition. People with a low self-concept are often pessimistic and make statements such as "Why should I try? I won't win." Constantly blaming and cutting down the accomplishments of others may also be signs of low self-concept. "I might have done better if Tom started better" or "Sally gets A's because she butters up the instructor" are examples of such statements. Moreover, people with low self-concepts frequently adopt a whining tone of voice when they are asked to explain their thoughts, feelings, or behavior. By contrast, people with a high self-concept look forward to the challenge of good competition; their statements show that they will give a good accounting of themselves whether they win or lose.

Moderator of Competing Internal Messages. A fourth, particularly interesting function of self-concept is to moderate internal messages. When you are thinking, you are in fact talking to yourself (some people even go so far as to do much of their thinking aloud). When you are faced with a decision, you may be especially conscious of the different and often competing voices in your head. Perhaps this morning when your alarm went off, you had a conversation much like Carl's: "There goes that blasted alarm. I'm so tired—maybe I'll just lie here a few more minutes. Hold on—if I don't get up now, I'll go back to sleep. Oh, who cares—I need sleep! If I slept just another fifteen minutes—no! It's already later than I wanted to get up. Come on, Carl, move it." Notice that several of the messages in this internal conversation are competing. What determines which voice Carl listens to? Self-concept is a moderator in the choice. If Carl feels good about himself and the day he has in store, he will probably get up right away. If, on the other hand, things aren't going well for him or there are important decisions to be made, Carl may seek to escape reality through sleep.

Eric Berne, a psychologist, developed a system of analyzing these internal messages called *Transactional Analysis (TA)*.[3] In brief, TA suggests that the kinds of thoughts Carl experienced come from three ego states: the *Parent*, the *Child*, and the *Adult*. Statements from the Parent ego state are critical evaluative statements; they are the voice of conscience. In effect, they are the kinds of statements that your parents were likely to have made to you when you were young, such as "Don't touch the stove, you'll get burned," "Cheating on tests is wrong," and "Eat your vegetables, they're good for you." Statements from the Child ego state are emotional reactions. If you are being criticized and you burst into tears and say, "Don't say another thing—I don't want to hear it," or if you are on a roller coaster and scream as you start down the steepest dip, you're giving voice to pure emotional reaction—you're literally becoming childlike. Statements from the Adult ego state, such as "Let me examine this carefully" or "I could go either way on this; I've got to see both sides clearly," indicate rational decision making.

Everyone listens to statements of each type on occasion. If you find, however, that you almost always react emotionally or that you almost always monitor your actions based on parental guidelines, your decision-making processes may be too narrowly focused and thus not meeting fully your personal needs. Especially when you are making a critical decision, you need to pay attention to those Adult voices of reason.

Although Transactional Analysis is not the only way to explain these competing voices in your head, our students have found some of its concepts helpful to understanding or identifying certain communication events. It is useful to know what kind of statements you are inclined to listen to and under what circumstances.

Influencer of Perception of Others. Your self-concept is important not only because of the way it influences your communication behavior with others but also because it affects how you perceive others.[4] This influence can be seen in three areas. First, the more accurate your self-concept, the more accurately you can perceive others. Second, the more you accept yourself—that is, have a positive self-concept—the more likely you are to see others favorably. Studies have shown that those people who accept themselves as they are tend to be more accepting of others; similarly, those with low self-concepts are more likely to find fault in others. Third, your own personal characteristics influence the type of characteristics you are likely to perceive in others. For example, people who are secure tend to see others as warm rather than cold.

Improving Perception of Self

To make any conscious change in self-concept, we have to be aware of our behavior in order to determine how self-concept influences it. How we behave is likely to depend on how extensively we monitor ourselves, that is, on whether we are a high or low self-monitor. At least to some extent, each of us decides who we will be in a given situation. The awareness of self and the ability to adapt self to situations is called *self-monitoring*.[5] According to Mark Snyder, a high self-monitor tends to adapt his or her self to the social situation; a low self-monitor tends to present a consistent image of self in every situation. For instance, suppose Dan, a very outspoken person who saw himself as rather happy-go-lucky, was attending a wedding. If Dan were a high self-monitor, he would perceive the nature of the situation and monitor his behavior accordingly. Thus, when the bride tripped slightly going down the aisle, he would not burst out laughing. If, on the other hand, Dan were a low self-monitor, he would be less likely to consider the solemnity of the situation and less likely to monitor his behavior. As a result, he might well burst out laughing when he noticed that the bride had tripped as she walked down the aisle.

In short, the two aspects of self-monitoring are (1) developing a consciousness of the social rules and guidelines for various situations and (2) being aware of when and how to react to situations based on those guidelines. As an exercise, for a few days you can monitor the different kinds of situations you face and the image you project in each. Which of your "selves" would have been most appropriate? Were you able to analyze the situation as it occurred and adjust your behavior to meet it? Of course, a low self-monitor may behave consistently because he or she doesn't really care whether the behavior is appropriate. We are assuming, however, that even if you are a strong low self-monitor, you may find it useful to adapt more consciously to a given situation. For instance, if you see yourself as a very informal person in dress and behavior, you may still wish to dress "up" for a job interview and communicate in a more formal style.

PRACTICE in Analyzing Self

By Yourself

1. How you see yourself: On a blank sheet of paper list characteristics that describe how you see yourself by completing the statement "I am _____" over and over again. List as many characteristics as you can think of. When you can think of no more, go back through the list. Label the positive statements with a P; label the negative statements with an N. How many statements are positive? How many are negative?

2. How others see you: On a second sheet of paper list characteristics that describe how others see you by completing the statement "Other people believe that I am _____" over and over again. When

you can think of no more, go back through the list and label and tally positive and negative statements.

3. How you wish you were: On a third sheet of paper list characteristics that describe how you wish you were by completing the statement "I wish I were _____" over and over again. When you can think of no more, go back through the list and label and tally positive and negative statements.

4. After you have compared the lists, noting similarities and differences, write a short statement that describes what you have learned about yourself and your self-concept.

Perception of and Communication about Others

When two people meet, they form quick impressions of each other. As they interact, their perceptions may be changed, reinforced, or intensified. What develops as a result of these impressions determines such things as how much they like each other and how well they will communicate with each other. Most of all, these perceptions lay the groundwork for defining their relationship.

Many psychologists believe that the brain creates cognitive models—structures for processing and organizing information—and then imposes them on the stimuli received. These cognitive structures are called *schema.*

Reflect on your own comments about others. Notice how often you verbalize impressions that are based upon limited information. For instance, after a party in which Sara talks briefly to Marty while they are at the buffet table making a sandwich, Sara later says, "Marty's a jerk" or perhaps, "That Marty's really got it together." This statement follows just a one- or two-sentence interchange! In some cases a person does not even need a live encounter to form an impression—merely looking at a photograph may produce a strong opinion. Show your friend a picture of your uncle or grandmother, and your friend may well form some perception of the person's personality on the basis of that photo alone!

Obviously, you form perceptions of people, and these perceptions are the bases of your communication with them. But what factors are

We often form impressions of other people on the basis of a single brief encounter—and sometimes on nothing more than a photograph. Such perceptions shape how well we will interact with others. Do you think you'd be comfortable talking with the two people shown here? Why or why not?

likely to affect the accuracy of your perceptions of others? We will discuss six such factors: emotional state, assumed similarity, selective perception, perceptual defense, halo effect, and stereotyping.

Emotional State. Your feelings at the moment affect the nature of your perception. If, for example, you are having a "down" day, your perception of a person you don't know will probably be more negative than if you were having a good day. When you receive a low grade on a paper you thought was well written, your perceptions of people around you will surely be colored by your negative feeling. If, however, you receive an A on an important paper that you weren't sure was any good, you're likely to perceive everything and everyone around you positively. So, regardless of whether your perception of another person is positive or negative, ask yourself before you act on it how your feelings may have affected that perception.

Assumed Similarity. Because it is easier to judge others if you assume they are like you, people usually perceive other personalities as similar to their own. If you are a very sociable person and like parties, you will probably perceive another person as sociable if that person is your own age and sex and from a similar background. When this perceptual shortcut is used extensively, a person's observations about others will correspond more to his or her personality than to the actual personalities of the others. In observing others who are genuinely like them, people are quite accurate, not because they are more perceptive but only because they always judge others as being similar to themselves.

Selective Perception. You also are likely to think highly of a person whom you would like to be with. If Donna sees Nick as a man with whom she would like to develop a strong relationship, Donna will perceive Nick positively. That is, Donna will look only at the positive side of Nick's personality and overlook or ignore the negative side that is apparent to others. A person in love is often oblivious to the loved one's faults. Once two people have married, however, they may begin to see the negative traits of their partners, traits that were perhaps obvious to others all along.

Perceptual Defense. When people wish something about others, they are likely to behave as if the wish were reality. In other words, through perceptual defense we tend to ignore or distort information that is personally threatening or culturally unacceptable. Consider the following situation: Don loves Jane, so Don wants to perceive Jane as loving him; that is, he wishes she would. His belief that Jane probably really loves him is wrong, but Don looks for ways to confirm it, however bizarre his efforts may seem to others. Jane can tell Don she does not love him, she can insult him to his face, yet Don may see every one of her insults as a reinforcement of his wish. Matthew says, "Don, she doesn't love you—she's refused to go out with you five times in a row, she won't talk with you on the phone, and she crosses to the other side of the street when she sees you!" Don replies, "She loves me all right—she's just trying to play hard to get. Give her time—she loves me; you'll see." Seeing the world through rose-colored glasses has not improved the accuracy of Don's perceptions of Jane's feelings. Although this example is certainly extreme, it illustrates how people actually do behave.

Halo Effect. You may often find yourself forming complex perceptions of someone based on observing a single central trait and then allowing that cue to influence your impressions of that person's other characteristics without further verification. This tendency is known as the *halo effect*. For instance, Nancy sees Marsha as a warm person. Nancy correlates warmth with goodness, and goodness with honesty, so she may perceive Marsha as both good and honest as well as warm.

Because people recognize a strong, dominating trait, they allow that trait to influence their perceptions of other traits and qualities whether such perceptions are warranted or not. For example, Marsha may be warm, but she may also be dishonest. Thus, if someone accuses Marsha of some dishonest act, Nancy is likely to defend Marsha because of her perception of Marsha's goodness. A halo effect can work to a person's advantage or disadvantage, depending upon whether the perception is positive or negative. Yet Hollman[6] has found that negative information about people more strongly influences impressions of others than does positive information.

Halo effects seem to occur most frequently under one or more of three conditions: (1) when the perceiver is judging traits with which he or she has limited experience, (2) when the traits have strong moral overtones, and (3) when the perception is of a person that the perceiver knows well.

Stereotyping. Perhaps the most commonly known barrier to our accurate judgment of others is our tendency to stereotype. *Stereotyping* consists of assigning characteristics to a person solely on the basis of their class or category. Secord, Backman, and Slavitt[7] suggest that stereotyping has four distinct phases. First, a person distinguishes some category or class of people, for example, economists. Second, the person observes that one or more of the individuals in this category exhibit certain traits, for example, dullness. Third, the person generalizes from this perception that everyone in this category possesses these characteristics; for example, all economists are dull. Finally, when confronted with an individual the person is not acquainted with but knows to be, for example, an economist, the person stereotypes this individual as dull.

Stereotyping constitutes a judgment about an entire group with little or no regard for individual differences within the group. You are likely to develop generalized opinions about any group you come in contact with. Your opinions may, in a very broad sense, be true, partially true, or totally false, depending on the accuracy and breadth of your perceptions. When you learn that a person is a member of a given group (recognition may come as a result of perception of skin color, a religious medal, grey hair, or any of a number of other signs), you may automatically project your generalized opinions onto the individual. Suppose Allen stereotypes a group as pushy, greedy, and insensitive. As soon as he learns that Dave is a member of that group, he automatically perceives Dave as pushy, greedy, and insensitive.

People can form stereotypes from an amazingly small amount of information. For example, one research study found that teachers tended to give higher grades to elementary school essays allegedly written by students named Michael or David than to the same papers supposedly authored by Hubert or Elmer.[8] Evidently, there are even commonly held stereotypes associated with certain names!

Stereotyping is a major problem for two obvious reasons. First, the original stereotype of a group is probably wrong. Just because one person or five persons who happen to belong to a particular group are greedy does not mean that all members of the group are greedy. Yet people often perceive some characteristic of one or two persons and generalize to a conclusion that the entire group has those characteristics. Second, those who stereotype compound the problem by assuming that a different person has the same characteristics just because that person happens to be a member of the same group. So even if 90 percent of a particular group are greedy, that does not mean that Dave is greedy just because he is a member of that group.

If stereotypes are often inaccurate, why do they persist? There are at least two good reasons. First, people look for shortcuts. It is easier to work with an inaccurate stereotype of a person or group of people than to take the time to really learn about the individuals involved. Second, people believe that stereotypes are helpful.[9] In unfamiliar social settings stereotypes help people to classify others and thus guide their behavior in what they hope are socially acceptable ways. For example, a young man may stereotype an older, well-dressed woman as being old-fashioned. Not wanting to offend her, he may use his stereotypical view of older women to guide his behavior. Thus, he quickly steps ahead of her to open the door for her when she is ready to leave.

All of these perceptual factors—emotional state, assumed similarity, selective perception, perceptual defense, halo effects, and stereotyping—contribute to inaccuracies in our perceptions of others. In the next section we will discuss ways that these can be overcome.

PRACTICE in Analyzing Perceptions of Others

With Others in Class

1. Your instructor will ask for three volunteers, who will leave the classroom. One at a time they will reenter the room and describe to

the class a full-page magazine ad that the instructor has given them. On the basis of their descriptions, you are to form a mental picture of the people in the advertisement. As each volunteer describes the ad, write five adjectives about the person or persons in the picture. When all three have finished, your instructor will show you the ad.

A. What were the differences among the three descriptions?

B. Which of the three descriptions helped you form the most accurate picture? How did your image differ from the actual picture? How can you account for the differences?

C. Now that you have seen the picture, write five adjectives. Did your five adjectives about the person or persons in the picture change after you actually saw the picture? If so, how and why?

2. For each of the following situations, determine which of the six factors discussed in this section contributed to the inaccuracy of the initial perception of others. Be able to defend your answers in class.

Tom was really disgusted. Jim had failed to show up again! His original perception that Jim was really compatible may have been inaccurate. Tom and Jim had met three weeks before when they were introduced at a party. They quickly discovered that they both enjoyed racquetball, old movies, and rock music. In addition, both Tom and Jim had been raised in military families and had moved frequently during their childhoods. Several days later Tom found himself sitting in the same lab section of a biology course as Jim. The professor announced that the next experiment was to be done with a partner. Tom had previously agreed to work with Stan, the fellow who lived down the hall from him, but decided to try to switch and work with Jim. Because they were so much alike, Tom reasoned that they would work better together. Now, two weeks later, Tom wasn't so sure. The project was due tomorrow and they had still not finished their observations.

Joan was depressed. She had flunked her art history exam, she had just been informed that her work hours were being cut back, and her mother was facing possible surgery. On her way home from campus, she stopped at the dry cleaner to pick up her laundry. There was a new man working the counter. From looking at him Joan could tell he was quite old. She thought to herself that he could be a problem. When she requested her laundry, he asked to see her claim check. Because no one had ever asked her for this before, Joan responded that she had thrown the receipt away. The man firmly replied, "Well, I'm not able to give you clothes without a claim check. It's store policy." After demanding to see the manager and being informed that she had left for the day, Joan stormed out of the store. "I'll get him," she fumed to herself. "Isn't it just like an old man to act so rigidly!"

Improving Perception

Because inaccuracies in perception are common and influence how we communicate, improving our perceptual accuracy is an important first step in becoming a competent communicator. The following guidelines can aid you in constructing a more realistic impression of others as well as assessing the validity of your own perceptions.

   1. *Actively question the accuracy of your perceptions.* Too many people insist that "I was there—I know what I saw"; that is, they act on their perceptions as though they are reality. Questioning accuracy begins by saying "I know what I *think* I saw, heard, tasted, smelled, or felt, but I *could* be wrong. What else could help me sort this out?" By accepting the possibility of error, you may be motivated to seek further verification. In situations where the accuracy of perception is important, take a few seconds to double-check. It will be worth the effort.

   2. *Seek more information to verify perceptions.* Once you have drawn a conclusion about others, you begin to behave in accordance with that conclusion. Has your perception been based on only one or two pieces of information? If so, try to collect further information before you allow yourself to form an impression so that you may increase the accuracy of your perceptions. It helps to mentally note that your perception is tentative, that is, subject to change. You can then make a conscious effort to collect more data in order to determine whether the original perception is accurate.

   3. *Talk with the people about whom you are forming perceptions.* The more information you have to work with, the more likely your perceptions are to be accurate. And the best way to get information about people is to talk with them. If you've perceived someone as inconsiderate on the basis of one experience, hold that perception as tentative until you have a chance to really talk with the person. As you talk with people, you get to know them. Some of your perceptions about people may still be inaccurate, but you will increase the likelihood of accuracy.

4. *Realize that perceptions of people need to change over time.* Suppose that two years ago you saw a person put down the accomplishments of a friend of yours. From this experience you may develop the perception that the person is mean. This one incident may have led you to *expect* mean behavior from this person at all times. Willingness to change means making an effort to observe this person's behavior at other times. If the person shows a different kind of behavior under different circumstances, you should be willing to change your perception of that person. People often saddle themselves with perceptions that are based on old or incomplete information yet find it easier to stick with a perception, even if it is wrong, than to change it. It takes strength of character to say to yourself or others, "I was wrong." But your communication based on outdated, inaccurate perceptions can be more costly than revising your perceptions.

5. *Check perceptions verbally before proceeding.* How can you be sure that the meanings others get from your nonverbal cues are accurate? Before you act on any conclusion you draw from other people's behavior, you should make a perception check. A *perception check* is a verbal statement that reflects your own understanding of the meaning of another person's nonverbal cues.

Because some people do not verbalize what they are thinking or feeling and because what they do say sometimes seems at odds with other clues they are sending, we, as receivers, must interpret not only the words but also the actions. There is no way of judging the accuracy of our perceptions without putting them to the test. The procedure for perception checking is quite simple:

1. Watch the behavior of the other person.

2. Describe the behavior to yourself or aloud.

3. Ask yourself, "What does that behavior mean to me?"

4. Put your interpretation of the behavior *into words* to verify whether your perception is accurate.

Examine the following situations and the efforts at using perception checking.

Vera comes walking into the room with a completely blank expression. She neither speaks to Ann nor acknowledges that Ann is in the room. Vera sits on the edge of the bed and stares into space. Ann says, "Vera, I get the feeling that something has happened that put you in some kind of a shock. Am I right? Is there something I can do?"

Gerry, speaking in short, precise sentences with a sharp tone of voice, gives Bill his day's assignment. Bill says, "From the sound of your voice, Gerry, I can't help but get the impression that you're upset with me. Are you?"

Ted, the company messenger, delivers a memo to Mary. As Mary reads the note, her eyes brighten and she breaks into a smile. Ted says, "Hey, Mary, you certainly seem pleased. That must have been good news. Am I right?"

In each of these examples, the final sentence is a perception check intended to test the receiver's perceptions of the behavior of the sender. Notice that body language sometimes provides the clues, while at other times the tone of voice does. Also notice that the perception-checking statements do not express approval or disapproval of what is being received—they are purely descriptive statements of the perceptions.

When should you check your perceptions? Whenever the accuracy of your understanding is important (1) to your current communication, (2) to the relationship you have with the other person, or (3) to the conclusions you draw about that person. Most of us use this skill far too little, if at all. People *assume* that we have a perfectly accurate understanding of the meaning of another's behavioral cues; too often they are wrong. Especially in new relationships you will find perception checking an important skill to use.

Let's see what might happen when we respond without checking the accuracy of our perceptions. We'll examine a rather typical conversation based on the situation described in one of the examples given above.

If, in place of the descriptive perception check ("I can't help but get the impression that you're upset with me. Are you?"), Bill were to say, "Why are you so upset with me?" Bill would not be describing his perception—he would be making a judgment based upon his perception. Replying as if his perception is "obviously" accurate involves reliance on mind reading. Unfortunately, few people can read minds that well. When mind reading is substituted for perception checking, communication breakdowns are likely to occur. Perhaps you are thinking, "Well, I know when another person is upset (or happy, angry, and so on) with me." Perhaps you are correct in thinking you can properly identify such feelings as anger or happiness most of the time. But if you do not check it out, you are still guessing that you know how the other person is feeling or that the person's anger or happiness is centered on you. If you choose the judgmentally phrased reply, the person you are addressing may be defensive about the feelings that you appear to be challenging. In response, that person might say, "Who said I'm upset?" or, more harshly, "What the hell are you talking about?" Such responses might lead to further emotional outbursts, and very little communication takes place when communicators lose their tempers.

Because a perception check is descriptive rather than judgmental, the original sender—the object of the perception check—is less likely to become defensive. The purpose of checking out any perception of behavior is to bring the meaning that was received through the nonverbal cues into the verbal realm, where the meaning that has been received can be verified or corrected. Let's carry through with Gerry and Bill's conversation. When Bill says, "I can't help but get the impression that you're upset with me. Are you?" Gerry may say either (1) "No, whatever gave you that impression?" in which case Bill can further describe the cues that he received; (2) "Yes, I am," in which case Bill can get Gerry to specify what has caused the feelings; or (3) "No it's not you, it's just that three of my team members didn't show up for this shift." If Gerry is not upset with him, then Bill can deal with what caused him to misinterpret Gerry's feelings; if Gerry is upset with him, then Bill has the opportunity of changing the behavior that caused Gerry to be upset.

A perception check may not always eliminate defensive behavior. There are times when a person's emotional stress is so great that calm, logical communication is nearly impossible. Through the selective use of perception checking, however, you can reduce the likelihood of misinterpreting another's nonverbal cues and thus the likelihood of defensiveness. As with most skills, in order to become competent you must practice.

PRACTICE in Perception Checking

By Yourself

1. Write down your responses to the following situations with well-phrased perception checks:

Marsha comes rushing into her room, throws her books on the floor, and sits at her desk with her head in her hands. You say:

Bob comes home from the doctor's office with pale face and slumped shoulders. Glancing at you with a forlorn look, he shrugs his shoulders. You say:

As you return the tennis racket you borrowed from Jim, you smile and say, "Here's your racket." Jim stiffens, grabs the racket, and starts to walk away. You say:

In the past, your advisor has told you that almost any time would be all right for working out your next term's schedule. When you tell him you'll be in Wednesday afternoon at 4 P.M. he pauses, frowns, sighs, and says "Uh," and nods. You say:

2. Compare your written responses to the guidelines for effective perception checking discussed above. Edit your responses where necessary in order to improve them. Now say them aloud. Do they sound "natural"? If not, revise them until they do.

Work In Groups

Working with others in groups of three, A and B should role-play a situation while C observes. During the conversation A should intentionally give off various nonverbal cues to his or her feelings. B should use perception checking to determine if his or her perception of A's behavior is accurate. When they have finished, C should discuss the behaviors observed and provide an analysis of the effectiveness of B's paraphrases. The exercise continues until each person in the group has a chance to be A, B, and C. After completing the exercise, the participants should discuss how the skill of perception checking affected the accuracy of the communication.

Summary

Perception is the process of gathering sensory information and assigning meaning to it. People's perceptions are a result of their selection, organization, and interpretation of sensory information. Inaccurate perceptions cause people to see the world not as it is but as they would like it to be.

A person's self-concept is a collection of perceptions that relate to every aspect of that person's being. The self-concept is formed by views of self and experiences and by other people's comments about self and behavior. The self-concept is then presented publicly through the roles played. The self-concept serves at least five basic communication functions: It predicts behavior, it filters messages from others, it influences word selection and tone of voice, it moderates competing internal messages, and it affects perception of others.

Perception also plays an important role in forming impressions of others. Because research shows that the accuracy of people's perceptions and judgments varies considerably, your communication will be most successful if you do not rely entirely on your impressions to determine how another person feels or what that person is really like. You will improve (or at least better understand) your perceptions of others if you take into account your emotional state, assumed similarity, selective perception, perceptual defense, halo effect, and stereotyping.

You can learn to improve perception if you actively question the accuracy of your perceptions, seek more information to verify perceptions, talk with people to help correct perceptions, realize that perceptions of people need to change over time, and check perceptions verbally before you react.

Notes

1. Russell H. Fazio, Steven J. Sherman, and Paul M. Herr, "The Feature-Positive Effect in the Self-Perception Process: Does Not Doing Matter as Much as Doing?" *Journal of Personality and Social Psychology* 42 (1982): 411.

2. In "Developing a Healthy Self-Image," Don Hamachek offers a lengthy analysis of the symptoms of inferiority and self-acceptance as shown through the tone of voice. See Don Hamachek, *Encounters with the Self* (New York: Holt, Rinehart & Winston, 1971), pp. 232–237.

3. See Eric Berne, *Games People Play: The Psychology of Human Relationships* (New York: Grove Press, 1964).

4. S. S. Zalkind and T. W. Costello, "Perception: Some Recent Research and Implications for Administration," *Administrative Science Quarterly* 9 (1962): 218–235.

5. Mark L. Snyder, "Self-Monitoring Processes," in Leonard Berkowitz, ed., *Advances in Experimental Social Psychology*, 12 (New York: Academic Press, 1979), pp. 86–131.

6. T. D. Hollman, "Employment Interviewer's Errors in Processing Positive and Negative Information," *Journal of Psychology* 56 (1972): 130–134.

7. P. F. Secord, C. W. Backman, and D. R. Slavitt, *Understanding Social Life: An Introduction to Social Psychology* (New York: McGraw-Hill, 1976).

8. H. Harari and J. W. McDavid, "Name Stereotypes and Teachers' Expectations," *Journal of Educational Psychology* (1973): 222–225.

9. Kay Deaux and Larence S. Wrightsman, *Social Psychology in the 80's*, 4th ed. (Belmont, Calif.: Wadsworth, 1984), p. 90.

Chapter 3

Verbal

Communication

Objectives

After you have read this chapter, you should be able
to define and/or explain:

Uses of language in human
communication

Syntax, pragmatics, and
semantics

Problems of denotation and
connotation

A semantic differential

Selection of precise words

Selection of specific/concrete
words

Selection of appropriate
words

Dating generalizations

Indexing generalizations

You were very worried about how well you had done on the midterm, but to your surprise, when the test was returned, your grade was better than you expected. As you leave class, you say to another student, . . .

As you leave a highly touted movie, you feel disappointed: The film started so brilliantly but failed to come to grips with any of the powerful issues it raised. Nonetheless, the acting was superb. As you walk to the car, you say to your companion, . . .

As you cross campus one day, you see a friend who borrowed twenty dollars from you two weeks ago but has yet to return it. After you share greetings, you say to your friend, . . .

In each of these situations you are planning to share your ideas and feelings verbally. How effectively you communicate will depend largely on both your verbal and nonverbal skillfulness. In this chapter we will examine the nature and role of verbal communication; in the next chapter we will examine nonverbal communication. We begin by discussing how people use language. Next, we examine three aspects of language study that will help you analyze and understand your own verbal effectiveness. We then discuss various complications that arise in using words. Finally, we present skills that are helpful for increasing your effective use of language.

The Nature and Use of Language in Human Communication

Language represents the systematic means of communicating ideas or feelings by the use of sounds and symbols that have commonly understood meanings. Some scholars believe that the human capability to think and communicate symbolically best distinguishes us from other species. Language is used for several purposes in human communication.

1. *Through language people designate and define.* We use language symbols to designate, label, and define thoughts, feelings, objects, people, and experiences in order to share them with others. There are, however, certain limitations inherent in the use of language symbols. The symbols we select have meaning for us, but by their very nature they cannot accurately represent the exact object, person, experience, or thought. You may define a classmate as "a young adult," "a student," "a singer," or "a basketball player." Whichever label you choose, you are calling attention to some particular aspect of that person; in addition, you are suggesting how others should perceive and act toward that person. For instance, people will perceive, and act somewhat differently toward, a person labeled as a *singer* than toward a person labeled as an *athlete*.

   2. *Through language people evaluate.* Language scholars emphasize the value-laden characteristics of language: We give a person, a place, or an action a positive or negative slant simply by how we *talk* about it. For instance, if you observe Hal taking his time to make a decision, you could speak of Hal as either "thoughtful and deliberate" or "wishy-washy." Likewise, you can call what your friend is cooking on the grill either "chopped steak" or "hamburger." The value-laden nature of language makes it almost impossible to communicate objectively. For example, the seemingly simple descriptive statement "The chairs in the classroom are brown" may be perceived as a judgment of these chairs. The inherent capacity of language to convey evaluations of the thoughts, feelings, objects, people, and experiences it defines means that language functions as a form of control over the perceptions and behaviors of people.

   3. *Through language people can discuss things outside their immediate experience.* Language enables us to speak hypothetically. It permits us to talk about past and future events and experiences and to communicate about people who are not present. For instance, because of language you can talk about what you would like to be doing five years from now or about what you did in high school. Moreover, you can talk about someone who is not present. Language enables us to learn from others' experiences, to share a common heritage, and to develop a shared vision for the future.

   4. *Through language people can talk about language.* Language is "self-reflexive"; in other words we can use language to reflect on or talk about language. For example, we can discuss how we phrased a question and consider whether better phrasing would have resulted in a more precise question—and answer.

   Each of these four uses of language has important implications for our interpersonal communication. Through language we create, maintain, and alter our environments. We can choose to give or seek information or we can choose to avoid doing so. Through language we can be clear or ambiguous—we can disclose what we are thinking or feeling or we can hide those thoughts or feelings. And perhaps most importantly, through language we can affect every aspect of our relationships.

Language Domains

Linguistic theorists (scholars who study language) have developed a vocabulary that helps us analyze various language domains, including syntax, pragmatics, and semantics.[1] These domains are different types of knowledge about language that aid effective interpersonal language use. Although linguistic theory identifies several other domains as well, knowledge of these three is most critical for interpersonal communication effectiveness.

Syntax

Syntax is the study of the architecture of phrases, clauses, and sentences; it is the study of word order. Syntax focuses not on the *meanings* of words or sentences but on the *rules* that must be followed for a sentence to be accepted as grammatically correct. The sentence "Tom was shot in the arm by the robber" is syntactically acceptable English; "Tom in the arm by the robber was shot" is not. Although syntax rules specify word orders that help us process language symbols, these rules still permit flexibility for the speaker. For example, we can say either "Tom was shot in the arm by the robber" or "the robber shot Tom in the arm." Both are acceptable. They differ only in that in the first sentence the relationship between the subject and verb is passive—"Tom *was shot*"—whereas in the second sentence the relationship between the subject and the verb is active—"The *robber shot.*"

Syntactic rules of a given language help members of that language community anticipate and process the verbal utterances of others. Thus, designing messages using proper syntax is an important aid in communication, one that you have studied throughout your formal education.

Pragmatics

Pragmatics is the study of how language is used to communicate. Pragmatics goes beyond the meanings implied in individual words and the order of words to consider how we use sentences when we talk. Pragmatics addresses such questions as *why* we phrase a sentence one way rather than another in a given context. For instance, a study of pragmatics enables us to explain how an individual comes to understand that "Can you pass the sugar?" is not a query about whether you have the physical ability necessary to perform the act but rather a request that you *do* perform it. These intentions of speech are called *speech acts.*[2]

Much of the meaning of our statements is guided by what are called regulative rules. Suppose you heard the words "That was a great idea." At face value the statement is one of praise for your idea. Yet, depending on the context in which it was uttered, the purpose of the speaker, and the relationship between you and the speaker, that simple utterance could have several meanings. For instance, a man might make the statement to a woman not just to praise her thinking process but to help him develop a better relationship with her. Or a friend might make the statement in a sarcastic tone to suggest that it was a rotten idea and both you and your friend know it. Or a teacher might make the statement to a third-grade student to encourage that student to make other statements. Thus, in verbal communication, for a response to be appropriate, a person must be sensitive to both potential and actual meanings. Throughout this book we are concerned with pragmatic issues.

Semantics

Semantics is the study of linguistic meaning. Semantics seeks to explain, for example, how two sentences may have the same meaning even though they use different words. Although semantics is a broad field that covers many areas, we will concentrate on meanings derived from the use of words. A critical question for students of interpersonal communication, one that scholars of semantics cannot agree on how to answer, is "Do words mean or do people mean?"

In this book we will help you develop skills that will aid your effectiveness of communication regardless of the answer to this question. On the one hand, we advocate the need to build a good vocabulary, because speakers of a language must learn conventional meanings for words if they are going to use words in such ways that they will be understood by others in that language community. It does us very little good to learn that *terse* means "short" and "abrupt" if, when we see it in a sentence, we are told that the writer meant "wordy"! In this sense skillfulness of communication based on building a vocabulary suggests that words have meaning. On the other hand, many words have multiple meanings, and even some words with specific meanings may not be correct in given contexts. So, when we talk about semantic meaning, we are referring to how two people arrive at shared meanings through the ways words are used. Many of the skills we present throughout this book are designed to aid you in using language effectively to share the meanings you wish to convey.

Several specific aspects of semantics can help to explain the relationship between language and meaning.

The Arbitrary Nature of Language Symbols. The meaning given to a word is a matter of choice. Whether the word is *chair, sister,* or *predilectory,* we know that someone at some time had to choose to use those letters (sounds) in that order for the first time. But, even though someone chose to use "sister," for example, to convey the idea of a female sibling, the use of the word *sister* as a generally accepted symbol with some specific meaning wasn't possible until others agreed to use that word when they wanted to express the idea of a female sibling.

Frequently, people form new words using certain sound patterns to stand for meaning; the word does not become a part of the language until other people have used it often enough that it develops some shared meaning. For instance, *zit,* slang for "skin blemish," became part of the language in the early sixties; *disk drive,* meaning "a device that enables data to be read from or written on a magnetic disk pack or floppy disk," became part of the language in the early seventies.

The Learning of Language. Each new generation must learn the language anew. Children's brains enable them to think, and they have a vocal mechanism that allows them to form any number of sounds. By the time children are between three and five years old, they have learned enough vocabulary to communicate almost all their basic ideas and feelings and have mastered enough grammar to be understood. From then on, they enlarge their vocabulary and sharpen their understanding of grammar. But how to determine which sounds go together to form which words must be taught from generation to generation.

How do people learn? Blaine Goss lists four principles that guide language learning.[3] First, development proceeds from simple to complex. Thus, one-syllable words that denote familiar objects and people are likely to be learned first.

Second, language acquisition is overgeneralized. Notice how children will say "I *goed* (rather than *went)* to the store." They hear *play/played* or *walk/walked* and so they generalize that all verbs become past tense by adding *-ed.* Later in the learning process they learn to differentiate verbs that do not follow this rule.

Third, our listening capabilities exceed our speaking capabilities. We all understand more than we can verbalize—our reading vocabulary, for instance, is much larger than our speaking vocabulary. This principle of language learning is at the heart of the teaching philosophy expressed in this book. You may already *know* many of the skills we will discuss, but you are likely to find that you do not *use* them very well or, in some cases, that you do not use them at all.

Fourth, people pay attention to the nonverbal as well as the verbal aspects of communication. In this chapter we emphasize the verbal aspect of meaning; in subsequent chapters, as we discuss various communication skills, we will stress both language and the tone of voice, gestures, and facial expressions that accompany the words.

The fact that meanings are learned implies that people do not learn exactly the same meanings for words, nor do they learn exactly the same words. You must never assume, therefore, that another person will know what you are talking about just because you have used the "right" word.

The Creative Nature of Language. When you speak, you use language to create new sentences that represent ideas you are thinking about or feelings you are experiencing. Although you may, on occasion, repeat other people's constructions to represent what you are thinking or feeling, most of your speech differs significantly from anyone else's. Language creativity is especially noticeable in children's usage. When children don't know the common designation for a thought, they create one out of the context. For instance, children may refer to restaurants as "meal stores" or sirens as "scary whistles." But all of us create different ways of expressing shared experiences. To test this out, have three people who witnessed the same event describe what they saw. Although there will be many similarities, each description will reflect unique, creative approaches to the details.

The Interrelationship of Language and Perception. Clearly, perception affects language. If we encounter a situation that no word in our vocabulary can describe, we are likely either to form a new word or to use an old word in a new way to describe it. Likewise, if we see an object that is different from any other known object, we choose a new word to label it.

That the words in our language shape our perceptions is more controversial. The idea that language shapes perception was developed by Benjamin Lee Whorf with contributions from Edward Sapir.[4] In the early 1950s Whorf presented what is now called the Sapir-Whorf Hypothesis, which suggested that your perception of reality is determined by the language system that controls your thought system. For instance, Eskimos have a wide variety of words for different kinds of snow, such as *gana* (falling snow) and *akilukak* (fluffy fallen snow), whereas in English we say simply *snow*. We can add modifiers, such as fallen, fluffy, or hard-packed, but in each case the word *snow* is included. The Sapir-Whorf Hypothesis asserts that, when confronted with many different samples of frozen moisture, the typical American will perceive all the different sizes, shapes, and

According to the Sapir-Whorf Hypothesis, your perceptions are determined by the language you use. Some languages express the concept of "dry cleaning" more clearly than do others, which may lack such a term. Be aware that your words and notions may mean something else to a person from another culture. Chevrolet created cross-cultural misunderstanding on a large scale when it marketed its Nova model in Latin America. Sales were terrible because Chevrolet didn't realize that *no va* means "no go" in Spanish.

densities as *snow*. Eskimos, on the other hand, perceive snow in many different ways because they have the language flexibility to do so.

The Sapir-Whorf Hypothesis allows us to see how different people from different places will *think* differently and *communicate* differently because of differences in both language and perception. Although you are not likely to be communicating much with Eskimos unless you live in Alaska, a lot of your communicating does cross cultural and socioeconomic boundaries. As a result, you must not assume either that the words you use will mean the same thing to others as they mean to you or that you will see the same realities that others see.

PRACTICE in Creating New Words

In Pairs

Each person in class should create a new word to express a meaning. The word should be written on the front of a 3 × 5 card. On the opposite side of the card write a dictionary-type definition of the word and one sentence from which the meaning of the word might be deduced.

At the beginning of class each person should submit the notecard to the instructor, who will shuffle the cards and give one card to each student. Study carefully the card you receive.

Divide into pairs. You and your partner should have a five-minute conversation during which each of you must use your new word. You may *not* tell your partner what your word means, but you may use it more than once in order to help your partner understand it. At the end of the five minutes each person should write a definition of the new word their partner used.

How many people were able to learn the definition of the new word through the conversation? What factors affected your success or failure in learning the meaning of the word?

Complications in Word Usage

Science fiction writers have worked for years on the premise that advanced societies will develop some form of telepathy so that a person will be able to share meanings directly with another. But until such a time, we must share our ideas and feelings indirectly through an often imperfect system of symbols—through words. Because words carry both denotative and connotative meanings, you need to be able to distinguish between them and understand the complications related to each.

Denotation

Denotation is the direct, explicit meaning or reference of a word; in short, denotations are dictionary meanings. Although knowing dictionary definitions facilitates effective interpersonal communication, even with a dictionary at hand communication effectiveness cannot be guaranteed. Why? Let's examine a few of the problems associated with the denotative meanings of words.

Dictionary Differences. Very few words are defined exactly the same way in each of the most popular American dictionaries. And even though most of the differences are minor ones, they illustrate the problems we face when we rely on them for meaning. Take the word *dog. Webster's New World Dictionary* defines a dog as "any of a large and varied group of domesticated animals related to the fox, wolf, and jackal."[5] *Webster's New Collegiate Dictionary* (published by another company even though the word *Webster's* is in both titles) defines a dog as "a carnivorous domesticated mammal, type of the family *Canidae.*"[6] Which definition is better?

Why do such differences occur? Most dictionaries are compiled in the same way: Companies survey printed materials to see how people use words. Then, based upon these surveys, someone writes a definition. Depending upon *what* printed materials are surveyed and *who* writes the definition, some definitional differences will occur. In this case both definitions of *dog* classify and differentiate. Nevertheless, if the only knowledge you had about a dog was from these two dictionary definitions, you might be confused about what a dog actually was.

Multiple Meanings. Even more confusing is the fact that a great many words we use daily have more than one distinct meaning. If we looked up the 500 most commonly used American words in any dictionary, we'd be likely to find more than 14,000 definitions! Some of the many definitions for a given word would be similar to one another, but others would be quite different. The word *low* is a good example of the problems that result from multiple meanings. You probably think you know what is meant by the word *low. Webster's New World Dictionary* offers the following twenty-six meanings for *low*:[7]

1. Of little height or elevation

2. Depressed below the surrounding surface of normal elevation

3. Of little depth; shallow

4. Of little quantity, degree, intensity, value

5. Of less than normal height

6. Below others in order, position, rating

7. Near the horizon—the sun was low

8. Near the equator

9. Cut so as to expose the neck or part of the shoulders, chest or back

10. Prostrate or dead—in hiding or obscurity

11. Deep; profound

12. Lacking energy; enfeebled; weak

13. Depressed in spirits; melancholy

14. Not of high rank; humble; plebeian

15. Vulgar; coarse; debased; undignified

16. Mean; despicable; contemptible

17. Poor; slight; unfavorable

18. Containing less than a normal amount of some usual element

19. Not advanced in evolution, development, complexity; inferior

20. Relatively recent

21. Designating or of that gear ratio of a motor vehicle transmission which produces the lowest speed and the greatest power

22. Not well supplied with; short of—not having any or much money; short of ready cash

23. Of little intensity; not loud

24. Designating or producing tones made by relatively slow vibrations; deep in pitch

25. Very informal and permissive in matters of ceremony, doctrine, etc.

26. Phonet. Produced with the tongue held relatively low in the mouth

When a person says, "I'm low," without other cues you may not know what the person means. Forgetting this simple fact may lead to misunderstandings—little and big—that can result in minor embarrassment, career problems, or even loss of friendship.

Less common words have fewer meanings. Ironically, then, our most common words usually get us into the most trouble. These common words have so many different meanings that unless we provide additional cues, the listener may get the wrong idea. Yet, if a person uses a less common though more precise word, the listener may not be familiar with it.

Changes in Meanings. Over time, words both acquire and lose meanings. According to W. Nelson Francis, in the 700 years the word *nice* has been in the English language, it "has been used at one time or another to mean the following: foolish, wanton, strange, lazy, coy, modest, fastidious, refined, precise, subtle, slender, critical, attentive, minute, accurate, dainty, appetizing, agreeable."[8]

If you think about it, you can probably come up with some words that have changed their meaning over a relatively short period of time. Communication is most affected when these changes are quick and/or dramatic. Take the word *gay*, for instance. In the fities and sixties people spoke of having a "gay old time," of Jack being a "gay blade," and the state of "being gay" as being happy. In each case *gay* meant joyous, merry, happy, or bright. Today having a "gay time," being a "gay blade," and the state of "being gay" are most likely to refer to a person's sexual preference. Although *gay* meaning joyous is still heard sometimes, it is becoming obsolete. If you describe another person as "gay" and you mean happy or joyous, you will probably be totally misunderstood.

The Influence of Context. The position of a word in a sentence and the total meaning derived from this word in conjunction with other words around it may change the denotative meaning of the word. When a young girl says, "Dad, you owe me a dime," the meaning is somewhat different from when she says, "Dad, I need a dime for the machine." In the first case she is looking for either two nickels, ten pennies, five pennies and a nickel, or a single ten-cent piece; in the second case she is looking specifically for a dime.

Examples of the influence of context abound. Think of the difference between "George plays a really *mean* drum" and "The way George talked to Sally was downright *mean*."

Connotation

Whereas denotation refers to the standard dictionary meaning given to a word, *connotation* refers to the feelings or evaluations associated with a word. For example, earlier we stated that the word *dog* denotes a domesticated animal. But for you the real meaning of *dog* likely depends on your experiences with dogs. Suppose that as a child you had a dog that was a constant companion, that slept with you at night, greeted you when you came home from school, lay at your feet as you watched television, and wagged its tail at the sight of you. The connotations of the word *dog* would be far different for you than for a person who had never had a dog for a pet, had been bitten six times by dogs for "no reason," and who was allergic to dog hair.

So, when Carl says to Paul, "I'm buying a dog this week," Carl must understand that his sentence denotes the purchase of a domesticated mammal—a denotation that Paul is likely to share. But it also carries a connotation that will be shared only if Carl and Paul have had similar experiences with dogs and, as a result, feel much the same way about them. In short, the meaning when Carl says *dog* may be different from the meaning when Paul says *dog*, because Carl and Paul are likely to have different connotations for *dog*. Thus, Carl ought not be surprised if Paul's response is "Why did you want to do *that?*"

Semantic Differentiation. Because people's feelings about words do vary considerably, scientists have been trying to find ways of measuring the nature and intensity of those feelings. Let us briefly describe one method that has gained popularity among psychologists and communication specialists. Charles Osgood and his associates developed an approach to word connotation that focuses on dimensions of meaning, or *semantic differentiation*. Each dimension of meaning is a part of the total feeling a person has about a word. The method used by Osgood involves describing feelings about words through *bipolar adjectives* (adjectives that are the opposite of each other).[9]

Why did Osgood and his associates focus their study on adjectives? If you list the responses that come to mind when someone says words like *dog, camp,* or *home,* you will see that many, if not all, of the words you use are adjectives. You may think of *dog, camp,* or *home* in terms of pleasant or unpleasant, big or small, happy or sad, attractive or unattractive.

As they studied the various responses, Osgood and his associates grouped them in identifiable categories called *dimensions.* Of the dimensions, the three most common are adjectives of evaluation, adjectives of potency or intensity, and adjectives of activity or movement. Thus, good-bad, awful-nice, ugly-beautiful, and valuable-worthless are pairs that can be used to measure the *evaluation dimension;* strong-weak, light-heavy, and large-small can be used to measure the *potency dimension;* and hot-cold, active-passive, and fast-slow can be used to measure the *activity dimension.* The end result of their word was a Semantic Differential Test that can be administered to groups and individuals alike.[10] A test based only on the ten pairs of adjectives just cited can be used to evaluate how one person or group feels in comparison to another person or group in terms of a specific word like *dog, camp,* or *home.*

The value of such a test is that it allows us to compare one person's feelings about a word with another's. For example, is one person's feeling about the word *home* more or less positive? Stronger or weaker? More or less active? Second, it enables us to compare a person's reactions to several different words. Does the person see *home* differently from *resort, farm, camp,* or *trailer?* Third, it permits us to compare a person's feelings about a word at different times. Does a person feel differently about *camp* after spending six weeks at one?

What is the value of this kind of knowledge to you in your verbal communication? If you know how others feel about the words they use, you can better understand and communicate with them. Consider a schoolteacher who wants to develop a teaching unit on the theme "A community is a group of people who help one another." The teacher would benefit from discovering how the class feels about such words as *community, home, police,* and *businessperson* before beginning the unit. Or consider the value of the semantic differential to the congresswoman who would like to know how the people in her district feel about words like *abortion, nuclear weapons,* and *taxes* before she begins preparing her campaign speeches.

PRACTICE in Denotation and Connotation

By Yourself

1. Make a list of current slang or "in" words. How do the meanings you assign to these words differ from the meanings your parents or grandparents assign?

2. Write your own definition of each of the following words, then go to a dictionary and check to see how closely your definition matches the dictionary's.

    glass   ring
    building   love
    freedom   justice
    peace   success

In Groups

Working with others in groups, select several common words like *home* and *dog*. Each person should list at least five adjectives that he or she associates with the word. When you have finished, compare the results. In what ways are your meanings different?

Interpersonal Language Skills

While nearly every skill discussed in the remainder of this text helps you develop effective communication habits, in this section we present skills that deal with language itself.

Clarity in Language

Clarity is tremendously important to effective interpersonal communication. Unclear language gives a listener so much possible meaning to choose from that shared meaning may be impossible; furthermore, unclear language runs the risk of frustrating the listener and conveying emotional reactions that are not intended.

Clarity in interpersonal communication is achieved through three skills: selecting the most precise word; selecting the most specific/concrete word; and selecting the most appropriate word. Let's first discuss what is meant by precision, specificity/concreteness, and appropriateness, and then let's see how you can improve these skills.

Precision. For any idea or feeling you wish to communicate, you have many words from which to choose. *Precision* in word selection means choosing words that are recognized by others in our culture as symbolizing certain thoughts and feelings. Because meaning is affected by various aspects of denotation and connotation, you can never be completely sure that your use of a word will create a meaning in the minds of others that is the exact meaning you intend. But the less precise your word choices, the greater the potential for confusion. Suppose that in order to catch the bus for work this morning, you had to move as fast as you could

These Vietnamese refugees have just arrived in California. Although they know some French and English, they can express themselves most clearly through their native tongue. Clarity in interpersonal communication means using the most precise, concrete, and appropriate words. As these young men expand their English vocabularies, they'll encounter an extraordinarily rich variety of words borrowed from many languages.

from your home to the bus stop. If, in a conversation later in the morning, you told a friend, "I had to amble to the corner to catch the bus," your friend would probably have an incorrect mental picture of your movement. Why? Because the word *amble* means a leisurely walk. Had you said to your friend, "I had to run as fast as I could," or "I had to sprint all the way," the meaning conveyed would be more precise.

The problem of precision is multiplied by the shades of meaning that many words carry. Take the simple verb *said*. Notice the changes in meaning when a person substitutes another word such as *stated, averred, growled, indicated, intoned, suggested, pleaded, shouted, purred, answered,* or *asked*. Effective communication requires an understanding of words— not only what they mean in general but also how they relate to one another.

Specificity/Concreteness. Precise words are those that give the best or most correct image; *specific* and *concrete words* focus that image—they indicate a single item within a category or a single representation of an abstract concept or value. In a conversation you may feel pressured to use words that are more general and abstract than they should be, thereby forcing the listener to choose from many possible images rather than conveying the single intended image. The more listeners are called upon to provide their own images, the more they will see meanings different from what you intended. *General* means an entire category; *specific* means one item within a category. When someone says "car" to you, you may see any number of four-wheeled vehicles used primarily to transport people: a large car or a small one, a two-door or a four-door, a sedan or a hatchback, and so on. If, on the other hand, someone says a "sedan," the number of possible images you can picture is reduced. If the person says "new, red, two-door sedan," you and the person doing the talking are far more likely to be picturing the same image.

Whereas the terms *general* and *specific* refer to objects you can see, *abstract* and *concrete* refer to ideas or values. Concrete language turns an abstract idea or value into clearly pictured behavior. When people say they are "loyal," for instance, you may think of the dictionary definition of faithful to an idea, person, company, and so on. The meaning of *loyal* in a particular situation, however, is difficult to pinpoint. What is an act of loyalty to Jim or to Sarah may not be an act of loyalty to you. To avoid ambiguity and confusion, a person might say, "Bill is very loyal to his company, he always buys his company's products." On hearing such a statement, you would have a better idea of what the speaker meant by loyalty. Why? Because the speaker has expressed the abstract concept of loyalty in terms of a concrete, observable action.

Semanticists speak of levels of abstraction. In many instances you can take an idea from a general, abstract level and move it to a specific concrete level through a series of words. For example, in talking about cars, we could write down a sequence that moved from the general term *vehicle*, to *motor vehicles*, to *passenger cars*, and so on, as shown in Figure 3.1.

Appropriateness. Words are *appropriate* when they are adapted to the people with whom you are talking and to the context of the conversation. You

Figure 3.1 Levels of abstraction.

Vehicles

Motor vehicles

Passenger cars

Ford passenger cars

Ford Escorts

Red, two-door Ford Escort sedan

should, of course, be reasonably certain that the listener will know the meaning of words you use. Moreover, you must be sure that a word does not have a potential for a strong connotation that will color the meaning. For instance, if you say the pigs picked you up last night for speeding, the people you are talking with will probably know that *pigs* is slang for *police*. The problem is that *pigs* has many connotations, nearly all of which will so color the thinking of the listener that, unless you were trying both to use the most abusive word possible and to create a strong feeling, *pig* would surely be an unfortunate word choice.

In selecting appropriate words you must also be aware of double meanings, because much of our metaphoric language carries the potential for two opposite connotations. For instance, if, in referring to Alice's work habits, you say, "Alice is a real workhorse," some people may think you are referring to Alice's appearance. You will also convey a double meaning if what you say differs from how you say it. When you say "Ouch!" you are likely to have a pained expression on your face and a pained sound in your voice. But verbal and nonverbal messages are not always complementary. For example, a person may answer the question, "Do you still love me?" with the words, "Of course I do," but nonverbal signals may contradict the words. In this situation the listener will tend to pay more attention to the nonverbal cue than to the words. Why? Because words can be controlled much more easily than can facial expression or tone of voice. We'll explore ways nonverbal cues affect meaning in the next chapter.

"What seems to be the problem, officer?" Although this driver may feel like swearing, he chooses to use respectful language appropriate to this situation's context. He knows that "Yes, sir" is suitable here; aggravating a confrontation is not in his best interest.

Developing Clarity in Speaking

Developing precision, specificity/concreteness, and appropriateness involves two specific skills: vocabulary building and structured brainstorming.

Vocabulary Building. How clearly you speak, and therefore how well you will be understood, depends on your vocabulary. In general, the smaller your vocabulary, the greater the potential difficulty in communicating effectively. As a speaker a meager vocabulary gives you fewer choices from which to select the word you want; as a listener you are limited in your ability to understand the words used. Thus, the better your vocabulary, the more accurate your communication is likely to be. Although precise wording does not ensure effective communication (the person to whom you are speaking may not have a mastery of a particular word, or other contextual factors may interfere), you are more likely to communicate effectively if your choice is precise.

One way to increase your vocabulary is to use a basic vocabulary book such as *Test Your Word Power* by Jerome Agel.[11] Or you could complete the "Word Power" feature in *The Reader's Digest* magazine. By completing this monthly quiz and learning the words with which you are not familiar, you might increase your vocabulary by as many as twenty words per month.

A second way to increase your vocabulary is to take a more active role in working with the words you read and hear every day. You can begin by noting words that people use in their conversations with you that you are *not* able to define precisely. For instance, suppose Jack says, "I was *inundated* with phone calls today!" If you can't define *inundated*, you could ask Jack what he meant. Or, you could make a note of the word, look up its meaning at the first opportunity, and then go back over what Jack said to see whether the dictionary meaning matched Jack's statement. Most dictionaries define *inundated* with synonyms like *overwhelmed* or *flooded*. So if you then say to yourself, "Jack was inundated—overwhelmed or flooded—with phone calls today," you will tend to remember that meaning and apply it the next time you hear the word. You can follow the same procedure in your reading. As you are reading today's assignment in one of your courses, circle any words whose meanings you are unsure of, and, after you have finished the assignment, look them up. Most people are confronted with several words each day for which they are unable to supply a precise meaning. By following the practice of noting those words and then looking them up, you can increase your vocabulary.

Structured Brainstorming. Developing clarity in speaking also requires conscious use of structured brainstorming during practice sessions. *Brainstorming* is an uncritical, nonevaluative process of generating ideas, much like the old word-association process. Thus, when you are trying to think of more precise, more specific/concrete, or more appropriate words for *music*, you might brainstorm "rock," "punk," or "new wave."

You can increase your clarity in the following way:

1. Begin a practice session talking about how your day went, what you did in class, or some similar idea.

2. As you talk, quickly assess whether a word or phrase you used is less precise, specific/concrete, or appropriate than it should be.

3. Pause to mentally brainstorm alternative choices.

4. Select the more precise, specific/concrete, or appropriate word.

For example, if you were talking about registration, you might say, "Pre-registration is such a drag." At that point stop. What words would be better than *drag? Pain? Frustrating experience?* Then restate the sentence: "Preregistration is such a frustrating experience." Or suppose you were talking about a game. You might say, "The play was really lousy." Stop. What words would be better than *play? Offense? Defense? Shooting? Passing?* Then restate the sentence: "The passing was really lousy."

Improvement with language skills requires hard work, and the brainstorming process should only be done consciously in practice, at least initially. As you gain skill with the process, you may find that you are able to make such adjustments in your normal conversation. For instance, in your conversation you might state ideas in the following ways:

"I think that many of Mark's statements are very [split-second pause while thinking: I want the word that means know-it-all] dogmatic."

"Well, she was driving one of these vans—no, I'm sorry, I don't mean van. She was driving one of those extra-large station wagons."

"Mike, would you please bring up all my stuff—that is, would you please bring my briefcase and the books I brought home?"

"I think Dr. Carson is a good person to take a course from because she is fair—she treats everyone as equals."

Precise, specific, concrete and appropriate language will go a long way toward sharpening ideas presented. Now let's look at two skills that qualify information in ways that will add another dimension to clarity.

Dating Generalizations

Dating generalizations means including in your statements a specific time referent that indicates when a given fact was true. You draw conclusions based on information. If the information is accurate, the conclusions drawn from that information are likely to be accurate. When people share information, they often give the impression that the information they are providing is current when in fact it may be outdated. For instance, Parker says, "I'm going to be transferred to Henderson City." Bill replies, "Good luck—they've had some real trouble with their schools." On the basis of Bill's statement Parker may worry about the effect this move will have on his children. What he doesn't know is that Bill's information about this problem in Henderson City is *five years old!* Henderson City still may have problems, but then, it may not. Had Bill replied, "Five years ago I know they had some real trouble with their schools. I'm not sure what the situation is now, but you may want to check" Parker would look at the information differently.

The fact is that nearly everything changes with time. Some changes are imperceptible, others are so extensive as to make old information about the person, idea, or thing inaccurate, obsolete, and even dangerous. Dating generalizations enables you to increase the accuracy of your verbal statements through a simple, two-step process:

1. Before you provide information about an object, a person, or a place, consider when you knew this information to be true and whether it is still likely to be true.

2. If your statement is not based on current information, be sure to include in your statement a reference to when you knew the information was valid.

Consider each of the following examples, in which the speaker dates each generalization:

"When we were in Palm Springs *two years ago*, it was really popular with the college crowd."

"Professor Powell brings great enthusiasm to her teaching—at least she did *last quarter* in communication theory."

"*Four years ago* the Beast was considered the most exciting roller coaster in the country."

"You think Mary's depressed? I'm surprised. She seemed her regular high-spirited self when I talked with her *the day before yesterday*."

You have no power to prevent change. Yet you can increase the effectiveness of your messages through verbally acknowledging the reality of change if you date the statements you make.

Indexing Generalizations

Indexing is a companion skill to dating. Through dating you acknowledge differences caused by the passing of time; *indexing generalizations* allows you to acknowledge the innate differences among groups of people, objects, or places. *Indexing* is the mental or verbal practice of accounting for individual differences that guards against the tendency to make unwarranted generalizations.

Generalizing allows people to use what they have learned from one experience and apply it to another. So, when Glenda learns that tomatoes and squash grow better if the ground is fertilized, she reasons that fertilizing will help all her vegetables to grow better. Likewise, when Sam notices that his girlfriend seems to enjoy the fragrance of the new aftershave he is wearing, he is likely to wear it again when they are together. Glenda and Sam have used what they learned from one experience and applied it to another—they have generalized.

Misuse of generalization can cause at least two serious communication problems. First, you may take the characteristics of a group of people (or objects) and assign them to all the individual members within that group *without exception*. For instance, just because *men* have greater strength in general than do *women* does not mean that Max (one man) is stronger than Barbara (one woman). Likewise, just because a university is ranked among the top twenty in the nation does not mean that every department in that university is so ranked.

Second, you may transfer a characteristic of one person (or object) to another person (or object) just because that other person (or object) is within the same group. For instance, just because Jack, a German, is industrious does not mean either that all Germans are industrious or that Don, who is also German, is industrious. Similarly, just because one Chevrolet goes 50,000 miles without needing a brake job does not mean that all Chevrolets can.

Now that we've considered the need to account for individual differences, let's see how the skill of indexing is used. Technically, indexing calls for you to acknowledge differences by mentally assigning numbers to each member of a class. So in the class of men you have man_1, man_2, man_3, and so forth; in the class of Chevrolets you have $Chevrolet_1$, $Chevrolet_2$, $Chevrolet_3$, and so forth. Of course, in real life people don't index by number. The process of indexing actual statements goes as follows:

1. Before you make a statement about an object, person, or place, consider whether your statement is about that specific object, person, or place or whether it is a generalization about a class to which the object, person, or place belongs.

2. If your statement is a generalization, inform your listener that it is not necessarily accurate.

To illustrate the process of indexing, in each of the following cases we'll make a statement that involves generalization; then we'll make a similar statement that is properly indexed.

Generalization: Because men are stronger than women, Max is stronger than Barbara.
Indexed: In general men are stronger than women, so Max *is probably* stronger than Barbara.

Generalization: State's got to have a good economics department; the university is ranked among the top twenty in the nation.
Indexed: Because State's among the top twenty schools in the nation, the economics department should be a good one, *even though there's the possibility that it may not be.*

Generalization: Jack is sure to be outgoing; Don is, and they're both Joneses.
Indexed: Jack is likely to be outgoing because his brother Don is (they're both Joneses), *but Jack could be different.*

Generalization: Your Chevrolet should go 50,000 miles before you need a brake job; Jerry's did.
Indexed: Your Chevrolet may well go 50,000 miles before you need a brake job; Jerry's did, *but of course, all Chevrolets aren't the same.*

All people generalize at one time or another, but by indexing your statements you can avoid the problems that hasty generalization sometimes creates.

The Effect of Pressure on Language Use

When you are relaxed and confident, your word choice usually flows smoothly and is likely to be most effective. When you are under pressure, however, your ability to select the best symbols to convey your thoughts is likely to deteriorate. For example, in a large family you may have heard harried parents verbally list all their children's names before finally calling the child they want by the right name.

Your brain, like a computer, is a marvelous storage and retrieval system, but like a computer, it functions better under certain conditions. More often than not, your brain fails when you are under pressure or when you speak before you think. People sometimes think one thing and say something entirely different. For example, a math professor might say, "We all remember that the numerator is on the bottom and the denominator is on the top of the fraction, so when we divide fractions—" "Professor," a voice from the third row interrupts, "You said the numerator is on the bottom and—" "Is that what I said?" the professor replies. "Well, you know what I meant!" Did everyone in the class know? Maybe not.

PRACTICE in Language Skills

By Yourself

1. For each word listed, try to find three words or phrases that are more specific or more concrete.

   happiness   education   clothes

   colors   chair   bad

   implements   stuff   things

2. Make the following statements clearer by using one or more of the skills of being precise, being more specific/concrete, being more appropriate, dating, or indexing.

"You know I love basketball. Well, I'm practicing a lot because I want to get better."

"Paula, I'm really bummed out. Everything is going down the tubes. You know what I mean?"

"Well, she just does these things to tick me off. Like, just a whole lot of stuff—and she knows it!"

"I just bought me a beautiful outfit—I mean, it is really in style. You'll love it."

"I've really got to remember to bring my things the next time I visit."

In Groups

Have two members of the group discuss a topic from the ones listed here. The rest of the group should observe when dating and indexing are used, how well they are being used, and when they should have been used. Each person in the group should have an opportunity to practice.

cars	equal opportunity laws
food preferences	college course requirements
job interviewers	wedding rituals
politicians	minority groups in college

Summary

Language is a system of symbols used for communicating. Through language we designate and define, evaluate, talk about things outside our immediate experience, and talk about language.

The domains of language include syntax—the study of the architecture of phrases, clauses, and sentences; pragmatics—the study of how language is used to communicate; and semantics—the study of linguistic meaning.

You will be an effective communicator if you recognize that language symbols are arbitrary, that language is learned and is creative, and that language and perception are interrelated.

The denotation of a word is its dictionary meaning. Despite the ease with which we can check a dictionary meaning, word denotation can still present problems. Why? Because most words have more than one dictionary meaning, changes in meanings occur faster than dictionaries are revised, words take on different meanings as they are used in different contexts, and meanings can become obscured as words become more abstract.

The connotation of a word is the emotional and value significance the word arouses. Regardless of how a dictionary defines a word, we carry with us meanings that stem from our experience with the object, thought, or action the word represents. Connotations can be quantified and tested by comparing scores achieved on a Semantic Differential Test.

You can improve your use of language by selecting the most precise, the most specific/concrete, and the most appropriate word possible and by dating and indexing generalizations.

Notes

1. Frank Parker, *Linguistics for Non-Linguists* (Boston: Little, Brown, 1986), p. 11.

2. J. R. Searle, "The Classification of Illocutionary Acts," *Language in Society* 5 (1976), 1–24.

3. Blaine Goss, *Processing Communication* (Belmont, Calif.: Wadsworth, 1982), pp. 60–61.

4. B. L. Whorf, *Collected Papers on Metalinguistics* (Washington D.C.: Department of State, Foreign Service Institute, 1952).

5. *Webster's New World Dictionary,* Second College Edition (Cleveland, Ohio: William Collins & World Publishing Co., 1978), p. 414. Copyright © 1978 by William Collins & World Publishing Co., Inc. Used with permission.

6. *Webster's New Collegiate Dictionary* (Springfield, Mass.: G. C. Merriam Co., 1979), p. 334.

7. *Webster's New World Dictionary,* Second College Edition, p. 839. Copyright © 1978 by William Collins & World Publishing Co., Inc. Used with permission.

8. W. Nelson Francis, *The English Language* (New York: W. W. Norton, 1965), p. 122.

9. Charles E. Osgood, George J. Suci, and Percy H. Tannenbaum, *The Measurement of Meaning* (Urbana, Ill.: University of Illinois Press, 1957).

10. Ibid., pp. 36–38.

11. Jerome B. Agel, *Test Your Word Power* (New York: Ballantine, 1984).

Chapter 4

Nonverbal Communication

Objectives

After you have read this chapter, you should be able
to define and/or explain:

Contrasts between verbal and
nonverbal communication

The four most important functions of nonverbal
communication

The use of emblems, illustrators, affect displays, regulators, and adaptors to
communicate

Paralanguage and its major
elements

How your clothing, touching
behavior, and use of time
affect self-presentation

How use of space
communicates

The ways color, temperature,
and lighting affect
communication

Helen moves forward smoothly on the tennis court to take the high, easy bounce and put the ball away. Instead of the super shot she anticipates, she hits the ball into the net. She groans and throws her racket on the ground in disgust.

As he picks up his fifth card in the hand of draw poker, George breaks into a wide smile. Quickly, he looks around the table to see whether anyone caught the smile, and then he resumes his "poker face."

"No doubt about it, Maggie, you were terrific," Susan says with a sarcastic sneer in her voice.

"Allison, listen," Jack said in a soft but firm tone of voice. Riveting his eyes on hers, he continued, "I need your support on this. If you will stay with me, I know you'll see some things happening that you're really going to like."

In each of the preceding examples the people use nonverbal messages as their primary means of communication. Although nonverbal communication usually accompanies verbal communication, we discuss it separately in order to stress the unique features of the nonverbal code.

We have all heard—and said—that actions speak louder than words. Actions, or nonverbal communication elements, are so important to our communication process that researchers have estimated that in face-to-face communication as much as 90 percent of the social meaning may be carried in the nonverbal message.[1] Moreover, how we are perceived as a communicator is based in part on our ability to use nonverbal skills appropriately. Yet using and interpreting nonverbal cues effectively is not always easy, even though we do it instinctively. Most of what we know about nonverbal usage and understanding stems from social, cultural, and environmental factors—a result of what you might call "doing what comes naturally." Yet, what is "natural" may be neither effective nor appropriate. In this chapter we provide you with a framework for analysis of nonverbal communication. Throughout the chapter we emphasize both developing an understanding of the nonverbal code and learning to manage nonverbal elements to communicate effectively. We begin by studying the nature of nonverbal communication and the way verbal and nonverbal communication interrelate. We then look at the major elements of nonverbal communication.

The Nature of Nonverbal Communication

Nonverbal communication may cover any aspect of communication that is not purely verbal. More precisely, nonverbal communication can be viewed from two different perspectives. From one perspective nonverbal communication refers to people's actions or attributes *other than words*. In keeping with this perspective J. Burgoon and T. Saine define nonverbal communication as "those attributes or actions of humans, other than the use of words themselves, which have socially shared meaning, are intentionally sent or interpreted as intentional, are consciously sent or consciously received, and have the potential for feedback from the receiver."[2]

From another perspective, however, nonverbal communication also refers to elements that neither come from nor are part of people but that communicate through people's use of them. Thus, such artifacts as clothes and such environmental factors as furniture, lighting, temperature, and color also fall within the province of nonverbal communication. Later in this chapter we will examine elements drawn both from human attributes and actions and from various artifacts and environmental elements to see how they relate to the communication process.

Nonverbal/Verbal Contrasts

Because we are inclined to think of nonverbal communication as it differs from verbal, perhaps the best way to discuss the nature of nonverbal communication is in a series of contrasts.

1. *Nonverbal communication is more ambiguous.* The ambiguous nature of nonverbal communication cues results from their being either intentional or unintentional. For example, a person who smiles may intend to communicate a sense of friendliness, so when a receiver interprets that smile in that way, we say that communication has taken place. But that person's smile may in fact have no communication intent—the person may have had a random thought about something that happened earlier in the day that causes him to smile at a time when the people around him are talking about nuclear destruction. Those people may try to interpret the smile and attribute some meaning to it, but in the communication context it may be meaningless.

2. *Nonverbal communication is continuous.* Whereas verbal symbols begin only when sound comes from the mouth and end when that sound stops, nonverbal communication continues for as long as a person is in your presence.

3. *Nonverbal communication is multichanneled.* Verbal symbols—words—come to us one at a time, in sequence; we hear the spoken words, see the printed or written words. Nonverbal cues, however, may be seen, heard, felt, smelled, and/or tasted—and several of these cues may occur simultaneously. For instance, when you say the word *please*, it occurs in a context of nonverbal cues that include tone of voice, facial expression, hand movement, and possibly touch. We communicate nonverbally more than most of us realize.

4. *Nonverbal communication is the more trusted form when verbal and nonverbal messages seem to be in conflict.* Because verbal communication can be constructed purposefully to deceive, people place more stock in nonverbal cues. Although nonverbal communication cues can be masked, most of them are spontaneous and thus perceived as more revealing. Recall that as much as 90 percent of social meaning may be carried by nonverbal cues.

5. *Nonverbal communication gives more insight into emotional states.* Whereas people vary widely in their verbal descriptions of how they are feeling, their nonverbal messages likely will accurately reflect their true feelings. For instance, when you stub your toe, your body will show some nonverbal sign of pain. When something strikes you as funny, you may smile slightly or laugh loudly, depending on how funny it really is. When you are sad, the corner of your mouth may twitch or your eyes might fill with tears.

6. *Many types of nonverbal communication are recognized across cultures.* Even though verbal languages differ so much that people are unable to understand those from another country, those people may well be able to communicate in nonverbal signs. For instance, nodding and shaking the head, pointing, smiling, and frowning are but a few of the nonverbal signs that help people understand one another even when they speak different languages. Studies have shown that people from different cultures often share the same facial expressions for such emotions as happiness, anger, fear, surprise, and so forth.[3]

Functions of Nonverbal Communication

These contrasts between verbal and nonverbal elements are not meant to give the impression that you have two communication systems functioning independent of each other. Actually, verbal and nonverbal communication both operate as you send and receive messages. In conjunction with verbal communication, nonverbal behavior serves the following functions.

1. *Nonverbal behavior may supplement words.* That is, the nonverbal behavior gives additional support to the meaning. So, when you point to show the direction a car went, when you frown as you say, "I lost," when you pat your sister's back as you say, "It's up to you—we need you!" or when you say *now* in a louder voice in the sentence, "Come here now," each of the nonverbal cues supplements the verbal meaning.

2. *Nonverbal behavior may contradict your words.* For instance, when you slam the door behind you but say you don't care, when you perspire profusely but claim you are not nervous, when you shout and say you are not angry, your verbal and nonverbal messages are contradictory. Which is to be believed? In these circumstances the nonverbal messages you send are likely to override the verbal meaning—observers are more inclined to believe what is expressed nonverbally because it is less subject to conscious control. You are not likely to fool anyone if you say, "Oh, I'm sorry!" while a smile is twitching at the corners of your mouth. The contradiction between verbal and nonverbal messages is especially apparent when the tone of voice is sarcastic. Such statements as "Great play, George!" said in a sarcastic tone are always perceived as negative, regardless of the positive nature of the words themselves.

3. *Nonverbal behavior may regulate the flow of verbal interaction.* Eye contact, vocal pitch, gestures, and other nonverbal cues may tell people when to talk and when to be quiet. For instance, we may look directly at another person when we want them to speak or we may make a slight backward move in a chair when we have finished talking.

4. *Nonverbal behavior may take the place of words.* At these times meaning is generated solely through the nonverbal behavior. When the team comes into the dressing room after a game, the looks, posture, and tones of voice tell the story of who won the game—no one needs to ask. And when the umpire jerks his thumb into the air, you know the runner is out.

In the remainder of this chapter we will examine specific elements of nonverbal communication: body motions, paralanguage, self-presentation, and management of the environment.

PRACTICE in Analyzing Nonverbal Behavior

In Pairs

Working with a partner, try to communicate for five full minutes entirely through nonverbal communication. At the end of the five minutes analyze your efforts. What kinds of information did you find easiest to communicate nonverbally? With what kinds of information did you feel the greatest frustration in communicating?

By Yourself

Watch a television situation comedy with which you are familiar. Turn the volume off. At the end of five minutes try to summarize the plot and the emotional state of the characters. What aspects of nonverbal communication enabled you to feel confident of your summary? What frustrations, if any, resulted from not being able to hear the dialogue?

Body Motions

Of all nonverbal behavior you are probably most familiar with *kinesics,* the technical name for body motions. In this section we will identify the types of body motions. Then we will look at the way people use them to communicate.

Types of Body Motions

The major types of body motions are eye contact, facial expression, and gesture.

Eye Contact. *Eye contact,* also referred to as *gaze,* involves looking directly at the face of the listener while talking. In addition to meeting psychological needs, eye contact helps monitor the effect of people's communication. For instance, through your eye contact you can tell when a person is paying attention to your words, when a person is involved in what you are saying, whether what you are saying is causing anxiety, and whether the person you are talking with has something to hide.

The amount of eye contact used differs from person to person and from situation to situation. Studies show that people are likely to look at each other 50 to 60 percent of the time as they talk. For the talker the average amount of eye contact is about 40 percent; for the listener the average is nearer 70 percent.[4] You will generally maintain better eye con-

As with other aspects of interpersonal communication, eye contact is a two-way street. When you look at the person you're talking to, you express your concern in getting your message across. Eye contact also lets you monitor the effectiveness of your message. Is your listener bored? Uncomfortable? Distracted? Failure to make eye contact suggests deception and shame: "He can't even look me in the eye."

tact when you are discussing topics with which you are comfortable, when you are genuinely interested in a person's comments or reactions, or when you are trying to influence the other person. Conversely, you will tend to avoid eye contact when you are discussing topics that make you uncomfortable, when you lack interest in the topic or person, or when you are embarrassed, ashamed, or trying to hide something.

Because people often judge others by the degree of eye contact, you want to ensure that your eye contact behavior is perceived as appropriate. You may need to alter your behavior if you find that you maintain a less-than-normal amount of eye contact either when you are concerned about the person or topic of conversation, when you feel confident, or when you have no cause to feel shame or embarrassment.

You can improve your eye contact if you are willing to practice. Begin with a situation in which you are the speaker, and as you talk, concentrate on looking at the source of your attention. You can even practice by holding conversations with objects in your room. For a minute, talk with your book, then shift your attention to your lamp, and finally, talk to the window. Once you become conscious of maintaining eye contact with objects, you can continue to practice by having a close friend help you monitor the amount of your eye contact. For example, you might say to your friend, "As I'm telling you about the movie I saw, I'd like you to keep track of how much I look at you while I talk. When I'm done, tell me if you thought I looked at you 25 percent, 50 percent, 75 percent, or nearly all the time." You also need to practice eye contact in the listener or receiver role. Have your friend tell you about something that happened, then ask your friend how much you maintained eye contact while you were listening.

Remember, because your eye contact will be taken as a measure of your communication competence, you need to use your eye contact effectively.

Facial Expressions. *Facial expression* involves the arrangement of facial muscles to communicate emotional states or reactions to messages. The three sets of muscles that are manipulated to form facial expressions are the brow and forehead; the eyes, eyelids, and root of the nose; and the cheeks, mouth, remainder of the nose, and chin.[5] Your facial expression is likely to mirror your thoughts or feelings—as we mentioned earlier, Paul Ekman and W. V. Friesen have discovered that across cultures people recognize those expressions conveying six basic emotions: happiness, sadness, surprise, fear, anger, and disgust.

The significance of the role your facial expression plays in the communication of your ideas and feelings may depend on the intensity of those ideas and feelings. For instance, if you cannot see the sadness in a situation, you are not likely to register any sadness facially, but if you truly feel sadness, your facial expression will reflect it. Likewise, we can often tell when someone is lying, because the facial muscles that express emotions are not easily controlled consciously.[6] A person's facial expression becomes difficult to read only when it gives either no cues or totally inaccurate cues to thoughts and feelings.

Gestures. *Gestures* are the movements of hands, arms, and fingers that we use to describe or to emphasize. When a person says "about this high" or "nearly this round," we expect to see a gesture accompany the verbal description. Likewise, when a person says "Put that down" or "Listen to me," we look for a pointing finger, pounding fist, or some other gesture that reinforces the point. People do vary, however, in the amount of gesturing that accompanies their speech—some people "talk with their hands" far more than others.

The Use of Body Motions

An awareness of *how* body motions are used is crucial to your understanding of nonverbal communication. To the unobservant all body motion may appear to be random movement; however, body movements serve important communication functions. Ekman and Friesen[7] classify these movements under the headings of emblems, illustrators, affect displays, regulators, and adaptors.

Emblems. Body motions or gestures that supplement or replace words are termed *emblems*. Just as we learn what words mean, so we learn what various body motions or gestures mean. A North American dictionary of emblems would include such definitions as thumbs up for "everything is go," extension of first and second finger in a V shape for "peace," shaking the head from side to side for "no" and nodding for "yes," and shrugging the shoulders for "maybe" or "I don't care."

Our nonverbal vocabulary includes the same three classifications as our verbal vocabulary: emblems that we know and use regularly in our daily speech, emblems that we can recognize if others use them but that are not in our working vocabulary, and emblems for which we have to discover meaning. For example, nearly everyone in our culture employs the nonverbal emblem of nodding to signify "yes." Or people may recognize or understand certain obscene gestures but not use them themselves. And people may even come across many gestures that have no meaning for them, because many groups develop certain emblems whose meaning is known only to group members.

People use emblems when they are too far apart for speech to be heard, when noise prevents them from hearing, or when they just don't feel like verbalizing. Emblems are also used by the deaf (sign language is an elaborate language) and by people trying to exclude someone who is not a member of their group.

Illustrators. Movements or gestures used to accent or emphasize what is being said are called *illustrators*. When we say, "He talks with his hands," we mean that the person's verbal output and body movements are totally complementary. We use gestures to illustrate in at least five ways:

1. Illustrators can be used to *emphasize* speech: People may pound the table in front of them when they say, "Don't bug me."

2. Illustrators can show the *path* or *direction* of thought: People may move their hands on an imaginary continuum when they say, "The papers ranged from very good to very bad."

3. Illustrators can show *position:* People may point when they say, "Take that table."

4. Illustrators can be used to *describe:* People may use their hands to indicate size as they say, "The ball is about three inches in diameter."

5. Illustrators can be used to *mimic:* People may nod their heads as they say, "Did you see the way he nodded?"

Like emblems, illustrators are socially learned and can be taught. We are not advocating, however, that you learn and put into practice a set of illustrators. Our goal is to raise your awareness of them. Only if you use illustrators inappropriately or if your use calls attention to them rather than adding to meaning should you try to correct them.

Affect Displays. When you experience a pronounced physical sensation, you are likely to display the nature of that feeling through *affect displays,* that is, through some facial reaction and/or body response. For instance, if you stub your toe, you are likely to express the pain both verbally (perhaps by cursing) and nonverbally with some accompanying grimace. More often than not, these spur-of-the-moment displays are not intended as conscious communication. One reason for labeling such reactions as "displays" is that the reaction will take place automatically whether you are alone or whether someone else is present, and it will probably be quite noticeable.

Despite the automatic nature of these affect displays, most people develop recognizable patterns of usage.

1. *Some people deintensify the appearance of clues.* When these people are afraid, happy, or hurt, they attempt to look less afraid, happy, or hurt than they really are. For example, when deintensifiers bang their heads getting into their cars so hard that a bump appears, they may act as if the bump was only a minor injury.

2. *Some people overintensify or amplify.* When such people are only slightly afraid, happy, or injured, they are likely to display a much greater

amount of emotion than they really feel. Children who suffer a minor pain may scream as if they've been maimed.

3. *Some people take neutral positions.* Whether these people are happy, afraid, sad, or angry, their facial expressions and body movements tend not to vary. We call a neutral expression a "poker face," the kind of expression a poker player will show to bluff successfully.

4. *Some people mask clues.* These people have a totally different expression from what would normally be expected in a given set of circumstances. For instance, when maskers are hurt, they may smile.

Because of the patterns of displays people adopt, we need to be very careful about the conclusions we draw from them—we can be fooled. These display patterns may be learned at home or in a social group and may be in keeping with a self-image a person is trying to project. For example, if your family considers it bad form to show fear, then you may learn to deintensify your display, to show a "poker face," or perhaps to mask your response. Of course, the stronger the stimulus, the more difficult it may be to deintensify your feelings. When you step sleepily out of bed and stub your toe, the display is likely to be directly proportional to the amount of pain incurred.

Regulators. Nonverbal communication cues that are meant to control the flow of conversation are known as *regulators*. Regulators tell a person when to continue, repeat, elaborate, hurry up, and finish. We pick up communication cues from such movements as shifting eye contact, shifts in posture, raised eyebrows, and slight head motions. (You may have noticed, for example, that nodding the head represents both an emblem meaning "yes" and a regulator meaning "good, go on." Like words, nonverbal responses have different meanings in different contexts.)

The process of regulation occurs on the periphery of our awareness, and regulators may penetrate our consciousness only when their usage reaches a state that we describe as rudeness. For instance, if other people gather up their things, put on their coats, and start to leave while you are in the middle of a statement, an emphatic nonverbal cue has been provided. Usually, however, we do not know when we are using nonverbal cues to regulate communication, nor are we necessarily conscious of others using them. Nevertheless, we expect and need these regulators to monitor communication on a subtler level.

Adaptors. The most difficult of the body motion cues to define are *adaptors*, because, unlike other cues, they change not only from person to person but from situation to situation. Researchers view *adaptors* as efforts to satisfy personal needs that arise as people relate to each other. Just as you may change the manner in which you verbally communicate with another

Whether or not you're aware of it, you use kinesics all the time. Kinesics, or body language, includes facial expression, gesture, and posture. People in agreement sometimes mimic each other's movements. What do the stances of these men suggest about their relationship?

person based on previous conversations, so you change your body posture, gestures, facial expressions, and amount of eye contact.

You may be familiar with one or more of the popular books that discuss the use of adaptors in the nonverbal communication process. Some twenty years ago the first of many books appeared that encouraged people to "psych out" the hidden messages that people were unaware of or were trying to repress.[8] These books suggested that such body motions as people crossing their legs or arms may (or may not) have something to do with their attitude toward the people they are with or with their rejection of others' ideas. Usually, we just are not aware of our adaptive behavior.

Yet communication is greatly affected if people believe they sense something in our nonverbal behavior. When we talk with people, we often get a sense of what they are like, what they are thinking, or what they are feeling. Although such feelings may seem to arise intuitively, they actually derive from our perceptions, whether conscious or unconscious, of adaptive behavior. For instance, when bosses take off their coats, roll up their sleeves, and pitch in, they are revealing that they may differ from the bosses who dress rather formally, stand apart from their workers, and look disgusted at the thought of getting their hands dirty. Many times we say we are attracted to people because they exude sexuality or have a kind of grace or just make us feel comfortable. Conversely, we are sometimes repelled by people because they seem stern, strict, formal, or uptight. Many of these impressions are projected by adaptive behaviors on the part of the people in question.

PRACTICE in Analyzing Body Motions

In Pairs

1. Do you use many gestures when you speak? Enlist the aid of a friend in helping you complete the following analysis: List the emblems, illustrators, and affect displays you use most frequently and the nonverbal cues you give to regulate conversation to show others (1) that you want to talk and (2) that you have finished talking.

2. Observe others' nonverbal behavior in the same categories.

3. Determine the kinds of facial expressions, postures, gestures, and movements that are suggestive of being "sexy," "fun loving," "boring," and "pushy." What is it about these cues that give these meanings?

Paralanguage

In contrast to *kinesic behavior*, which relates to the bodily movements we see, *paralanguage*, or *vocalics*, relates to the sounds we hear. Paralanguage concerns *how* something is said rather than *what* is said. We have all developed some sensitivity to the clues people give through their voices. Let's consider two major categories of paralanguage.

Vocal Characteristics

The four major characteristics of voice are *pitch* (highness or lowness of tone), *volume* (loudness), *rate* (speed), and *quality* (the sound of the voice). Each of these characteristics, by itself or in concert with one or more of the others, either complements, supplements, or contradicts the meaning conveyed by the words themselves. For example, people talk loudly when they wish to be heard at great distances or in noisy settings, but some people also talk loudly when they are angry and softly when they are being loving. People tend to raise and lower vocal pitch to accompany changes in volume. They may also raise the pitch when they are nervous or lower the pitch when they are trying to be forceful. People may talk more rapidly when they are happy, frightened, or nervous and more slowly when they are unsure or are trying to emphasize a point.

In addition to combined changes in volume, pitch, and rate, each of us uses a slightly different quality of voice to communicate a particular state of mind. We may associate complaints with a whiny, nasal quality; seductive invitation with a soft, breathy quality; and anger with a strident, harsh quality. To each of these different qualities we assign some kind of a value judgment about how persons are feeling or what they are thinking.

Note, however, that none of these particular differences in voice quality necessarily has the meaning we assign. Some people have high-pitched or breathy or nasal or strident voices all the time. Perhaps some people use these different qualities for reasons other than what we perceive. Nevertheless, *how* people say what they say does convey meaning, whether intended or not. Our purpose here is to make you more aware of the meanings received through paralanguage, not to suggest the need for changes in your own paralanguage. If you have concerns about your vocal characteristics, talk them over with your professor.

Vocal Interferences

Sounds that interrupt or intrude into fluent speech, causing distraction and, occasionally, total communication breakdown, are termed *vocal interferences*. Excessive vocal interferences are bad speech habits that we develop over a period of time. The most common interferences include the "uh's," "er's," "well's," and "OK's" that creep into our speech and that nearly universal interrupter of conversation, "you know."

Vocal interferences are difficult to eliminate from our speech, but they can be reduced through a program of awareness and practice. Vocal interferences are often caused by a fear of momentary silence. Americans have been taught that it is impolite to interrupt another person until the flow of sound stops. A problem occurs for people when they pause for the right word or idea, because the second or two it takes for them to come

up with the word may be perceived by listeners as "dead air time." Therefore, they fill the dead air time with sound that, more often than not, has
no meaning. For some speakers the customary filler sounds are "uh" or
"er"; for others they may be "well uh" or "um." Although the fear of being
interrupted may be real (some people will seek to interrupt at any pause),
the intrusion of an excessive number of fillers is a high price to pay for
an occasional interruption.

Equally prevalent, and perhaps even more irritating than the "uh's"
and "um's," is the incessant use of "you know." Curiously, no matter how
irritating the use of "you know" may be, listeners are unlikely to acknowledge their irritation. Seldom if ever do people say openly to others anything like "your use of 'you know' at every break in thought is really very
annoying to me." Yet passages like the following are quite common: "You
know, Maxwell is, you know, a good uh, a good, you know, lecturer." In
addition to one "uh" and one repetition, the short sentence contains three
"you knows"! We wish such examples were exaggerations. Unfortunately,
they are not. If it seems appropriate, you might start pointing out this
irritant in others' speech; most importantly, you should request others to
tell you whether you are an offender.

In the normal give and take of conversation even the most fluent
speakers may use an occasional "uh" or "you know." Interferences become
a problem when they are perceived by others as "excessive," when they
begin to call attention to themselves and prevent a person from concentrating on meaning. With some practice you can *limit* the occurrence of
vocal interferences in your speech. Remember, although people may not
be willing to tell you about it, they are likely to be distracted or irritated
by your vocal interferences, or nonfluencies. So, what do you do?

1. *Train yourself to hear your interferences.* Even people with a major
   problem seem to be unaware of the interferences they use. You
   can train your ears in at least two ways:
   a. Tape-record yourself talking for several minutes about any
      subject—the game you saw yesterday, the course you plan to
      take next term, or anything else that comes to mind. Before
      you play it back, estimate the number of times you think you
      peppered your speech with "uh's," "you know's," and the like.
      Then compare the actual number with your estimate. As your
      ears become trained, your estimates will be closer to the actual
      number.
   b. Have a close friend listen to you and raise a hand every time
      you say "uh" or "you know." You may find the experience
      traumatic or nerve-wracking, but your ear will soon start to
      pick up the vocal interferences as fast as the listener.

2. *Practice to see how long you can go without using a vocal inter-ference.* Start out by trying to talk for fifteen seconds. Continue to increase the time period until you can talk for two minutes without a single interference. Meaning may suffer; you may spend a disproportionate amount of time avoiding interferences. Still, it is good practice.

3. *Mentally note your usage of interferences in conversation.* You will be making real headway when you can recognize your own interferences in normal conversation *without* affecting the flow. When you reach this stage, you will find yourself beginning to avoid or limit the use of interferences.

Ridding yourself of these habits is hard work—you will have to train your ear to catch your usages. But the work is worth it. Conversation would be a lot more pleasant if everyone would work to reduce vocal interferences by just 50 percent.

PRACTICE in Paralanguage

By Yourself

1. What happens to your voice in stress situations? When does your pitch go up? down? When do you talk loudly? softly? When are you likely to talk fast? slowly?

2. Are there any vocal interferences that you use frequently? Are you always aware of their use? Are you making some effort to reduce or eliminate their use?

In Groups

1. Working in groups, have two persons of the group role-play various situations. For instance, a student has received a low grade on her theme that she worked on for hours and she wishes to confront her instructor, a person who does not have much patience when talking with students. The rest of the group should listen for paralanguage.

2. Working in groups, each person should try to talk continuously for two minutes. When it is your turn, you can select your own topic—a movie you saw recently, the success of your school team, difficulties you are having with a particular course, and so forth. Whenever the speaker uses an interference, one of the members of the group should raise a

hand. At the end of two minutes count the number of times hands were raised. Give everyone two chances. See who can use the fewest interferences.

Self-Presentation

People learn a great deal about you from the way you choose to present yourself. Elements over which you have some control include choice of clothing, amount of touch, and the way you treat time.

Clothing

Although people's reactions to your appearance will vary in intensity, they will draw conclusions about you based on the way you dress. You need to determine what you are trying to say and then dress appropriately.

Sometimes, it is in our best interest to meet the expectations of others. For example, business managers generally have a clear idea of the images they want their businesses to project. If you are to succeed with those businesses, you must dress in a way that is in line with those images.[9] Thus, the woman who goes into an interview with a major oil company in sweatpants and a tanktop had better have a lot going for her if she expects even to be heard, let alone considered for the job. And a defendant charged with assault and battery runs a risk of alienating the jury if he shows up in the courtroom wearing a black leather jacket, jeans, and boots.

People have a right to their individuality. Nevertheless, remember that your clothes are perceived by others as clues to your attitudes and behaviors. Clothes do communicate, however accurate or inaccurate you may believe that communication to be.

Touch

Touch, known as *haptics*, is often considered to be the most basic form of communication; as such it is a fundamental aspect of nonverbal communication in general and of self-presentation in particular. We use our

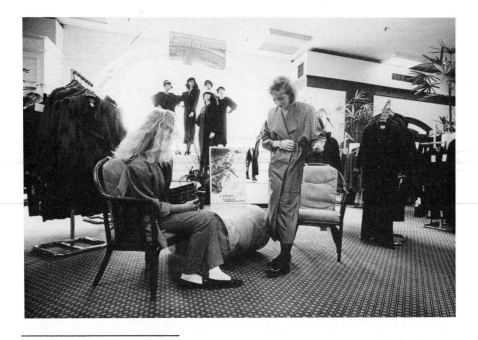

Weather, cost, and fashion are among the factors influencing how you dress. Some of these factors are within your control, some are not. You need to judge what is appropriate in context for your self-presentation, as you do for other areas of nonverbal communication. You know not to wear a sweatsuit to a wedding or go to the beach in a tuxedo, but you may be less certain about the clothes you select for a job interview.

hands to pat, slap, pinch, stroke, hold, embrace, and tickle. We employ such touching behaviors for a variety of reasons ranging from impersonal and random to intimate and purposeful. We shake hands to be sociable and polite, we pat a person on the back for encouragement, we hug a person to show love.

But whether people touch and like to be touched is a matter of individual preference. Although America as a culture is relatively non-contact-oriented, the levels and amounts of touching behavior within our society vary widely. Behavior that seems impersonal to one person may be very intimate or threatening to another. Appropriateness of touch will differ with context, so that a normally touch-oriented person may act differently in public or with a large group of people. Your own behavior at times will have to be tempered by the expectations of those with whom you interact.

Chronemics

Chronemics is the study of how we use and structure time. Its significance to our nonverbal behavior is that people perceive actions and reactions on the basis of time sequence.[10] Thus, how we manage time and how we react to others' use and management of time are important aspects of self-presentation.

Probably the aspect of time that is most important to interpersonal communication and the idea of self-presentation is what Edward T. Hall calls *informal time*,[11] time usages that are learned through observation and imitation. We will focus here on three aspects of informal time: duration, punctuality, and activity.

Duration refers to the amount of time that we regard as appropriate for certain events. For instance, people expect a sermon to last twenty to thirty minutes, a class to run fifty minutes, and a movie to be roughly two hours long. When the length of an event does not meet our expectations, that time becomes an obstacle to communication. We get angry with the professor who holds us beyond normal class time; we become hostile if someone asks us to cut short our lunch hour or coffee break.

Activity refers to what people perceive should be done in a given period of time, including the time of day that is considered appropriate for certain activities to take place. We work during the day, sleep at night, eat lunch at noon, and so on. Based on these habits we make judgments about people who consistently do things at times that differ from our perception of what is natural. For example, Joe is regarded as strange if he gets up at 4:30 A.M. daily; Laura is viewed as peculiar if she always eats dinner at midnight. *When* people do things also affects communication.

Punctuality, which refers to meeting a time expectation, may be the most important of these three aspects because we draw conclusions about people based on their relative punctuality. If your professor asks you to stop by her office at 10 A.M., her opinion of you may be affected if you knock on her door at 9:45, at 10:00, at 10:10, or at 10:30. Likewise, your perceptions of your professor might alter depending upon whether or not she is in her office when you get there.

Keep in mind, however, that any discussion of time is culturally based. Our perspective here derives from attitudes of general North American culture, yet within this dominant culture are subcultures that hold contrasting views of time. For instance, a southerner has a different concept of duration, activity, and punctuality than does an easterner; likewise, a black American perceives time differently than does a Hispanic American. Because time does communicate, we must be sensitive to our own perceptions of time as well as to those of others, so that the variable of time helps—or at least does not hinder—our communication.

PRACTICE in Analysis of Self-Presentation

By Yourself

1. Take a clothing inventory. Divide your clothes into three groups: those you wear for special occasions, those you wear for everyday activities, and those you wear for "grubbing around." Over the next week note how your interactions with others are affected by your clothing. Do you act differently when wearing one type of clothing as opposed to another? Do others treat you differently?

2. Next time you go to class, dress completely differently than you normally do. Notice what effect, if any, this has on your communication with those around you.

3. Analyze your reaction to people's time behavior. Describe an incident where someone's violation of your time behavior caused communication problems with you.

Communication Through Management of Your Environment

In addition to the way you use body motions, paralanguage, and self-presentation, you also communicate nonverbally through management of your physical environment. The principal elements of your environment over which you can exercise control are space, color, temperature, and lighting.

Space

How much control you have over space depends on whether you are dealing with structures, movable objects within space, or distance.

Management of Permanent Structures. The buildings in which you live and work and the parts of those buildings that cannot be moved fall in the category of permanent structures. Although you may not have much control over the creation of such elements, you do exercise control in your selection of them. For instance, when you rent an apartment or buy a condominium or home, you consider whether or not the structures are in tune with your life-style. People who select a fourth-floor loft may view themselves differently from those who select one-room efficiencies. Business people, doctors, and lawyers usually search with care to find surroundings that fit the image they want to communicate. In addition, specific features of that choice affect your communication within that environment. People who live in apartment buildings tend to become better acquainted with neighbors who live across the hall and next door than with those who live on other floors. Also, your chances of knowing people who live in your building are greatly enhanced if you live near an elevator, a staircase, or a main door.

Management of Objects Within Space. You have the opportunity to manage objects in space by arranging and rearranging them to create the desired atmosphere. Whether the space is a dormitory room, a living room, a seminar room, or a classroom, you can move the furnishings around until you achieve the effect you want. For example, in a living room you can arrange furniture in a way that contributes to conversation or that focuses attention on, say, a television set. A room with Victorian furniture and hard-backed chairs arranged formally will produce an entirely different kind of conversation from a room with a thick carpet, pillows, beanbag chairs, and a low, comfortable sectional sofa. In general, the more formal the arrangement, the more formal the communication setting.

A professor's office will give you clues about the kind of climate that professor is trying to establish just by the arrangement of the office and where you are expected to sit. A professor who shows you to a chair across the desk may be saying "Let's talk business—I'm the professor and you're the student." Such an arrangement, with the desk between you and the professor, lends itself to formal conversation. On the other hand, the professor who shows you to a chair at the side of his desk may be saying, "Don't be nervous—let's just chat." In this case the lack of any formal barrier between you and the professor, as well as the relatively small space, is designed to lead to much more informal conversation. Although such conclusions about the management of objects within space should not be regarded as absolute, the use of space nevertheless is one index of how people are going to treat you and how they expect you to treat them.

The effect of the arrangement of objects on communication can be illustrated by examining your various classrooms. The communication atmosphere of a classroom in which several rows of chairs face the lectern differs from that of a classroom in which chairs are grouped into one large circle or one in which there are four or five smaller circles. In the first environment most students anticipate a lecture format. In the second setting they might expect a give-and-take discussion between the instructor and members of the class. In the third one they might expect the class to work on group projects.

Management of Informal Space. The space around us or the space we are occupying at the moment is known as *informal space*. The study of informal space is called *proxemics*. Managing your informal space requires some understanding of attitudes toward both space around us and our territory.

You are probably aware that communication is influenced by the distances between people. Edward T. Hall, a leading researcher in nonverbal communication, has studied the four distinct, generally accepted distances for different types of conversations.[12] Intimate distance, up to eighteen inches, is appropriate for private conversations with close friends. Personal distance, from eighteen inches to four feet, is the space in which casual conversation occurs. Social distance, from four to twelve feet, is where impersonal business such as job interviews is conducted. Public distance is anything more than twelve feet. Note that these four distances were not determined arbitrarily; they represent descriptions of what many people consider appropriate in various situations. Individuals do, of course, vary.

Of greatest concern to us is the intimate distance, that which we regard as appropriate for intimate conversation with close friends, parents, and younger children. People usually become uncomfortable when "outsiders" violate this intimate distance. For instance, in a movie theater that is less than one-quarter full, couples will tend to leave a seat or more between them and another couple. If in such a setting a stranger sits right next to you, you are likely to be upset and may move away.

Intrusions into our intimate space are acceptable only when all involved follow the unwritten rules. For instance, when we're packed into a crowded elevator we do not react to the fact that a part of our body may be touching someone else: we try to stand rigidly, look at the floor or at the indicator above the door, and pretend that we are not touching.

Interpersonal problems occur when one person violates the behavioral expectations of another person who follows different rules of behavior. For instance, Paul may come from a family that conducts informal conversations with others at a range closer than the eighteen-inch limit that most Americans place on intimate space. So when Paul talks to Dan or Mary for the first time and moves in closer than eighteen inches, both Dan and Mary may back away from him during the conversation.

Another form of nonverbal communication is management of our physical environment. Although the space around us is called informal space—because it moves when we do—we carry strong feelings about our territory and the proper distances between us and others, particularly intimate distance. We manage permanent structures, objects within space, and the informal space around us. Notice how this couple manages objects within their environment.

Normally, our intimate or personal space moves when we move, because we tend to define these spaces in terms of our current location. Yet in many situations we seek to claim a given space whether we are occupying it currently or not. That is, we are likely to look at certain space as our *territory*, as space over which we may claim ownership. If Marcia decides to eat lunch at the school cafeteria, the space at the table she selects becomes her territory. Suppose that during lunch Marcia leaves her territory to get butter for her roll. The chair she left, the food on the table, and the space around that food are "hers," and she will expect others to stay away. If, when she returns, Marcia finds that someone at the table has moved a glass or a dish into the area that she regards as her territory, she is likely to feel resentful.

Many people stake out their territory with markers. For example, George, who is planning to eat in the cafeteria, finds an empty table and puts his books on the table and his coat on a chair *before* he gets his food. If someone comes along while George is gone, moves his books and coat to the floor, and occupies his space, that person is violating what George perceives as his territory.

As a student of nonverbal communication, you must understand, however, that other people may not look at either the space around you or your territory in quite the same way as you do. That the majority of Americans have learned the same basic rules governing the management of space does not mean that everyone shares the same respect for the rules or treats the consequences of breaking the rules in the same way.

Temperature, Lighting, and Color

Three other elements of environment that people seem sensitive to and over which they generally have considerable control are temperature, lighting, and color.

Temperature. Temperature acts as a stimulant or deterrent to communication. To illustrate the negative effect of temperature on communication, recall when the June or September heat made listening to the teacher in a stuffy classroom especially difficult. Or, if you live in the northern part of the country, think of how a sudden cold snap that caused buildings to be much colder than normal made concentration that much more difficult.

Lighting. Lighting can also act as a stimulant or deterrent to communication. In lecture halls and reading rooms bright light is expected—it encourages good listening and comfortable reading. By contrast, in a chic restaurant, a music listening room, or a television lounge you expect the lighting to be soft and rather dim, which makes for a cozy atmosphere and leads to intimate conversation.

Color. Differences in color seem to have a particularly significant effect on how people behave: We react to color both emotionally and physically. For instance, many people see red as exciting and stimulating; blue as comfortable and soothing; yellow as cheerful and jovial. Interior designers thus will decorate in blues rather than in reds and yellows when they are trying to create a peaceful, serene atmosphere, whereas, when they want to create a stimulating atmosphere for a playroom, they will decorate with reds and yellows.

Color has other associations as well. We describe a cowardly person as yellow, a jealous person as green with envy, an angry person as seeing red; we lament certain black days of our history; and Mondays are often seen as blue. The effect of color is most noticeable when the color violates our expectations. Mashed potatoes tinted green in honor of Saint Patrick's Day may nauseate diners who are not color-blind, even before they attempt to eat.

PRACTICE in Analyzing Effects of Environment

By Yourself

1. Are you territorial? Make a list of territories that you "own." What do you do when those territories are invaded?

2. Analyze your use of personal space. What are your expectations about space when you are talking with an instructor? When you are talking with a good friend? When you are talking with a stranger? How do they differ?

3. Change the arrangement of the furniture in your dorm room or a room of your home. Do these changes seem to affect the conversations of the people who are usually in these spaces?

With a Friend

1. Visit six different restaurants in your city. Choose several that specialize in fast food and several that specialize in more leisurely dining. Make notes on management of objects within space as well as on color and lighting. What conclusions can you draw?

2. Enlist the aid of a friend. Start on the opposite sides of the room (at least twenty feet apart) and begin to walk toward each other. (1) Stop when twelve feet apart and hold a conversation; (2) stop when seven feet apart and hold a conversation; (3) stop when one or two feet apart and hold a conversation; (4) continue moving closer and conversing until you feel uncomfortable. Step back until the distance seems comfortable. Notice how far apart you are. Compare your reactions to your friend's.

Summary

Nonverbal communication refers to how people communicate by nonverbal means, that is, through the use of body motions, paralanguage, self-presentation, and environment. The nature of nonverbal communication is revealed through its contrasts with verbal communication. Nonverbal communication is more ambiguous, is continuous, is multichanneled, is more trusted when verbal and nonverbal cues are in conflict, gives more insight into emotional states, and is often recognized across cultures.

Although verbal and nonverbal communication work together best when they are complementary, nonverbal cues may replace or even contradict verbal symbols.

Perhaps the most obvious of the nonverbal means is what and how a person communicates through body motions and paralanguage. Eye contact (looking directly at people while you are talking with them), facial expression, and gestures are three major types of body motions. Eye contact is especially important, because people will form judgments about you and your message based on the amount of eye contact you make. Body motions act as emblems, illustrators, affect displays, regulators, and adaptors. Likewise, a person's vocal characteristics and vocal interferences affect the meaning communicated.

Self-presentation, manifested in such factors as clothing, touching behavior, and use of time, further affects communication. The environment is an often overlooked aspect of nonverbal communication. Yet the way people arrange and react to space and the way they control or react to color, temperature, and lighting contribute to the nature of the communication that will occur.

Notes

1. Albert Mehrabian, *Silent Messages*, 2nd ed. (Belmont, Calif.: Wadsworth, 1981), p. 76.

2. J. Burgoon and T. Saine, *The Unspoken Dialogue* (Boston: Houghton Mifflin, 1978). This book provides a comprehensive analysis of nonverbal communication—still among the best books on the subject.

3. Paul Ekman and W. V. Friesen, *Unmasking the Face* (Englewood Cliffs, N.J.: Prentice-Hall, 1975), pp. 137–139.

4. Mark L. Knapp, *Essentials of Nonverbal Communication* (New York: Holt, Rinehart & Winston, 1980), p. 184.

5. Ekman and Friesen, *Unmasking the Face.*

6. Mark Knapp and Mark Comadena, "Telling It Like It Isn't: A Review of Theory and Research on Deceptive Communications," *Human Communication Research* 5 (1979): 270–285. For a very interesting study on the role of facial expression and deception, see Paul Ekman, *Telling Lies* (New York: W. W. Norton, 1985).

7. Paul Ekman and W. V. Friesen, "The Repertoire of Nonverbal Behavior: Categories, Origins, Usage, and Coding," *Semiotica*, Vol. 1 (1969): 49–98.

8. One of the first of these books was Julius Fast's *Body Language* (New York: M. Evans & Co., 1970). A more recent book of the same type is David B. Givens, *Love Signals: How to Attract a Mate* (New York: Crown Publishers, 1987).

9. There have been many books published recently that report the power of clothing. One of the most recent is Lois Fenton's *Dress for Excellence* (New York: Rawson Associates, 1986).

10. Mark L. Hickson III and Don W. Stacks, *NVC: Nonverbal Communication* (Dubuque, Iowa: Wm C. Brown, 1985), p. 122.

11. Edward T. Hall, *Beyond Culture* (Garden City, N.Y.: Doubleday, 1976).

12. Edward T. Hall, *The Silent Language* (Garden City, N.Y.: Doubleday, 1959), pp. 163–164.

Two

Developing Interpersonal Skills

This unit presents communication skills that can help you become a more competent communicator. We begin this unit with a discussion of the framework in which the development of skills is most relevant: developing interpersonal relationships. Then in the next five chapters we discuss the skills that are most appropriate for building effective interpersonal relationships—communicating ideas and feelings, listening, responding, influencing, and managing conflict. With an increased repertoire of interpersonal communication skills you can select the ones that are most appropriate for the particular communication situation.

Chapter 5

Communication
In Relationships

Objectives

After you have read this chapter, you should be able
to define and/or explain:

Life cycle of relationships

Communication in relationship life cycles

Interpersonal needs theory

Exchange theory

Johari window

Climates in which sound relationships thrive

Descriptiveness

Openness

Provisionalism

Equality

Because so many of the interpersonal skills we use are for the purpose of starting, building, and maintaining good, ongoing relationships with others, we begin Part Two with an analysis of relationships. An interpersonal relationship is defined as "a series of interactions between two individuals known to each other."[1] An effective relationship is composed of a series of satisfying interactions—on any level—with another person. What determines whether your relationships will grow, stabilize, or deteriorate? Do you have control over the success of your relationships? Relationships do not just happen, nor do they grow and maintain themselves automatically. In this chapter we will discuss the stages of communication that typically comprise the life cycle of a relationship, two theories of why relationships develop, and the functions of self-disclosure and feedback in relationship development. We will also examine the climate in which effective relationships are developed and maintained.

Communication in the Life Cycle of Relationships

Even though no two relationships develop in exactly the same manner, scholars who have studied a variety of relationships have noted that relationships do follow a "life cycle." Although these scholars agree in general about the elements of relationship development and deterioration, they often list different numbers of stages and give them different names.[2]

For the purposes of our discussion we will examine the life cycle of relationships in terms of getting acquainted, building friendships, developing intimate relationships, seeking stability, and coping with deterioration.

Getting Acquainted

The first stage of any relationship is forming an acquaintanceship, the getting-to-know-you stage. Distinct phases of the getting-acquainted stage include attraction, striking up a conversation, and applying appropriate types of communication.

Attraction. An old song lamented that "she lived on the morning side of the mountain, and he lived on the twilight side of the hill." The song suggests that two people may have characteristics that would be attractive to each other but that their potential compatibility would hardly matter if they never met. The point is obvious but well taken: People's lives must intersect in some way or they will never begin a relationship.

Attending college, working with a company, worshiping at a church or synagogue, or belonging to a club puts you in a context that helps you meet people. People who are in their first year of college or who are new to the town in which they are working try to immerse themselves in as many different contexts as possible in order to meet people. Which contexts you pursue will have some effect on the number and kinds of people with whom you come into contact.

Yet, whether you are in a course with twenty-five other students, an aerobics class of fifteen, a young adults group of thirty at your church or synagogue, or a business environment with hundreds of people, you may be attracted to only a small number of people out of that total. Why? At least six factors help to explain people's attraction to one another.

1. *People are attracted by another's physical characteristics.* People you find physically attractive are likely to catch your eye. Physical attractiveness is so important that advertisers spend millions of dollars in the various media to convince you that their products are most likely to develop, preserve, or increase your attractiveness. Still, as the old saying goes, beauty is in the eye of the beholder, so the issue is not whether a majority of people find a man or a woman attractive, but whether an individual finds some *specific* man or woman attractive.

2. *People are attracted by another's social similarities.* You are likely to be attracted to another person who enjoys the same activities you do. Although you may initiate a conversation with a person on the basis of physical characteristics, that attraction is likely to increase if you also discover you are socially compatible. For instance, if you could spend hours every night dancing, you will tend to be attracted to a person who shares your enthusiasm for dancing. Conversely, if you discover that the person really doesn't care for dancing that much, he or she may become less attractive to you.

3. *People are attracted by another's professional similarities.* You may be drawn toward a person on the basis of joint work interests. For example, when you find you enjoy working with a person on a research paper, you may begin to wonder whether you might also enjoy the person's company socially. For many people professional compatibility represents an important test of the possibility of a long-term relationship.

4. *People are attracted by another's similarities in background.* People who grew up on farms, who attended the same school (or the same kind of school), who spent their summers working at the beach, or who had parents in the armed services are likely to be attracted to each other.

Similarly, Americans visiting or touring in a foreign country may be attracted to other people from America simply on the basis of their common background.

5. *People are attracted by another's similarities in attitudes and values.* When you discover that people have the same feelings as you do about religion, ethics, premarital sex, welfare, and money, you are likely to be drawn toward them.

6. *People are attracted to others when they perceive a personality fit.* A relationship can be built on either similarities or dissimilarities in personality. The saying "Opposites attract" is as accurate as "Birds of a feather flock together." From a theoretical standpoint a relationship rests on mutual need fulfillment, so people can be attracted to those who are different from them as well as to those who are similar to them. Thus, opposites attract when the differences between the people are seen as *complementary.* If each person's set of personality characteristics differs from the other's but each is able to satisfy the needs of the other, then the two people complement each other. In this sense a very dogmatic person and a very shy person, though opposite in personality, may be attracted to each other because they "fit" together—each provides something the other needs. Likewise, an extrovert may be attracted to an introvert because together they are better equipped to face the pressures of the outside world. Nevertheless, in addition to these complementary needs, or dissimilarities, some basis of similarity upon which the relationship can grow must exist.

How do these facets of attraction explain the early stages of relationships? As we said, people are initially attracted to those whom they perceive as physically attractive. But physical attraction appears to be only a door through which people pass in order to enter into a relationship. Whether the relationship develops depends on social interests, work interests, background commonalities, attitude and value similarities, and personality fits. The more interests people have in common, the more they are attracted to each other. Yet what people believe to be true (based on initial perceptions) may not prove to be so. Moreover, even when the initial perceptions about common interests are correct, other factors, over time, may affect the relationship. And when the basis of attraction fades or proves invalid, the relationship will suffer.

Striking Up a Conversation. No matter how attractive you find another person, no relationship can begin until you talk with that other person. Yet one of the most difficult times for many people is the initial interaction with someone who, although attractive, is a complete stranger. Many people are so shy that, although they may be right next to the person

Of the six factors influencing why one person is attracted to another, four of them involve *similarity*. We tend to welcome friendship with people who are most like us because we're most comfortable with the familiar—those who share a similar background, job, or attitude. The more interests people share, the easier it is for them to communicate. Think of your newest friend—what brought you together?

whom they find attractive, they are unwilling or afraid to say a word. The first step to establishing a relationship, then, is building up the courage to say something.

In male-female encounters, same-sex encounters, and business encounters, what happens in the first few minutes of an initial conversation will have a profound effect on the nature of the relationship that develops. How do you go about striking up a conversation with strangers? For some people the advice given in this next section will be second nature.

For those who find starting conversations difficult, however, the following suggestions for initial interaction with a stranger may be some of the most important information in this chapter.

1. *Formally or informally introduce yourself.* Start a conversation with a person by introducing yourself (or by getting someone else to introduce you). For example, "Hi, my name is Gordon. What's yours?" may sound trite, but it works. Or you might have a friend introduce you by saying, "Doris, I'd like you to meet my friend Bill. Bill, Doris is Susan's sister."

2. *Refer to the physical context.* One of the safest ways of starting a conversation is by referring to some aspect of the physical context. Certainly, one of the oldest and most effective of these is a comment about the weather: "This is awful weather for a game, isn't it?" Other contextual references include such statements as "They've really decorated this place beautifully," "I wonder how they are able to keep such a beautiful garden in this climate?" and "Doesn't it seem stuffy in here?"

3. *Refer to your thoughts or feelings.* A very direct way to make contact is to comment on what you are thinking or feeling at the moment: "I really like parties, don't you?" or "I live on this floor too—do these steps bother you as much as they do me?"

4. *Refer to the other person.* "I don't believe I've ever seen you—have you been working here long?" "President and Mrs. Phillips have sure done a lovely job of remodeling this home. Did you ever see it before the renovation?"

None of these statements is particularly threatening, so if the person you want to meet feels the same way about you, chances are he or she will respond pleasantly.

Types of Communication in Acquaintanceships. Once two people have begun an interaction, they are likely to engage in relatively unthreatening conversations, that is, "small talk." Small talk typifies early stages of relationships and serves to meet many social needs with relatively low amounts of risk and disclosure of self and personal feelings. Moreover, small talk provides a basis on which to decide whether to move a relationship to the next level.

One common type of small talk is to refer to people you both know. Statements such as "Do you know Bill? I hear he has a really great job," "Would you believe that Mary Simmons and Tom Johnson are going together? They never seemed to hit it off too well in the past," and "My sister Eileen is really working hard at losing weight. I saw her the other day and all she talked about was the diet she's on" are all examples of small talk. This kind of small talk, often referred to as *gossip*, occurs during all phases of a relationship but is most common in the early phase because it is considered safe. You can gossip for a long time with another person without really saying anything about yourself or without learning anything about the other person. Gossip can be a pleasant way to pass the time of day with people you know but with whom you have no desire or need for a deeper relationship. It can also provide a safe way to explore the bases for attraction since it allows each person to see whether the other reacts similarly to the views expressed about the object of the gossip. Gossip can, of course, be malicious. More often than not, however, gossip represents a means of interacting amicably with others without becoming personally involved. This is why conversations at parties are comprised largely of gossip.

Another kind of small talk is simple idea-exchange. In *idea-exchange communication* people share information that contains facts, opinions, beliefs and that occasionally reflects values. Idea-exchange is a common type of communication between both new acquaintances and friends. At the office Dan may talk with Walt about sports, Martha may talk with Louise about new cars, and Pete may talk with Jack about landscaping. Or, on a more serious level, Jan may talk with Gloria about the U.S. role in the Far East and Dave may talk with Bill about abortion. Although the discussions of foreign policy and abortion are "deeper" than conversations about sports or cars, both sets of conversations represent idea-exchanges. This type of communication is important to early stages of relationships because you learn what the other person is thinking, reassess your attraction level, and decide whether or not you want the relationship to grow.

Building Friendships

As you interact with large numbers of people, you will be trying to identify some number of those acquaintances with whom you can build a friendship. *Friends* are people you like and who like you; friends seek each other out because they enjoy each other's company. Friends may go out of their way to help each other; they are concerned for each other's welfare. But friendships don't occur automatically—they develop from acquaintanceships through exploratory behavior and appropriate communication.

Exploratory Behavior. When people see the possibility of building a friendship with another, they explore to determine the kinds of satisfaction they get from being together. They seek information about each other and put together images about the other person based upon this information. For example, Tom, who is exploring his relationship with Nancy, takes Nancy to a museum, a place where he enjoys spending time. If Nancy doesn't seem to care about the exhibits, or if she can't discuss intelligently what they see, Tom may not pursue the relationship with Nancy as actively as he would have if the experience had been more satisfying.

Exploring for deeper relationships occurs in both opposite- and same-sex relationships. For instance, Mark may seek to develop a friendship with Derek because they both like to play racquetball. But if Derek can't get enough free time to play with Mark, or if Derek and Mark do not play at the same level of competence, the friendship may not develop.

Types of Communication in Friendships. In addition to engaging in some small talk, people who are exploring friendships will also begin to talk about more serious ideas and to share their feelings about important matters. Through the sharing of feelings and the process of self-disclosure you really come to know and to understand another person. Although it is unrealistic, and perhaps undesirable, to expect to share feelings with a great many others, the achievement of a feelings-sharing level of communication with a few people is a highly beneficial communication goal. And when people find that they get satisfaction out of being together and are able to share ideas and feelings, their friendship grows.

Establishing Intimate Relationships

Although most people have countless acquaintances as well as many friends, they are likely to have only a few very close, intimate friendships.

Characteristics of Intimate Relationships. Intimate relationships are built on trust and require a deep level of commitment. Friendships can evolve into intimate relationships in which people find satisfaction with each other on many levels and in which the degree of trust between them is quite high. As Richard Reichert has said, trust reflects an "ability to risk yourself, to put yourself in the hands of another, to put yourself at the service of another."[3] Trust almost always involves some risk. In effect, trust is a kind of prediction—a prediction that if you "put yourself in the hands of another," the result will be to your advantage. Close, intimate friends earn trust by doing what is expected of them. If a person can be relied on to deliver on a promise, to keep a secret, or to provide emotional support when needed, a relationship based on trust will grow.

Deep friendships also require *commitment*. Deep friendships are characterized by the extent to which a person gives up other relationships

People in relationships must learn to rely on each other for support. One measure of a relationship's strength is trust, which develops over time.

in order to devote more time and energy to the primary relationship. Especially when two people are testing the suitability of a deep or intimate friendship, they spend long periods of time together. During the early, euphoric stage of a deep relationship they rarely seem to notice the other's flaws or are willing to ignore them. They are also likely to develop their own language, pet names for each other, "in" jokes, and the like.

Later in this stage a certain amount of relationship evaluation takes place as questions concerning the permanency of the relationship are raised, especially in romantic relationships. For example, Jack and Margaret go out a few times and enjoy themselves. Each is benefiting from the relationship. The relationship progresses so well and the rewards are so high that they begin to spend every possible waking minute together. Although other relationships may be superficially maintained during this time (Margaret continues to visit her mother on Wednesday evenings), relationships of the same kind will be limited (Jack had been dating Nancy before he met Margaret, but he no longer sees her).

As relationships deepen, they gain strength and are often formalized in some way. This stage of a relationship is not really a process but an event. In a male-female relationship this stage is most often marked by marriage or cohabitation. In other relationships it could be marked by signing a contract, forming a partnership, or any other act appropriate for that particular situation.

A deep friendship has a great deal of strength. Sometimes, when one of the friends moves to another part of town or even to another city, the relationship remains unaffected. Some people see each other only once or twice a year but still consider themselves friends or intimates because they share ideas and feelings freely and rely on each other's counsel when they are together.

Types of Communication in Intimate Relationships. Although close friends and intimates may continue to engage in small talk, their relationships are characterized by the sharing of feelings and the disclosure of highly personal information. At this stage people are likely to seek out the other person for help with a problem. They may talk for hours, sharing both the joys and the sorrows of their lives.

As you may have noticed, the different kinds of communication that occur during the development of a relationship follow a continuum from impersonal-superficial to personal-deep. Because intimate relationships are time-consuming and require a level of mutual trust that is difficult to attain, people generally have only one or two truly intimate friends at any one time.

Stabilizing Relationships

When two people have a satisfactory relationship, whether as acquaintances, as friends, or as intimates, they look for *stabilization*—a means of maintaining the relationship at that level for some time. Some people find that they can keep many of the same acquaintances, friends, and intimates throughout much of their lives. For instance, you may have a friend with whom you play tennis or cards, with whom you attend professional conferences, or with whom you've gone to the theater for years.

Yet the stability of relationships, especially intimate ones, is under constant pressure. And when the energy that was used to build a relationship is withdrawn, the relationship will deteriorate.

Deteriorating Relationships

Most relationships change with time: Some get better, others do not. Although the deterioration phase of relationships has at least three distinct stages, movement through them can be so rapid that people miss the warning signs.

Reduction of Tolerance. The first sign of a weakening relationship is *reduction of tolerance*—people begin to lose interest in the opinions and feelings of other people. They change their orientation from *we* to *I*. Subjects that once were sources of free and open discussion become sources of discord, which limits the amount of sharing of personal feelings and ideas. The relationship begins to be characterized by an increase in "touchy" subjects, and people begin to have more unresolved conflicts.

Drifting Apart. As deterioration progresses, people begin to drift apart. Their communication changes from deep sharing of ideas and feelings to small talk and other "safe" communication. Not only are they no longer interested in exchanging significant ideas, they may begin to avoid each other altogether, seeking out other people with whom to share interests and activities. Hostility need not be present; rather, this stage is likely to be marked by indifference.

Ending. The ultimate outcome of a deteriorating relationship is an ending. If the relationship had no signs of formal commitment, the people simply stop seeing each other or living together. Formal commitments end in divorce or in the formal breaking of the contract.

PRACTICE in Identifying States of Relationships

By Yourself

1. Identify five people you consider to be your friends. In what kind of context did you first meet? What attracted you to them? What aspects of attraction have proved to be most important as the relationships developed?

2. Identify five people you consider to be acquaintances. List the ways in which communication with your acquaintances differs from communication with your friends.

3. Consider a recent relationship that has deteriorated. When did you notice that deterioration was taking place? What kinds of communication behavior marked the stages of deterioration?

Theories of Interpersonal Communication in Relationships

Although the old adage "If it ain't broke, don't fix it" has a lot of merit, many potentially strong and/or enduring relationships deteriorate and dissolve because people don't stop to analyze where the relationship is going right and where it is going wrong. The following discussion of interpersonal needs and exchange theory provides a useful rationale for analyzing your relationships and understanding their link to the process of communication.

Interpersonal Needs Theory

One method of analyzing your relationships is by assessing how well they meet your interpersonal needs.

Defining Needs Theory. The interpersonal needs theory hypothesizes that whether or not a relationship can be started, built, or maintained depends upon how well each person meets the interpersonal needs of the other. William Schutz identified three interpersonal needs that people have: affection, inclusion, and control.[4] His analysis demonstrates how interpersonal communication contributes to meeting these basic interpersonal needs.

The need for *affection* reflects a desire to express and to receive love. The people you know probably run the gamut of showing and expressing affection both verbally and nonverbally. At one end of the spectrum are the "underpersonal" individuals, who avoid close ties, seldom show strong feelings toward others, and shy away from those who show or who want to show affection. At the other end of the spectrum are the "overpersonal" individuals, who thrive on establishing "close" relationships with everyone. They think of all others as their close friends, immediately confide in persons they have met, and want everyone to consider them close friends. Somewhere in between these two extremes are "personal" people who can express and receive affection easily and who derive pleasure from their relationships with others.

The need for *inclusion* reflects a desire to be in the company of other people. According to Schutz, everyone has a need to be social. Yet people differ in the amount of interaction with others that will satisfy this need. At one extreme are the "undersocial" persons, who usually want to be left alone. Occasionally, they seek company or enjoying being included with others if specifically invited, but they do not require a great deal of social interaction to feel satisfied. At the other extreme are the "oversocial" persons, who need constant companionship and feel tense when they must be alone. If a party is happening, they must be there; if there is no party, they start one. Their doors are always open—everyone is welcome, and they expect others to welcome them. In reality, most people do not belong to either of these extreme types. Rather, they are sometimes comfortable being alone and at other times need and enjoy interacting with others.

The need for *control* reflects a desire to successfully influence the events and people around you. As with the other two interpersonal needs, people vary in how much control they require. At one extreme are persons who need no control, who seem to shun responsibility and do not want to be in charge of anything. The "abdicrats," as they are called by Schutz, are extremely submissive and are unlikely to make decisions or accept responsibility. At the other extreme are persons who like to be—indeed, who feel they must be—in charge. Such "autocrats" need to dominate others at all times and become anxious if they cannot. They usurp responsibility from those who may have the authority to control a situation, and they try to determine every decision. Again, most people fall somewhere between these two extremes. These "democrats" need to lead at certain times, but at other times they are content to follow the lead of others. Democrats can stand behind their ideas, but they also can be comfortable submitting to others, at least some of the time.

Applying Needs Theory. Through verbal and nonverbal communication behavior people display cues that reveal the level of their immediate interpersonal needs. As you interact with others, you can detect whether their needs for affection, inclusion, and control seem compatible with yours. Relationships develop and deteriorate in part because of interpersonal need compatibility. Thus, how you display your own interpersonal needs when you interact with others helps to determine the effectiveness of the relationship.

Schutz's theory of interpersonal needs is useful because it helps to explain a great deal of interpersonal behavior.[5] In addition, research on this model has been generally supportive of its major themes.[6] Interpersonal needs theory does not, however, explain *how* people adjust to one another in their ongoing relationships. The next theory we discuss will help us develop this understanding.

Exchange Theory

Another way of analyzing your relationships is on the basis of exchange ratios.

Defining Exchange Theory. John W. Thibaut and Harold H. Kelley, who originated exchange theory, believed that social relationships and the interaction between people can be understood in terms of the exchange of rewards and costs incurred during interaction.[7] *Rewards* are outcomes that are valued by the receiver. Some common rewards are good feelings, prestige, economic gain, and fulfillment of emotional needs. *Costs* are outcomes that the receiver does not wish to incur and include time, energy, and anxiety. For instance, Sharon may be willing to spend time talking with Jan if she anticipates feeling good as a result; she may not be willing to spend that time if she expects to be depressed at the end of the conversation.

According to Thibaut and Kelley, people seek interaction situations in which their behaviors will yield an outcome of high reward and low cost. For example, if Jill runs into Sarah on campus, several communication options are available to Jill: She can ignore Sarah, she can smile, she can say, "Hi!" in passing, or she can try to start a conversation. What Jill does will depend in part upon her appraisal of the *cost-reward analysis* of the outcome of the interaction. For instance, if Jill had been thinking about calling Sarah to arrange a game of tennis, she will probably take the time now to attempt to seek that outcome—she will be willing to pay the cost of taking time and using energy in hopes of receiving a suitable reward, a tennis date. If Jill and Sarah do talk, the duration of the interchange will continue until one or both realize that the interaction is falling below the satisfactory level. For Jill, this might mean until a tennis game is set. For Sarah, this might mean something else. Thibaut and Kelley suggest that the most desirable ratio between cost and reward varies from person to person and within one person from time to time.

If, over an extended period of time, a person's net rewards (reward minus cost) in a relationship fall below a certain level, that person will come to view the relationship as unsatisfactory or unpleasant. But if the net reward is higher than the level viewed as satisfactory, the person will regard the relationship or interaction as pleasant and satisfying. Moreover, if people have a number of relationships they perceive as giving them a good cost-reward ratio, they will set a high satisfaction level and will probably not be satisfied with low-outcome relationships. By contrast, people who do not have many positive interactions will be satisfied with relationships and interactions that people who enjoy high-outcome relationships would find unattractive. Thus, if Joan has four or five men she gets along well with, she is not likely to put up with Charley, who irritates her. If, however, Joan believes that Charley is the only man who can provide the benefits she seeks, she will be inclined to tolerate his irritating habits.

While the ratio of outcome to satisfaction level determines how attractive or unattractive a relationship or an interaction may be to people, it does not indicate how long a given relationship or interaction will last. Although it seems logical to terminate a relationship or an interaction in which costs exceed rewards, circumstances sometimes dictate that people will stay in a relationship that is plainly unsatisfactory.

Thibaut and Kelley's explanation for such a situation involves what they call the *comparison-level of alternatives*. They suggest that the decision to continue in a relationship may depend on what alternatives or other choices a person perceives as being available. Thus, durability of a relationship is also dependent upon possible alternatives. If the outcome level a person is experiencing drops below the level that person can attain elsewhere, the person will leave the relationship or interaction in order to engage in the next-best alternative. However, a person who is not satisfied with the outcome level may continue in the relationship or interaction because no viable alternative exists. The experience, as unsatisfactory as it may seem, is the best this person believes can be attained *at that time.*

Applying Exchange Theory. Like Schutz's interpersonal needs theory, Thibaut and Kelley's exchange theory helps illuminate important aspects of relationship development. Yet critics of this theory point out an important limitation. Exchange theory suggests that people *consciously* and *deliberately* weigh the costs and rewards associated with any relationship or interaction. That is, people *rationally* choose to continue or terminate relationships. Thus, the theory assumes that people behave rationally from an economic standpoint: they seek out relationships that benefit them and avoid those that are costly.[8] In fact, although people may behave rationally in most situations, rational models such as Thibaut and Kelley's cannot always explain behavior. Nevertheless, it is useful to examine your relationships from a cost-reward perspective. Especially if the relationship is stagnating, you may recognize areas where costs are greater than rewards. If so, you may be able to change some aspects of the relationship before it deteriorates completely.

PRACTICE in Analyzing Interpersonal Communication

By Yourself

1. Consider a person with whom you have a close interpersonal relationship. Analyze it on the basis of meeting interpersonal needs and in terms of its costs versus its rewards.

2. On a 1 to 5 scale (1 low, 5 high) how would you rate yourself on the following?
   a. need to show affection
   b. need to receive affection from others
   c. need to be included with others in bull sessions, informal gatherings, and parties
   d. willingness to include others in leisure-time activities
   e. need to be in charge of situations
   f. willingness to allow others to be in charge of situations

With a Friend

1. Ask a close friend to rate you on these same six criteria.

2. Have the friend indicate the verbal and nonverbal behaviors you use for the following:
   a. to show affection
   b. when you receive affection from others
   c. to get included with others in bull sessions, informal gatherings, and parties
   d. when you try to include others in leisure-time activities
   e. to take charge of situations
   f. when you want others to take charge of situations

3. Discuss the contrast (if any) between your and your friend's ratings.

Self-Disclosure and Feedback in Relationship Development

A healthy interpersonal relationship, especially one on a friendship or intimate level, is marked by a balance of self-disclosure (sharing biographical data, personal ideas, and feelings that are unknown to another person) and feedback (the mental and physical responses to people and/ or their messages) within the relationship. Consider a close interpersonal relationship you currently enjoy. As you examine your relationship, you may believe that both parties perceive it as being a good one. If so, you and your friend probably maintain a mutually satisfying blend of self-disclosure and feedback.

Johari Windows

How can you tell whether you and another are sharing enough to keep the relationship growing? The best method is to discuss it. As the basis for a worthwhile discussion we suggest the use of a Johari window, named after its two originators, Joe Luft and Harry Ingham. The Johari window is a tool for examining the relationship between disclosure and feedback.[9]

The window is divided into four sections or panes, as shown in Figure 5.1. The first quadrant is called the "open" pane of the window, where everything about people that is known and freely shared with others, as well as others' observations of their behavior, is placed. For instance,

Figure 5.1 The Johari window.

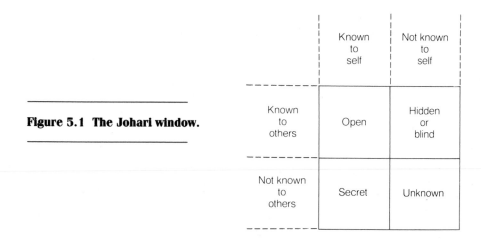

most people are willing to discuss where they live, the kinds of cars they drive, the activities they enjoy, and countless other items of information. Moreover, most people are aware of certain of their mannerisms that others observe. People may be well aware that they get red when they are embarrassed or that they wrinkle their noses when they are not sure of something. If you were preparing a Johari window that represented your relationship with another person, you would include in the open pane all the items of information about yourself that you would feel free to share with that other person.

The second quadrant is called the "secret" pane, where all those things people know about themselves that they do not normally share with others, for whatever reason, are placed. This information may run the gamut from where Tim keeps his pencils or why he does not care for green vegetables to deep secrets that seem very threatening to him. If you were preparing a Johari window that represented your relationship with another person, you would include in the secret pane all the items of information that you were unwilling to share with that other person. Secret information moves into the open part of the window only when you change your attitude about revealing that specific information. If, for example, Angela was engaged at one time but usually does not let people know that fact, it would be placed in the secret part of her window. If for some reason she decided to disclose this information to you, it would move into the open part of the Johari window.

The third quadrant is called the "blind" pane, where information others know about people that the people are unaware of is placed. Most people have blind spots. For example, if Charley snores when he sleeps, if he mumbles to himself when he is concentrating on something, or if he gets a gleam in his eye when he sees a girl he would like to meet, these may well be nonverbal behaviors that he is blind to. Information in the blind area of the window moves to the open area through feedback from others. If you were preparing a Johari window that represented your relationship with another person, the size of the blind pane would include your guess as to the amount of information the other person holds about you either that the person is reluctant to share or that you are unwilling to hear. For instance, if Ken is Charley's roommate at the dorm, he may not tell Charley that he has bad breath. If he does tell Charley directly or indirectly through some nonverbal response, Charley may not choose to "hear" what Ken tells him. In both cases the blind spot continues. If Charley is receptive to such feedback, however, the blind pane becomes smaller, and the open pane larger.

The fourth quadrant is called the "unknown" pane, where aspects of a given person that are not known to anyone—neither to the people themselves nor to others—are placed. If, for instance, you have never tried hang-gliding, neither you nor anyone else knows how you might react at the point of takeoff—you might chicken out or you might follow through, do it well, and love every minute of it. Once you had tried, your feelings and abilities would be known by you and, probably, by at least a few others.

Thus, as you can see, with each bit of self-disclosure or feedback the sizes and shapes of the various window panes change. For any relationship you have with another person, you can construct a window that represents the ratio of openness to closedness. Let's look at four different representations of Johari windows and consider what they mean.

Figure 5.2a shows a relationship in which the open area is very small. The people are not sharing much information about themselves and are blind to what other people know or think about them. This pane might represent your relationship with another person during the first stages of getting to know that person. It is also typical of people who keep to themselves and who do not want, desire, or need to interact on more than a superficial level with others.

Figure 5.2b shows a relationship in which people are willing to share their thoughts and feelings but get or are receptive to very little

Figure 5.2 Four Johari windows. (a) Willing to share information and receptive to feedback. (b) Seeking feedback but unwilling to share information. (c) Willing to share information but blind to feedback. (d) Unwilling to share information and blind to feedback.

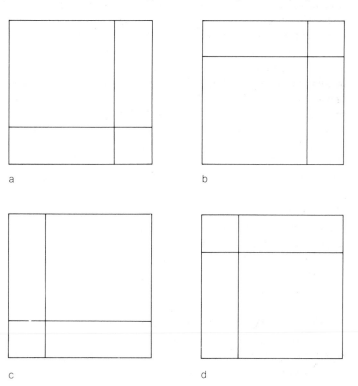

a

b

c

d

feedback from others. Such people may perceive themselves as being very open in their communication. Yet their communication is limited by their unwillingness to learn or their lack of interest in learning about what others observe.

Figure 5.2c shows a relationship in which people seek out and are very receptive to feedback but are quite reluctant to share much of themselves. They want to hear what others have observed, but they are unwilling or afraid to disclose their own observations or feelings.

Figure 5.2d shows a relationship in which people both seek out and are very receptive to feedback and are willing to share information and feelings they have. This kind of pane would usually depict a close relationship of friends or intimates. Even though Figure 5.2d represents the best model of communication for friends and intimates, the other windows also depict many types of acceptable communication relationships. Although people need not share every idea or feeling with others, nor need they be receptive to every reaction to them, having a relatively large open pane is helpful for good interpersonal communication.

PRACTICE in Drawing Johari Windows

With a Friend

Working with a friend, each of you should draw a window that represents your perception of your relationship with the other. Then each of you should draw a window that represents what you perceive to be the other's relationship with you. Share the windows. How do they compare? If there are differences in the representations, talk with your friend about them.

Skills for Creating Positive Communication Climates

At this point in your life you will be beginning, testing, and modifying relationships. The remainder of this chapter will focus on communication skills you can use to create a climate in which relationships thrive. Currently, you may have relationships in all phases of the life cycle. Let's look at communication skills that are most likely to lead to satisfying relationships.

Descriptive Communication

Relationships grow best in a climate in which communication is descriptive rather than evaluative.[10] Being descriptive simply means stating what you see or hear in objective language, but it is deceptively difficult to do. Why? Because when you think you are describing, you may in fact be evaluating or judging.

Many people might perceive the following examples as being *descriptive* when in fact they are *evaluative*.

As Molly leaves a student senate meeting, she runs into a friend and says, "I just came from the dullest meeting!"

As Arnold recounts the basketball game he saw the night before, he says, "Grover kept making ridiculous passes!"

After Jack eats his fifth enchilada, he turns to Marian and says, "I'm going to die."

In reality, each of these statements is more evaluative than descriptive. Calling a meeting "dull" does not describe what did or did not happen; calling passes "ridiculous" does not describe what the passes were actually like; and saying "I'm going to die" does not accurately describe the feeling of having eaten too much. What, then, is descriptive language? If Molly had said, "I've just come from a two-and-a-half-hour meeting. We heard four reports, none of which was under fifteen minutes, and we debated for an hour on a topic that ended up passing unanimously," she would have described a meeting that might well be evaluated as dull.

How does evaluation affect the relationship climate? First, evaluation does not inform; it places a judgment on what has been said or done. Misunderstandings often result from a shortage of information. Before an evaluation can be understood, a person must have the data on which it was based. In conversation, however, people are inclined to skip over the information (the description). At the basketball game Arnold watched Grover repeatedly force passes into crowds of players under the basket, resulting in turnovers; he watched Grover try behind-the-back passes that went out of bounds; and he watched Grover make passes when he had a good open shot. Arnold has all this information, but when he talks about the game the next day, he says, "Grover kept making ridiculous passes!" Nick, the person Arnold is talking to, wasn't at the game—he has no mental picture of the passes. He has no data upon which to judge the accuracy of Arnold's remark, and the remark itself doesn't really tell him anything. Had Arnold said, "Grover kept passing into crowds, throwing behind-the-back passes that went out of bounds, and passing off when he had the best open shot," Nick would have been able to understand Arnold's evaluation of Grover's game.

Second, evaluations are likely to make other people defensive, especially if the evaluation is personal, negative, or contrary to the other person's perception. *Defensiveness* is a negative feeling and/or behavior that results when a person feels threatened. For instance, as Henry and Susan leave a musical comedy, Henry thinks to himself, "That was a really enjoyable show—the songs were great, the sets were good, and every major part was well acted." Suddenly, Susan turns to him and says, "What a miserable excuse for a professional production." Her statement is almost sure to draw a defensive reaction from Henry because it is both negative and contrary to his opinion. Henry may sharply contradict Susan, or he may withdraw in anger from further communication with her. In either case the climate for effective communication between them is likely to be spoiled—at least for the moment.

The descriptions you will want to use are of two types: (1) descriptions of behavior ("Did you know your eyes sparkle when you're happy?") and (2) descriptions of feelings ("When you look at me like that, I feel warm inside"). Guidelines for the skill of describing behavior will be presented on page 229, and guidelines for the skill of describing feelings will be discussed on pages 163–170.

Open Communication

Relationships grow best in a climate where the *agenda*—the subject of the conversation or the purpose for the communication—is readily apparent. When Carson, the account executive, calls Sanders in to talk about his progress on the Morris account, the reason for the meeting—the agenda—is to discuss progress of that account. By contrast, in normal conversation we expect agendas to be made up as we go along.

Occasionally, however, participants in a conversation may have a secret underlying motive, known as a *hidden agenda*. For instance, if Carson calls Sanders in to talk about the Morris account but she really wants to find out whether Sanders is writing his own reports, Carson's hidden agenda would be finding the answer to this question.

Interpersonal communication works best when the people involved understand what is going on. When people aren't honest about their reasons for talking, a potential for communication barriers between the people exists. In some cases people use hidden agendas as a matter of tact, propriety, or lack of nerve. Suppose Collins suspects Jones is taking home company material (paper, paper clips, pencils) for his personal use; Collins may call Jones into her office to talk about a report and indirectly try to get at the subject of misappropriation. In this case the hidden agenda may appear to be beneficial to Collins, but when the real subject is revealed, her attempt to keep it below the surface may become a bigger issue than the theft. When hidden agendas are discovered, the fragile bond of trust may be frayed or even broken, and with it the chance for good working relationships. Thus, approaching a difficult problem directly is usually the best tactic. If Collins suspects Jones is taking office supplies—or if she has seen him do it—she would be wiser to say, "Jones, I called you in here today because I believe you may be taking office supplies home for your personal use, and I'd like to talk to you about this issue." Dealing with the issue may prove difficult, but at least the difficulty will be the issue itself and not something else.

Hidden agendas also can turn into psychological games that can be very destructive. A game is one person's attempt to manipulate another person's behavior until the manipulator gets some payoff, usually a predictable behavior. Notice the hidden agendas in the following two examples:

Glen knows that Judy gets angry when he smokes in the bedroom, so he lights up in the bedroom and acts amazed when Judy loses her temper.

Rachel knows that Steve is likely to become very uncomfortable when his former girlfriend, Doris, is mentioned. So in his presence Rachel "innocently" asks, "Say, has anyone seen Doris lately?"

In both cases the person's hidden agenda is to create a painful experience for the other person. If the behavior elicits the desired response, that person "wins." It is this win-lose element that makes such statements games.

Provisionalism in Communication

Relationships grow best in a climate where people are willing to state their beliefs, but there is a difference between stating a belief provisionally and stating it dogmatically. *Provisional* wordings suggest that the ideas expressed are thought to be correct but may not be; *dogmatic* wordings leave no room for discussion. Whereas provisional language helps create or maintain a good communication climate, dogmatic statements stop discussion and tend to create defensiveness.

Consider the differences between the two sentences in each of the following pairs:

If I remember rightly, Dalton holds the record for most sales in a month.
I'm telling you, Dalton holds the record for most sales in a month.

It's my opinion that this is no time to buy a house.
Everybody knows this is no time to buy a house.

What differences did you notice? The first sentence of each pair is stated provisionally; the second is stated dogmatically. Why are the first sentences more likely to result in better interpersonal communication? First, the tentativeness of the phrasings as compared to the second sentences is likely to be less antagonistic. Second, they acknowledge that the words come from the speaker—who may have it wrong. "I'm telling you" leaves no room for possible error; "If I remember rightly" not only leaves room for error but also shows that it is the speaker's recollection and not a statement of universal certainty. Both sets of statements are asserting the "truth." Although the first set considers facts that are a matter of record (they can be validated by looking at company records), neither sentence, as stated, is *necessarily* true. The second set of statements deals with matters of opinion, or inferences drawn from facts, but again, neither sentence is necessarily true.

Speaking provisionally may seem unassertive and wishy-washy, and, if carried to extremes, it can be. But there is a world of difference between suggesting what you think to be true and stating your views in a way that is likely to arouse hostility. Speaking provisionally allows for conflicting opinions. On certain topics it acknowledges that something that seems to be true under certain circumstances may not be entirely true or may not be true at all under different circumstances.

The procedure for phrasing ideas provisionally is as follows:

1. Consider what you are about to say.

2. Determine whether it contains a wording that shows an attitude of finality, positiveness, or "allness" of concept that is not warranted.

3. If it does, add a qualifying statement that recognizes (a) that the statement is your opinion or (b) that the statement may not be entirely true or is only true under these circumstances.

Adults and children can talk most easily when they relate on the same level. You can create a positive climate for communication by talking to others as equals regardless of differences in age, status, and experience. But equality in interpersonal communication does not mean treating everyone alike—you must remain sensitive to each individual's unique perspective.

Equality in Communication

Relationships grow in climates where the people are seen as equals rather than in climates where one person is perceived as superior to another. Some people believe that their positions make them superior to those around them. Heads of departments or oldest members of the family may think that these designations make them better people. Whatever the basis for the assumption of superiority, however, projecting it often results in a negative rather than a positive communication climate, particularly when others involved are not all convinced of that superiority.

A positive communication climate may be achieved by choosing language that conveys an attitude of equality rather than an attitude of superiority. *Equality* implies that two people exist on the same level, that they perceive each other as being of similar worth. Equality is usually shown by the exclusion of any words or nonverbal signs that might indicate the opposite.

One way to alter statements that project personal superiority is to make statements issue-related. Instead of saying, "Listen, I know that LLG is the top stock to buy—I'm an expert in these kinds of things," try something like "LLG looks like a good stock to buy; it has paid solid dividends exceeding bank interest rates for the last eight years." A second way is to be very conscious of the effects of your tone of voice, facial expressions, dress, and manners. Through both words and actions you need to show that you are a person—no better and no worse than others. By listening to others' ideas, by pitching in and working, and by respecting what others say, you can demonstrate an attitude of equality.

The procedure for showing equality is as follows:

1. Consider what you are about to say.

2. Consider whether it contains words or phrases that indicate or imply that you are in some way superior to those you are speaking to.

3. If there are signs of superiority, recast the sentence to change the tone.

PRACTICE in Analyzing Climates

By Yourself

1. Label the following statements as E (evaluative), D (dogmatic), or S (superior). In each case rephrase the statement so that it is descriptive, provisional, or equal. We have done the first one for you.

___D___ 1. "Maud—turn that off! No one can study with the radio on!"
"Maud—I'd suggest turning the radio down or off. You may find that you can study better without the distraction."

_____ 2. "Did you ever hear of such a tacky idea as having a formal wedding and using paper plates?"

_____ 3. "That advertising program will never sell."

_____ 4. "Oh Jack—you're so funny wearing plaids with stripes. Well, I guess that's a man for you!"

_____ **5.** "Paul—you're acting like a baby. You've got to learn to use your head."

_____ **6.** "A Walt Disney show? I don't want to see any kids' movie!"

_____ **7.** "You may think you know how to handle the situation, but you are just not mature enough. I know when something's right for you."

ANSWERS: 1. D; 2. E; 3. D; 4. S; 5. E; 6. E; 7. S

2. Share your revisions with other members of the class.

3. Think of the last time you had a long discussion with another person. Which aspects of climate helped or hindered the effectiveness of that discussion?

Summary

An effect of—if not the primary reason for—communication is developing and maintaining relationships. Although at times we seem to fall into and drift out of relationships for no particular reason, identifiable elements do underlie the success or failure of a relationship. A good relationship is any mutually satisfying interaction, on any level, with another person.

Relationships have an identifiable life cycle composed of development, (acquaintanceship, friendship, and deep or intimate friendship), stability, and deterioration. Each of these phases can be characterized by the dominant types of communication and the amount of self-disclosure that takes place. Many different theories have been set forth to explain how relationships work. Schutz sees relationships in terms of ability to meet the interpersonal needs of affection, inclusion, and control. Thibaut and Kelley see relationships as exchanges: People evaluate relationships through a cost-reward analysis, weighing the energy, time, and money invested against the satisfaction gained.

The Johari window is a particularly useful means for analyzing the amount of self-disclosure that occurs in a relationship.

Relationships are likely to develop best in climates of descriptiveness rather than evaluation, climates of openness rather than deceit and manipulation, climates of provisionalism rather than dogmatism, and climates of equality rather than superiority. Many of the communication skills presented in later chapters can be used to create healthy climates.

Notes

1. Steve Duck and Robin Gilmour, eds., *Personal Relationships* (London: Academic Press, 1981), p. 2.

2. For instance, whereas Mark Knapp, one of the first communication researchers to study building and deteriorating relationships, describes the development of a relationship as having five stages (which he labels initiating, experimenting, intensifying, integrating, and bonding), Dalman A. Taylor and Irwin Altman describe the development of a relationship as having four stages—orientation, exploratory, effective exchange, and stable exchange. Similarly, although both Knapp and Steve Duck describe deteriorating relationships in four or five steps, they use different labels. Knapp calls them circumscribing, stagnating, avoiding and terminating; Duck calls them breakdown phase, intrapsychic phase, diadic phase, social phase, and grave-dressing phase. See Mark L. Knapp, *Interpersonal Communication and Human Relationships* (Boston: Allyn & Bacon, 1984); Dalman A. Taylor and Irwin Altman, "Communication in Interpersonal Relationships," in Michael E. Roloff and Gerald R. Miller, eds., *Interpersonal Processes: New Directions in Communication Research* (Beverly Hills, Calif.: Sage, 1987), p. 259; and Steve Duck, "How to Lose Friends Without Influencing People," in Roloff and Miller, eds., *Interpersonal Processes: New Directions in Communication Research*, pp. 290–291.

3. Richard Reichert, *Self-Awareness through Group Dynamics* (Dayton, Ohio: Pflaum/Standard, 1970), p. 63.

4. William Schutz, *The Interpersonal Underworld* (Palo Alto, Calif.: Science & Behavior Books, 1966), pp. 18–20.

5. Stephen W. Littlejohn, *Theories of Human Communication*, 2d ed. (Belmont, Calif.: Wadsworth, 1983), p. 180.

6. Marvin Shaw, *Group Dynamics: The Psychology of Small Group Behavior*, 3d ed. (New York: McGraw-Hill, 1981), pp. 228–231.

7. John W. Thibaut and Harold H. Kelley, *The Social Psychology of Groups* (New York: Wiley, 1959), pp. 100–125.

8. Littlejohn, *Theories of Communication*, p. 208.

9. From *Group Processes: An Introduction to Group Dynamics*, by Joseph Luft. By permission of Mayfield Publishing Company (formerly National Press Books). Copyright © 1963, 1970 by Joseph Luft.

10. A good background of descriptive versus evaluative, provisional versus dogmatic, and equal versus superior is laid in Jack R. Gibb, "Defensive Communication," *Journal of Communication* 11 (September 1961): 141–148.

Chapter 6

Communication of

Ideas and

Feelings

Objectives

After you have read this chapter, you should be able
to define and/or explain:

Sharing ideas   Crediting others

Self-disclosure   Owning feelings

Guidelines for disclosing   Asking for criticism

Describing feelings   Serial communication

Differences between express-   Information overload
ing feelings and describing
feelings

Jan has just read an account of another terrorist attack on an American diplomat abroad. Totally absorbed in her thoughts, she approaches a group of her friends and tries to begin a conversation on the subject. She says . . .

Gordon is reading a letter that explains why his favorite uncle won't be able to hire him for the summer job he has had for the past several years. This totally unexpected news so late in the year is devastating to Gordon. He turns to his roommate Phil and says . . .

Jan and Gordon are about to communicate. But the nature of their messages will be qualitatively different. Why? Jan will be sharing her *ideas* on terrorism, so the effectiveness of her communication will depend on the quality of information that she presents. Gordon will be sharing his *feelings* about the bad news, so the effectiveness of his communication will depend on his ability to disclose sensitive information about himself and describe his feelings.

Although communication is a dynamic, transactional process between people in relationships, one of the persons involved in the process must introduce topics of conversation. Moreover, even in the midst of a give-and-take interaction, one person may be focusing on the presentation of his or her own ideas and feelings rather than on a response to the ideas presented. In this chapter we consider the sender skills of sharing ideas, self-disclosure, describing feelings, crediting, and asking for criticism.

Sharing Ideas

Years ago, Dale Carnegie made a fortune with a book entitled *How to Win Friends and Influence People*. The premise of the book was that a person can gain fame, wealth, friends, and admiration through the power of conversation. As they did in the past, people continue to look for those who are interesting to talk with. Surprisingly, despite their years of education, most college students believe they are not very stimulating to talk with. In fact, anyone can learn to initiate and participate in meaningful exchanges of ideas.

In the previous chapter we talked about how you go about initiating conversations with people you wish to meet. We recommended that to break the ice you employ such strategies as introducing yourself and referring to physical context, to thoughts or feelings, and to the other person. Once people begin to converse, however, the effectiveness of their interchange and the satisfaction they receive often depend on how stimulating they perceive the exchange to be. Most people gravitate toward others whom they regard as interesting to talk with. Sometimes, they don't really expect to do much of the talking—they are more interested in hearing what the others have to say on a particular subject. Yet almost everyone aspires to be a stimulating conversationalist. Thus, we begin our study of communication skills in this chapter by examining those skills designed to help initiate and maintain conversations.

Characteristics of an Effective Conversationalist

Effective conversationalists are likely to share at least the following five characteristics.

1. *Effective conversationalists have quality information.* The key to solid, stimulating conversation is to have information that others value. In a recent study Claire Brunner and Judy Pearson found that men in particular judge others as competent communicators on the basis of their knowledge.[1] In late September before the 1988 general election we were with a group of people, one of whom had just finished conducting a major opinion poll on a political issue. For an hour that person was the center of attention. Why? Because she had information that people wanted to hear about.

Although you cannot be an expert in every area, the more you know, the greater the chance that you will be a good conversationalist. Do you read at least one newspaper a day (not just the comics or the sports)? Do you read at least one news or professional magazine a week? Do you watch television documentaries and news specials as well as entertainment and sports programs? Do you engage knowledgeable people in conversation on topics about which they have expert information? Do you go to the theater, concerts, and so on? If you answered no to all of these questions, you probably do not have much to contribute to social conversations. Only when you expose yourself to a broad array of information experiences can you develop ideas that others will find interesting and provide grist for the conversation mill.

2. *Effective conversationalists enjoy the give-and-take of informal discussion.* The best conversations usually occur when people enjoy interacting. Do you enjoy listening to the ideas presented by others? Do you like to comment on, discuss, and even disagree with what they say? If you do, then you probably enjoy the conversations you have. In addition, those you converse with can sense this enjoyment through the nonverbal messages you send.

3. *Effective conversationalists ask good questions.* There are times when you will be the center of attention, when the conversation will focus on your ideas. Many times, however, the quality of your conversation will depend on how well you can draw out the other person. Even when you are the major source of information in a conversation, you want other people to react to the issue being discussed. To do this you need to develop your skill as a questioner. Both in Chapter 8 and Module E we will discuss asking questions in some detail.

4. *Effective conversationalists listen to others' ideas.* A conversation represents an interaction between people, not a one-way broadcast. Although some people regard a conversation as successful when they do all the talking, effective conversations are characterized by the development of shared meaning. In a normal conversation, then, you can expect to be the listener at least half the time. In Chapters 7 and 8 we consider the topics of listening and appropriate response skills, respectively.

5. *Effective conversationalists are willing to try.* You cannot become interesting, witty, provocative, and stimulating overnight. You must be willing to practice. Thus, at every opportunity you should engage in conversation with others.

Guidelines for Effective Conversation

Of the number of guidelines for effective conversation, the following two are most relevant.

1. *Have a plan of operation.* Most conversation has some purpose, so you should have a conversational plan, "some consciously constructed conceptualization of one or more sequences of action aimed at achieving a goal."[2] Because conversation is a dynamic process for which you cannot plan for every possible response, the plan usually involves an opening approach and some idea of how to proceed given the most likely listener reactions. So, if your goal is to explain the steps of a process, you should have planned the sequence of steps in advance, and you also should have some idea of how you might answer questions about various steps.

2. *Adhere to the goal of the conversation.* Good conversation occurs when you are committed to furthering the goals of that conversation. Thus, you ought to make a contribution to conversation "such as is required, at the stage at which it occurs, by the accepted purpose or direction of the talk exchange [in which you are engaged]."[3] How is this done? You should contribute neither more nor less information than is required; you should state only that which you believe to be true or for which you have considerable evidence; and you should state information as clearly as possible.

PRACTICE in Preparing for Conversation

By Yourself

1. List the five subject areas you believe you know the most about. Is there some variety in your repertoire of knowledge?

2. For the next few days keep a log of your conversations with others. At the end of each day make note of the people you talked with and the topics you talked about. Pay special attention to topics you discussed with people you just met or with people you do not know very well.

3. Try to work for greater variety in conversations with others. How well are you able to develop and maintain such conversations? Are they more or less satisfying than conversations on weather, sports, and daily happenings? Why?

Self-Disclosure

As we pointed out in the previous chapter, effective communication involves some degree of self-disclosure. *Self-disclosure* means sharing biographical data, personal ideas, and feelings that are unknown to another person. Statements such as "I was 5'6" in seventh grade" reveal biographical information—facts about you as an individual. Biographical disclosures are the easiest to make, for they are, in a manner of speaking, a matter of public record. By contrast, statements such as "I don't think prisons ever really rehabilitate criminals" disclose personal ideas and reveal what and how you think. And statements such as "I get scared whenever I have to make a speech" disclose feelings.

Self-disclosure enables other people to get to know you. Usually the more people know about a person, the better the chance that they will like that person. Yet self-disclosure does carry a degree of risk, for just as knowing a person better is *likely* to result in closer interpersonal relations, learning too much about a person *may* result in alienation. The statement "Familiarity breeds contempt" means that some people can learn too much about another person; eventually, they learn something that detracts from the relationship. Because some people fear that their disclosures could have negative rather than positive consequences, they prefer not to disclose in the belief they will get no reaction at all.

Although a risk-free life (probably impossible to attain) might be safe, some risk is vital to achieving satisfying interpersonal relationships. At the same time, too much risk can be more costly than we wish. The following are guidelines for determining an appropriate amount of self-disclosure in interpersonal encounters.

1. *Self-disclosure should begin with the kind of information you want others to disclose to you.* When people are getting to know others, they look for information that is generally shared freely among people, such as talking about hobbies, sports, school, and current events. These are the kinds of disclosures that you should make early in a relationship.

2. *Self-disclosure of more intimate information should come when you believe the disclosure represents an acceptable risk.* There is always some risk involved in disclosing, but as you gain trust in another person, you perceive the disclosure of more revealing information as "safe." Incidentally, this guideline explains why people sometimes engage in intimate self-disclosure with bartenders or with people they meet in travel. They perceive the disclosures as safe (representing reasonable risk) because the person either does not know them or is in no position to use the information against them. Unfortunately, these people apparently cannot trust their husbands, wives, or other members of the family enough to make the disclosures to them.

3. *Self-disclosure should move gradually to deeper levels.* Because receiving self-disclosure can be as threatening as giving it, most people become uncomfortable when the level of disclosure exceeds their expectations. As a relationship develops, the depth of disclosure increases as well.

4. *Intimate or very personal self-disclosure is most appropriate in ongoing relationships.* Disclosures about deep feelings, fears, loves, and so forth are most appropriate in close, well-established relationships. When people disclose deep secrets to acquaintances, they are engaging in potentially threatening behavior. If disclosure is made before a bond of trust is established, the person making the disclosure risks alienating the acquaintance. Moreover, people are often embarrassed by and hostile toward others who try to saddle them with personal information in an effort to establish a relationship where none exists.

Self-disclosure simply means sharing information about yourself that's unknown to another person. Although interpersonal communication always involves some self-disclosure, determining the appropriate level of disclosure is critical to its effectiveness. Intimate disclosures about your feelings should be reserved for relationships in which others are comfortable sharing the same level of disclosure.

5. *Intimate self-disclosure should continue only if it is reciprocated.* When people disclose, they expect disclosure in return. When it is apparent that self-disclosure will not be returned, you should limit the amount of disclosure you make. Lack of return generally suggests that the person does not feel the relationship is one in which extensive self-disclosure is truly appropriate.

6. *People's attitudes about disclosure vary, so what you would consider appropriate or inappropriate may not be so to someone else.* When the response to your self-disclosure tells you that the disclosure was inappropriate, ask what led to this effect. You can learn from a previous mistake and can avoid the same kind of mistake in the future.

PRACTICE in Determining Self-Disclosure Guidelines

By Yourself

People's perceptions of appropriate self-disclosure vary. The following exercise will help you recognize the variations in what people see as appropriate and provide you with a useful base of information from which to work. Label each of the following statements L (low risk), meaning you believe it is appropriate to disclose this information to almost any person; M (moderate risk), meaning you believe it is appropriate to disclose this information to persons you know fairly well and with whom you have already established a friendship; H (high risk), meaning you would disclose such information only to the few friends you have great trust in or to your most intimate friends; or X (unacceptable risk), meaning you would disclose it to no one.

_____ **a.** Your hobbies, how you like best to spend your spare time

_____ **b.** Your preferences and dislikes in music

_____ **c.** Your educational background and your feelings about it

_____ **d.** Your personal views on politics, the Presidency, and foreign and domestic policy

_____ **d.** Your personal religious views and the nature of your religious participation

_____ **f.** Habits and reactions of yours that bother you at the moment

_____ **g.** Characteristics of yours that give you pride and satisfaction

_____ **h.** The unhappiest moments in your life—in detail

_____ **i.** The occasions in your life when you were happiest—in detail

_____ **j.** The actions you have most regretted taking in your life and why

_____ **k.** The main unfulfilled wishes and dreams in your life

_____ **l.** Your guiltiest secrets

_____ **m.** Your views on the way a husband and wife should live their marriage

_____ **n.** What to do, if anything, to stay fit

_____ **o.** The aspects of your body you are most pleased with

_____ **p.** The features of your appearance you are most displeased with and wish to change

_____ **q.** The person in your life whom you most resent and the reasons why

_____ **r.** Your favorite forms of erotic play and lovemaking

_____ **s.** The people with whom you have been sexually intimate and the circumstances of your relationship with each

In a Group (Optional)

Working in a group, discuss your labeling of the statements. You are not required to make any of the disclosures, only to discuss why or why not you would make them and under what circumstances, if any. The purpose of the discussion is to see how people differ in what they view as acceptable disclosure.

Dealing with Feelings

Everyone has feelings. But people differ in how they handle the feelings they have. Three ways that people deal with their feelings are (1) to withhold them, (2) to express or display them, and (3) to describe them.

Withholding Feelings

One way people deal with their feelings is by withholding them. *Withholding feelings* means keeping feelings inside and not giving any verbal or nonverbal cues that might reveal those feelings to others. Withholding feelings is best exemplified by the good poker player who develops a "poker face," a neutral look that is impossible to decipher. The look is the same whether the player's cards are good or bad. Unfortunately, many people use poker faces in their relationships. Whether they hurt inside or are extremely excited, no one knows. For instance, Doris feels very nervous when Candy stands over her while Doris is working on her report. And when Candy says, "That first paragraph isn't very well written," Doris begins to seethe, yet she says nothing—that is, she withholds her feelings.

Psychologists believe that when people withhold feelings, they can develop physical problems such as ulcers, high blood pressure, and heart disease, as well as psychological problems such as stress, neuroses, and psychoses. Moreover, people who withhold feelings are often perceived as cold, undemonstrative, and not much fun to be around.

Is withholding ever appropriate? When a situation is inconsequential, you may well choose to withhold your feelings. For instance, a stranger's inconsiderate behavior at a party may bother you, but because you can move to another part of the room, withholding may not be detrimental. In our example of Doris seething at Candy's behavior, however, withholding could be costly to Doris.

Expressing or Displaying Feelings

The second way of dealing with feelings is to express or to display them. *Expressing or displaying feelings* means giving an immediate nonverbal and/or verbal cue that reveals the feelings. Cheering over a great play at a sporting event, booing the umpire at a perceived bad call, patting a person on the back when the person does something well, and kicking a chair when you stub your toe are all expressions or displays of feelings.

An open expression or display of positive feelings will tend to benefit you both psychologically and interpersonally. For example, if someone does something nice for you, a smile, a thank you, or some such reaction is likely to be well received. Squeals of delight, exclamations of "Wow" or "Great," and the like represent verbal expressions of positive feelings. A pat on the back, a hug, or just a touch may be nonverbal expressions of positive feelings. At times, some people even need to be more demonstrative. The bumper sticker "Have you hugged your kid today?" reinforces the point that love and affection need to be demonstrated constantly for a person to understand that they still exist.

An open expression or display of negative feelings may be good for you psychologically but bad for you interpersonally. If someone steps on your toe and hurts you, you may have an urge to lash out at that person either nonverbally with a sudden slap or punch or verbally with "Watch where you're putting your stupid feet!" Such behavior, however, is not likely to improve your interpersonal relationship with that person. Likewise, had Doris lashed out at Candy by saying, "Who the hell asked you for your opinion!" she might have felt better, but it would certainly have created interpersonal problems with Candy.

We deal with our feelings by withholding them, displaying them, or describing them. While openly showing positive feelings is usually good for you psychologically and interpersonally, handling negative feelings is more difficult.

Describing Feelings

The final way people handle their feelings is by describing them. *Describing feelings* simply means putting your immediate emotional state into words. Describing feelings is often the best strategy for dealing with feelings, not only because it gives you the best chance for a positive outcome, but also because it gives people clues as to how you wish to be treated. Let us emphasize this point. Describing feelings represents a starting point in educating others about you and your feelings. Consider the following statements: "Cliff, I get really angry with you when you borrow my jacket without asking." "Rick, you may not mean anything by it, but I feel embarrassed when you tease me about my accent." "Martha, I resent it that you leave the kitchen when I start to wash the dishes." "Paul, I'm pleased that you take the time to stop by to see me when you are in town."

When you identify your feelings, people are in a better position to know whether they should change their behavior toward you. If you tell Paul that you really feel flattered when he visits you, such a statement should encourage Paul to visit you again. Likewise, when you tell Cliff that you feel very angry when he borrows your jacket without asking, he is more likely to ask to borrow it the next time.[4] Thus, you exercise a measure of control over others' behavior toward you.

Note, however, that describing feelings is not a perfect method for controlling behavior; it will not always get people to change their behavior toward you. For instance, Paul might not want to stop by each time he is in town, and Cliff might not care whether you get angry or not. Still, a great deal of what we're talking about in our discussion of skill development involves increasing the *probability* of desirable outcomes. If, therefore, you can raise the chances of desirable behavior by describing feelings, isn't it worth a try? And even if people do not behave as you would like, at least they will know the consequences of their behavior— they will have a rational base for what they do.

Keep in mind that describing and expressing feelings are not the same. Many times people think they are describing feelings when in fact they are expressing them. For instance, saying in an angry tone of voice, "Why the hell do you need to yell at me when I don't play the card you think I should?" would be expressing your feelings. Saying, "When you yell at me like that in front of everyone, I feel humiliated—instead of helping my play, those comments just make me want to strike back at you" is an example of describing your feelings. The first part of the communication practice at the end of this section focuses on developing your awareness of the difference between expressing or displaying and describing feelings.

If describing feelings is so important to effective communication, why don't more people do it regularly? There seem to be at least four reasons why many people don't describe feelings.

1. *Many people don't have a very good vocabulary of words for describing the various feelings they are experiencing.* People can sense that they are angry; however, they may not be able to distinguish between feeling annoyed, betrayed, cheated, crushed, disturbed, envious, furious,

Describing how you feel about something that has happened to you can be even more difficult than describing your feelings about a painting. This kind of sharing is important for maintaining close relationships.

infuriated, outraged, or shocked. Each of these terms describes a slightly different aspect of what many people lump together as anger. The second part of the communication practice at the end of this section focuses on developing your vocabulary so you can describe your feelings more precisely.

2. *Many people believe that describing their true feelings reveals too much about them.* If you tell people what hurts you, you risk their using the information against you when they want to hurt you on purpose. Although this may be true, the potential benefits of revealing your true feelings far outweigh the risks. For instance, if Pete has a nickname for you that you don't like, and you tell Pete that calling you by that nickname upsets you, Pete has the option of calling you by that name when he wants to hurt you, *but* he is more likely to stop calling you by that name. If, on the other hand, you don't describe your feelings to Pete, he's probably going to call you by that name all the time because he doesn't know any better. By saying nothing you reinforce his behavior. The level of risk varies with each situation, but you will more often improve a relationship by describing feelings than be hurt by it.

3. *Many people believe that if they describe feelings, others will make them feel guilty about having such feelings.* At a very tender age we all learned about "tactful" behavior. Under the premise that "the truth sometimes hurts," we learn to avoid the truth by not saying anything or by telling "little" lies. Perhaps when you were young, your mother said, "Don't forget to give grandma a great big kiss." At that time you may have blurted out, "Ugh—it makes me feel yucky to kiss grandma. She's got a mustache." If your mother then responded, "That's terrible—your grandma loves you. Now you give her a kiss and never let me hear you talk like that again!" then you probably felt guilty for having this "wrong" feeling. The point is that the thought of kissing your grandma made you feel "yucky," whether it should have or not. In this case the issue was the way you talked about the feelings—not your having the feelings. In Chapter 8 we will introduce skills that will help you to respond better to others' feelings.

4. *Many people believe that describing feelings causes harm to others or to a relationship.* If it really bothers Max when his girlfriend Heather bites her fingernails, Max may believe that describing his feelings to Heather may hurt her so much that the knowledge will drive a wedge into their relationship. So it's better if Max says nothing, right? Wrong! If Max says nothing, he's still going to be irritated by Heather's behavior. In fact, as time goes on, Max's irritation probably will cause him to lash out at Heather for other things because he can't bring himself to talk about the behavior that really bothers him. Heather will be hurt by Max's behavior, but she won't understand why. By not describing his true feelings, Max may well drive a wedge into their relationship anyway. But if Max does describe his feelings to Heather, she might quit or at least try to quit biting her nails; they might get into a discussion in which he finds out she doesn't want to but that she just can't seem to stop, and he can help her in her efforts to stop; or they might discuss the problem and Max may see that it really is a small thing and it may not bother him as much. In short, describing feelings yields a better chance of a successful outcome than does not describing them.

Now let's outline the procedure for describing feelings:

1. Experience and identify your feeling. This sounds easier than it sometimes is. When people experience a feeling, they will sometimes express it without thinking about it. To describe a feeling, you must be aware of exactly what you are feeling.

2. Put that emotion you are feeling into words—and be specific. The second part of the communication practice at the end of this unit provides a vocabulary of emotions so that you can develop your ability to select the specific words that describe your emotions.

3. Indicate what has triggered the feeling. The feeling results from some behavior, so identify the behavior.

4. Make sure that you indicate that the feeling is yours.

Here are two examples of describing feelings: (1) "Thank you for your compliment *[trigger]*; I *[the person having the feeling]* feel really gratified *[the feeling]* that you noticed the effort I made"; (2) "When you criticize my cooking on days that I've worked as many hours as you have *[trigger]*, I *[the person]* feel very resentful" *[the feeling]*.

To begin with, you may find it easier to describe positive feelings: "You know, your taking me to that movie really cheered me up" or "I really feel delighted when you offer to help me with the housework." As you gain success with positive descriptions, you can try describing negative feelings attributable to environmental factors: "It's so cloudy; I feel gloomy" or "When the wind howls through the crack, I really get jumpy." Finally, you can move to negative descriptions resulting from what people have said or done: "Your stepping in front of me like that really annoys me" or "The tone of your voice confuses me."

PRACTICE in Describing Feelings

By Yourself

1. In each of the following sets of statements, place a D next to the statements that describe feelings, and place an X next to the statements that express or display feelings or that show the effects of feelings without actually describing them (such statements can be called judgmental or evaluative).

a. ——(1) That was a great movie!

   ——(2) I was really cheered up by the story.

   ——(3) I feel this is worth an Oscar.

   ——(4) Terrific!

b. ——(1) I feel you're a good writer.

   ——(2) Your writing brings me to tears.

_____ **(3)** [As you pat the writer on the back] Good job!

_____ **(4)** Everyone likes your work.

c. _____ **(1)** Yuck!

_____ **(2)** If things don't get better, I'm going to move.

_____ **(3)** Did you ever see such a hole!

_____ **(4)** I feel depressed by the dark halls.

d. _____ **(1)** I'm not adequate as a leader of this group.

_____ **(2)** Damn—I goofed it.

_____ **(3)** I feel inadequate in my efforts to lead the group.

_____ **(4)** I'm depressed by the effects of my leadership.

e. _____ **(1)** I'm a winner.

_____ **(2)** I feel I won because I'm most qualified.

_____ **(3)** I did it! I won!

_____ **(4)** I'm ecstatic about winning that award.

2. The following is a list of more than two hundred adjectives that you can use to describe your feelings. For your convenience they have been grouped under several broad headings. As you look at each adjective, say, "I feel . . ." and try to identify the feeling this word would describe. Which words are meaningful enough to you that you could use them to help make your communication of feelings more precise?

Words related to **anger:**

aggravated	agitated	angry	annoyed	bitter
cranky	cruel	enraged	exasperated	frenzied

| furious | hostile | incensed | indignant | infuriated |
| irritated | outraged | resentful | steamed | vicious |

Words related to **happiness:**

amused	beautiful	blissful	calm	charmed
cheerful	contented	delighted	ecstatic	elated
excited	fantastic	giddy	glad	gratified
happy	high	joyous	jubilant	pleased
proud	soothed	thrilled	tickled	turned on

Words related to **hurt:**

abandoned	abused	awful	cheated	deprived
deserted	desperate	dismal	dreadful	forsaken
ignored	isolated	hassled	jealous	oppressed
pathetic	rejected	rotten	scorned	slighted
snubbed	terrible	trapped	upset	wiped out

Words related to **belittled:**

betrayed	crippled	defeated	deflated	foolish
helpless	incapable	incompetent	inadequate	inept
inferior	insulted	intimidated	persecuted	powerless
run down	unfit	unworthy	useless	worn out

Words related to **loving:**

| affectionate | amorous | aroused | gentle | gracious |
| heavenly | passionate | sensitive | tender | vivacious |

Words related to **embarrassed:**

anxious	awkward	chagrined	conspicuous	disgraced
doomed	humbled	humiliated	jittery	overwhelmed
regretful	ridiculous	silly	troubled	thwarted

Words related to **disgust:**

| disgusted | repulsed | revolted | sickened | wary |

Words related to **energetic:**

assured	bold	brave	clever	confident
determined	eager	firm	frisky	genial
hardy	inspired	lively	peppy	potent
robust	secure	strong	tough	vigorous

Words related to **loneliness:**

abandoned	alone	bored	cheated	deserted
empty	forsaken	ignored	jilted	lonely
lost	rejected	scorned	slighted	snubbed

Words related to **surprised:**

astounded	baffled	bewildered	confused	distracted
flustered	jarred	jolted	mystified	perplexed
puzzled	rattled	shocked	startled	stunned

Words related to **sad:**

blue	burdened	dejected	depressed	downcast
frustrated	gloomy	let down	low	melancholy
miserable	moody	pained	troubled	weary

Words related to **fear:**

alarmed	boxed in	cornered	fearful	frightened
jittery	jumpy	nervous	petrified	scared
shaken	terrified	threatened	troubled	uneasy

Words related to **helpful:**

agreeable	amiable	caring	compassionate	cordial
gentle	aiding	neighborly	obliging	supportive

In Groups

1. One person in the group will role-play a situation (for example, Tom's roommate borrows Tom's car without asking permission; the roommate comes into the room later and, giving Tom the keys, says, "Thanks for the car") and then tell how he or she feels about it. Other members of the group should question what was said until feelings have been described fully. The exercise continues until each member of the group has practiced describing feelings.

2. Each person in the group should develop a list of contexts and arrange them from "contexts in which I am unlikely to describe feelings" to "contexts in which I would easily describe my feelings." Then share your lists in the group, discussing both similarities and differences.

Crediting Ideas and Feelings

When you write a term paper, you give credit to authors you have quoted or paraphrased by footnoting the sources. Similarly, when you use words or ideas of others in your oral communication, you should give verbal footnotes. Verbal footnoting is called *crediting.* In interpersonal communication you credit others and you credit yourself.

Crediting Others

People get along better with others when they believe that their ideas and feelings have been properly recognized. Yet at times we may, through neglect or thoughtlessness, chip away at the very relationships we are trying to build or maintain. *Crediting others* means verbally footnoting the source from which you have drawn your ideas. Consider the following situation: Tina and Mike are discussing ways their organization might make money. Mike suggests selling raffle tickets on a product they have bought at discount. Tina tells Mike that she thinks the idea is a good one. The next day at a meeting of the group's fund-raising committee Tina says, "What about buying a television at discount and selling raffle tickets? We could probably make a couple of hundred dollars!" The group responds immediately with such comments as "Great idea, Tina!" and "Tina, you always come up with good ideas." At this point Mike, the originator of the idea, will probably be hurt or resentful that Tina is taking credit for his idea. But if he says, "That was my idea," the group may think less of him for quibbling over whose idea it was. In this instance it was Tina's *responsibility* to give credit to Mike for originating the idea. Had Tina just said, "Mike had a great idea—what about buying a television at discount and selling raffle tickets?" the group probably would have reacted in the same way, but Mike would have felt much better for receiving credit for his idea. You can understand the importance of crediting if you think of the times you were hurt because an idea of yours was not credited.

Crediting Yourself—Owning Feelings

In addition to crediting others, you should also get in the habit of crediting yourself. Instead of owning their feelings, people tend to wrap them in impersonal or generalized language or attribute them to unknown or universal sources. *Crediting yourself,* or *owning feelings,* means making "I" statements to identify yourself as the source of a particular idea or feeling. An "I" statement can be any statement that has a first person pronoun such as *I, my, me,* or *mine.* For accuracy of information, as well as to help the listener understand fully the nature of the message, it is essential to own feelings by making "I" statements. Consider the following paired statements:

"The Forty-Niners are a great team."
"I believe the Forty-Niners are a great team."

"Everybody thinks Collins is unfair in his criticism."
"I think Collins is unfair in his criticism."

"Lots of people love to watch television."
"I love to watch television."

"Nobody likes to be laughed at."
"I don't like to be laughed at."

Each of these examples contrasts a generalized or impersonal account with an "I" statement. Why do people use vague referents to others rather than owning their ideas and feelings? There are two basic reasons.

1. *To strengthen the power of their statements.* Saying "Everybody knows the Forty-Niners have the best team" means that if listeners doubt the statement, they are bucking the collective evaluation of millions of Americans. Of course, not everybody knows the Forty-Niners are best. In this instance the statement really means that one person holds the belief. Yet because people may think that their feelings or beliefs will not carry much power, they may feel the need to cite unknown or universal sources for those ideas or beliefs.

2. *To escape responsibility.* Similarly, people use collective statements such as "everybody agrees" and "anyone with any sense" to escape responsibility for their own feelings and thoughts. It seems far more difficult for a person to say, "I don't like Herb" than it is to say, "No one likes Herb."

The problem with such generalized statements is that at best they are exaggerations and at worst they are deceitful. To be honest with others, you should own your feelings. People have a right to their own opinions and feelings. If what you are saying is truly *your* opinion or an expression of how *you* really feel, then let others know, and be willing to take responsibility for it. If you don't, you may alienate people who would have accepted your opinions or feelings even if they didn't agree with them.

PRACTICE in Crediting Ideas and Feelings

By Yourself

1. Are you likely to credit statements of others? Of your own? Under what circumstances?

2. Write down five opinions, beliefs, or feelings you have. Check to make sure each is phrased as an "I" statement. If not, correct each one. For example, "Nobody likes a sore loser" becomes "I don't like a sore loser."

Asking for Criticism

One way of improving your communication is by identifying and correcting mistakes you make. But how do you know when you have made a mistake? Because monitoring your own communication behavior is very difficult, you need to solicit the reactions of other people. Good communication includes knowing when and how to ask for constructive criticism. *Asking for criticism* means asking others for their reaction to you or to your behavior.

You can obtain some information from others by being very sensitive to their nonverbal cues. If you tell a joke and someone laughs, that laughter signals your effectiveness; however, if no one laughs, or if a person frowns, the lack of laughter and/or the frown are nonverbal cues that say the joke was not funny—or not in good taste.

When you can't read nonverbal cues, or when you don't know what people are thinking, you may have to ask for criticism. For instance, after you told your joke and no one laughed, you might say to a friend, "I told one of the funniest jokes I know, but no one laughed. Why not? Is the joke just not funny? Or was there something else that I missed?"

Although asking for constructive criticism represents the most direct way of finding out how you are doing, people are often reluctant to do that, mainly because they feel threatened by criticism. One reason people feel more comfortable relying on nonverbal cues is that they regard such indirect criticism as much less threatening. Unfortunately, relying heavily on nonverbal reactions is unlikely to help you understand why your behavior

How can you learn from your mistakes when you don't understand what you did wrong? You can ask for constructive criticism. Such feedback can help you see why your behavior may be ineffective and how to correct it. Asking for criticism involves more than saying, "What do you think?" And knowing how to ask for criticism can enhance the quality of the comments you receive.

is ineffective. Nor will such cues help you decide what changes are needed in order for you to improve your communication. By employing the verbal skill of asking for criticism you accomplish these two objectives.

The following guidelines should help you learn to ask for constructive criticism.

1. *Ask for criticism so you will avoid surprises.* If you take the initiative in asking for criticism, you prepare yourself psychologically to deal with the criticism.

2. *Think of criticism as being in your best interest.* No one likes to be criticized, but through valid criticism we often learn and grow. When you receive a negative appraisal—even when you expected a positive one— you should not look upon it as critical of you personally but as a statement that reveals something about yourself that you did not know. Whether you will do anything about the criticism is up to you, but you cannot make such a decision about altering negative behavior if you do not know that the negative behavior exists.

3. *Outline the kind of criticism you are seeking.* Rather than asking very general questions about ideas, feelings, or behavior, ask specific questions. If you say, "Marge, is there anything you don't like about my ideas?" Marge is likely to consider this a loaded question. But if you say, "Marge, do you think I've given enough emphasis to the marketing possibilities?" you will encourage Marge to speak openly to the specific issue.

4. *Ask for criticism only when you really want an honest response.* If you ask a friend, "How do you like this coat?" but you really only want the friend to agree with your appraisal, you are not being honest. Once others realize that in requesting an appraisal you are actually fishing for a compliment, they will be unlikely to offer constructive—and valuable—criticism.

5. *Try to avoid contradictions between your verbal and nonverbal cues.* If you say, "How do you like my paper?" but your tone of voice indicates that you do not really want to know, the other person may be reluctant to be honest with you.

6. *Give positive reinforcement to those who take your requests for criticism as honest requests.* If you ask your friends how they like your ideas for the ad campaign and get the response "The idea seems a little too understated," and you get annoyed and say, "Well, if you can do any better, you can take over," your friends will learn not to give you honest appraisals even when you ask for them. Instead, reward the person for the criticism. Perhaps you could say, "Thanks for the opinion—I'd like to hear what led you to that conclusion."

7. *Make sure you understand the criticism.* Don't jump to conclusions about the meaning of the criticism. When a person offers an appraisal of your behavior, ideas, or feelings, be careful that you don't read into that criticism things that are not there. In Chapter 8 we will consider the skills of questioning and paraphrasing—skills you should use to ensure that you have understood what is being said.

Asking for criticism does not require that you always act on every comment. You may decide against making a change in what you've said or done for other good reasons. But asking for honest criticism enables you to choose consciously and rationally whether or not to change your behavior.

PRACTICE in Asking for Criticism

By Yourself

Write down one to three specific attitudes or behaviors of yours that you would like to have criticized. For instance: Does the way I dress make me look younger than I am? Do I talk too much at meetings? Did my analysis of Paul's plan help the discussion?

With a Close Friend

Ask a close friend for criticism on one or more of the attitudes or behaviors you have listed. Note how you react to the criticism.

Problems Related to the Communication of Ideas and Feelings

We've examined several of the skills that will help you communicate ideas and feelings effectively. Let's conclude this chapter with a brief look at two common problems related to communicating ideas and feelings.

Serial Communication

Communication is likely to be most effective when it is person to person. If for any reason you find yourself using serial communication, your communication is likely to suffer. In a *serial communication* one or more people intervene between the sender of a message and the receiver. If Tom tells Susan to tell Charley to call him, Tom is engaging in serial communication. You've probably played the game called "Gossip" (or "Telephone"), in which one person whispers a statement to another, who in turn whispers what he thinks he heard to another, who whispers what she thinks she heard to the next person, and so on through five, six, seven, or more transfer stations. By the time it reaches the last person, the message may be so garbled that it is unintelligible.

Why is serial communication to be avoided? First, because of the very nature of the system. Let's consider an example. Dora, the originator of a message, may have all the information needed to communicate her idea. When she encodes the idea into language, she has already simplified, limited, and perhaps interpreted the original idea. Glen, to whom she directly communicates this message, does not have the benefit of the entire background for the idea. All he has is the words Dora used. Glen may not be able to remember all the words, he may not understand all the words, and he may be distracted by semantic noise. Nevertheless, he communicates what he now *perceives* as the message to Pauline, who then communicates what she perceives. As the message moves on down the line, each person in the chain further selects and interprets the message. If there are enough intervening people (and it does not take many), the message may be totally lost.

Unscrupulous persons have used the technique of serial communication purposely to spread rumors. *Rumors* are statements that are passed from person to person and that are usually embellished along the way. Furthermore, messages containing many facts are not only distorted in serial communication but also shortened, which means important information may be lost. By contrast, messages that are storylike, with a plot and maybe even dialog, usually are expanded—certainly they are distorted.

You need to avoid serial communication. Be sure, whenever possible, to give information directly to those who need it. If you are caught in the middle of serial communication, you will need to work very hard checking the accuracy of your ideas. And you should not pass a message until you have taken the opportunity to make sure you have it right.

Information Overload

With people as with computers, there is a limit to the amount of information they can process at any given time. If they are forced to receive more information than they can absorb, *information overload* can result, and part or even all of the message may be lost.

Sometimes, in the interests of accuracy or objectivity, people pack so much information into a single message transmission that their receivers lose nearly everything. Very few people can truly understand a given procedure—a recipe, directions, rules to a game—if they hear them only once. In general, the more new information you attempt to communicate, the more careful you must be.

You have probably had the experience of trying to obtain directions to a particular place in an unfamiliar area. When you think you are at least in the right area, you stop a pedestrian and ask, "How do you get to the stadium from here?" If he says, "Go three blocks north, turn to the right, and it's down a block or two on the left-hand side," you can probably process the information easily enough and will reach your destination with little difficulty. But what if you ask for directions and the local character says to you, "Well, let's see, go three blocks north, turn right at the diner, go five blocks until you come to a Texaco station, turn left until you hit the third stop sign, turn left again, . . ." If you are like most people, you will probably go part of the way, wonder where you are, and then seek new directions. Regardless of how well you listen, you can be overloaded with details.

As the sender of information you can protect against overload by limiting the details of the message, by grouping ideas, and by emphasizing the key points verbally or nonverbally. Of course, the more information you elect to send, the greater the likelihood for overload.

Summary

In this chapter we discussed communicating ideas and feelings. Communicating ideas begins with initiating a conversation. People gravitate toward individuals who are knowledgeable, who enjoy interaction, and who are willing to converse.

Sharing feelings begins with self-disclosure statements, which reveal information about yourself that is unknown to others. Describing feelings is the skill that helps teach people how to treat you. Although expressing feelings may psychologically benefit the person doing the expressing, describing feelings represents a sounder way of handling feelings, interpersonally.

Crediting is a skill that clarifies the source of ideas. Crediting contributes to the quality of a relationship by avoiding negative feelings from the person who originated an idea. Asking for criticism is the skill of verbally requesting another person to express an opinion or make an observation about your behavior. Although criticism is usually threatening, it provides direct feedback that can aid us in changing behavior.

People must also be aware of the potential problems arising from transmitting information from person to person serially and from overloading information.

Notes

1. Claire Brunner and Judy Pearson, "Sex Differences in Perceptions of Interpersonal Communication Competence." Unpublished paper presented at Speech Communication Association annual meeting, Chicago, November 1984.

2. J. R. Hobbs and D. A. Evans, "Conversation as Planned Behavior," *Cognitive Science*, 1980, p. 349–377.

3. H. P. Grice, "Logic and Conversation," in P. Cole and J. Morgan, eds., *Syntax and Semantics, Vol. 3: Speech Acts* (New York: Academic Press, 1975), p. 45.

4. Carol Tavris, *Anger: The Misunderstood Emotion*. New York: Simon & Schuster, 1982. Tavris draws on a great deal of recent research to show that most of our information about anger and dealing with anger is inaccurate. She points out that as a mature person you can handle anger in a way that is best for both you and those around you. She provides a detailed rationale for much of the analysis of dealing with feelings in this chapter.

Chapter 7

Listening

Skills

Objectives

After you have read this chapter, you should be able
to define and/or explain:

Attending   Evaluating

Understanding   Remembering

Interpreting

During the last ten years a great deal has been written about the much neglected communication skill of listening. This chapter focuses on the first five factors that most scholars consider fundamental to listening; the next chapter considers the response skills that complete the communicative listening process.

Listening Behaviors

If you were to examine your own communication behavior over the next few days, you would probably find that in your daily communication you spend more time listening than you do speaking, reading, or writing. One study of the communication habits of college students found that college students spend 22 percent of their time speaking, 20 percent reading, 8 percent writing, and 50 percent listening.[1] Yet of these four skills, most of us are likely to be least effective as listeners, even though we hear satisfactorily. Note that hearing, the receiving and attending to of audio stimuli, represents only one part of the total listening process. Research studies have shown that most people listen with only 25 to 50 percent efficiency.[2]

Listening is a six-step process that begins with hearing and progresses through understanding, interpreting, remembering, evaluating, and responding. By definition *listening* is the process of making sense out of what you hear. To illustrate the entire listening process, and to show common listening problems attendant to each phase, let's see what might interfere with your listening.

1. *You may not hear what a person is saying.* Many times we miss key ideas in and even large sections of spoken communication because of a momentary physical or psychological problem. If we've had some deep emotional trauma like a death in the family, the loss of a friendship, or a low grade on an assignment, we can be completely distracted while someone is trying to explain something to us. Even a simple head cold can distract us. You will recall that in Chapter 1 we discussed such factors that interfere with meaning as *noise* in the communication process.

2. *You may hear what is said but be unable to understand it.* For instance, you might hear every word someone is saying, but if that person is speaking in French and you don't know French, you may be unable to decode the message. The speaker need not be talking in a foreign language, however, for this to occur. If the person talking uses words that you don't know or uses them in a way that you don't recognize, you won't understand the message. Suppose the person told you that "the superfluity of your verbosity is prodigiously redundant" would you understand that the person is telling you you talk too much?

3. *You may understand what is said, but you may assign it a meaning different from that intended by the originator.* This happens because the meanings you infer for words may differ from the inferences of the originator. For example, the person says that a hotel is "within walking distance" of the convention center. Four miles later, when you stumble exhausted into the hotel dragging two suitcases, you know that your interpretation of "walking distance" differs from that of the person who provided directions.

4. *You may hear and understand the message but behave inappropriately because you did not evaluate it properly.* For instance, you may recommend that the family buy stock in a company on the basis of an appeal made by a broker. But when you study the basis of the appeal, you discover that the recommendation was illogical.

5. *You may interpret accurately but forget it.* Suppose you accept an invitation to dinner on a specific date but fail to show up because you forgot it. Yet when called and questioned about your absence, you remember having made the date.

6. *You may fully understand what was said, but respond inappropriately.* For example, you may understand what your co-worker means when he says that his candidate for office supports direct payments to welfare recipients, but you may reply, "That's a stupid plan," an inappropriate response that causes your co-worker to become defensive.

Because each of the six phases of listening requires distinct, specific skills, we are going to discuss each in detail—the first five in this chapter and the sixth, responding, in the next chapter.

Hearing (Attending)

Hearing is the physical process of receiving sound waves and the perceptual process of attending to them. Stop reading for a minute and try to be conscious of all the sounds occurring around you. Perhaps you notice the humming of an electrical appliance, the rhythm of street traffic, the singing of birds, the footsteps in the hall, a cough from an adjoining room. Yet, while you were reading, you may have been unaware of these sounds and perceived your environment as quiet. In fact, we seldom function in an environment of silence. But whereas some sounds intrude sharply on our consciousness, others go entirely unnoticed. Why is it that we "hear" some sounds and not others?

Although the physical mechanisms in our ears may respond to any sound waves emitted within our hearing range, our brain does not attend to them all, because we exercise a certain amount of psychological control over the sounds we choose to hear. Sounds range from those that almost always get our attention to those that we can block out or control. Unexpected loud noises such as alarms and other warning signals almost always take precedence over other sounds. When a fire alarm goes off in our building, we hear it and immediately focus our attention on its meaning. Likewise, the ring of telephones and doorbells, the howl of ambulance sirens, and shouts of "Look out" or "Fire" usually get our attention.

With most sounds, however, there are both times when we receive and attend to them and times we receive them but don't attend to them. For instance, as you and a friend are chatting while you walk to class, you both receive and attend to each others' words. At the same time you *may* physically "hear" footsteps behind you, the chiming of school bells, and/ or birds singing. But even if you physically receive them, you don't attend to them—you block them out, treat them as background noise. In fact, you may be so unconscious of background noise that you would deny that certain sounds occurred. The phenomenon of receiving one sound while you are attending to others is called *dichotic listening.*[3]

Poor listeners exercise very little control over which sounds they attend to. Improving your listening skills therefore begins with learning how to select some sounds to bring to the foreground while keeping others in the background. People who have developed this skill are able to focus their attention so well that only such sounds as a fire alarm, a car crashing into a post, or the cry of their child can intrude.

Let's consider what you can do to consciously focus your attention.

1. *Adopt a positive listening attitude.* There's no reason why you cannot be more attentive if you want to be. It's up to you to decide that listening is important and that you are going to do whatever it takes to listen better.

2. *Get ready to listen.* You can start to increase your listening effectiveness by being physically and mentally ready to listen. Because physical alertness often encourages mental alertness, you need to stand or sit in a way that will help you listen. Also, you should look people in the eye when they talk with you. The visual bond established between you and the speaker helps form a mental bond that improves listening effectiveness.

Mentally, you need to direct all your attention to what a person is saying; you must make a conscious decision to block out the thousands of miscellaneous thoughts that constantly pass through your mind. When people are talking with you, their ideas and feelings compete with whatever's on your mind at the moment—a basketball game, a calculus test, a date you're excited about, a movie you recently saw. And what you're thinking about may be more pleasant to attend to than what someone is saying to you. Attending to these competing thoughts and feelings is one of the leading causes of poor listening.

3. *Adjust your hearing to the listening goals of the situation.* Listening is similar to reading in that you need to adjust how you listen to the particular goal you wish to achieve and to the degree of difficulty of the material you will be hearing. The intensity with which you attend to a message should depend on whether your purpose or goal consists primarily of achieving pleasure or appreciation, learning or understanding, evaluating or critiquing, or responding helpfully to the needs of another.

Listening for pleasure requires the least conscious attending. For example, listening to music or to a casual social conversation is usually

"I'm all ears" indicates your readiness to listen, but hearing what someone is saying is only the first step of listening, the process of understanding what you hear. When listening, as with reading, you must adjust your level of concentration according to the goal of the situation. When the goal of listening is to understand or evaluate, close attention is vital.

done for pleasure. When we listen to music on the car radio, we are aware of the music as "background" sound—we find it soothing, relaxing, and generally pleasant. Similarly, we listen to a conversation for pleasure. For instance, when Tom listens to Paul talk about the game he saw on television, Tom doesn't need to attend intensively to the elaborate play-by-play details that Paul provides.

Unfortunately, many people approach all situations as if they were listening for pleasure. Yet how you listen should change qualitatively when you listen to understand or to evaluate. Listening to understand requires greater intensity. For college students classroom lectures represent a situation requiring this type of listening. Likewise, in other situations such as attending to directions (how to get to a restaurant), to instructions (how to shift into reverse in a foreign car), and to explanations (a recounting of the new dorm rules), the goal of understanding requires more careful attending. In the next section of this chapter we consider several skills for improving understanding.

By far the most demanding challenge in attending is when our goal or purpose for listening is to evaluate. Every day we are flooded with countless messages designed to influence our behavior. In order to choose wisely in these situations, we must be able to recognize the facts, weigh them, separate out emotional appeals, and determine the soundness of the conclusions presented. Various procedures necessary to improve critical listening are considered later in this chapter.

A special challenge is listening to enable us to give helpful responses. Each day people come to us to share their problems and concerns. Sometimes, they simply want someone to talk with; other times they come to us for help. Many of the skills we cover in the next chapter are response skills that will work for you in helping situations. In this type of listening more than in any other, you must be conscious of nonverbal cues because they frequently will tell you much more than what the person is expressing in words.

4. *Make the shift from speaker to listener a complete one.* In the classroom where you listen continuously for long stretches, it is relatively easy to develop a "listening attitude." In conversation, however, you are called upon to switch back and forth from speaker to listener so frequently that you may find it difficult to make the necessary shifts. If, instead of listening, you spend your time rehearsing what you're going to say as soon as you have a chance, your listening effectiveness will take a nosedive. We have all experienced situations in which two persons talked right past each other—both of the participants in a conversation broadcasting and neither one receiving! Especially when you are in a heated conversation, take a second to check yourself—are you "preparing speeches" instead of listening? Although shifting from the role of speaker to that of listener may be difficult for you to put into practice consistently, you must work at it.

5. *Hear a person out before you react.* Far too often, because we "know what a person is saying" before the person has finished, we may stop listening before the person has finished speaking. Always let a person complete his or her thought before you stop listening or before you try to respond. Until the person has finished, you don't have all the data necessary to form an appropriate response.

In addition to prematurely stopping listening, we often let certain words interfere with our attending. We even may say that certain words "turn us off." Are there any words or ideas that act as red flags for you? Does the mere utterance of these words cause you to lose any desire to listen attentively? For instance, do you have a tendency to turn off when people use such terms as *male chauvinist, gay, Commie, Mafia, Jesus freak, redneck, yuppie,* or *housewife?* Often, poor listeners (and occasionally even good listeners) receive an emotional jolt from a speaker who emits such semantic noises. At this point all you can do is be wary. When the speaker trips the switch to your emotional reaction, let a warning light go on before you cease to attend. Instead of tuning out or getting ready to fight, overcome this "noise" by working that much harder to be objective. If you can do it, you will improve your listening.

6. *Analyze and, if possible, eliminate physical impediments to attending.* Nearly 15 million Americans suffer from some hearing impairment that may be significant enough to affect their ability to listen.[4] If you are among this number, you may wear a hearing aid or you may have learned to adapt to the problem. If you often miss spoken words and have to ask that they be repeated, however, you may have a hearing impairment that you are unaware of that limits your listening effectiveness. If you suspect you may have a hearing problem, have a complete hearing test. Most colleges have facilities for testing hearing acuity. The test is painless and is usually provided at small, if any, cost to the student.

PRACTICE in Attending

By Yourself

Select an information-oriented program on your public television station (like "NOVA," "The McNeil-Lehrer Newshour," or "Wallstreet Week"). Watch at least twenty minutes of this show while lounging in a comfortable chair or while stretched out on the floor with music playing on a radio in the background. After about twenty minutes quickly outline what you have learned. Now, make a conscious decision to be attentive to the next twenty minutes of this show. Turn off the music and sit in a straight-back chair as you watch the program. Your goal is to increase your listening intensity in order to learn, so block out other distractions. After this twenty-minute segment you should again outline what you remember.

Compare your notes. Is there any difference between the amount or quality of the information you retained? Discuss your results with your classmates. Are their results similar or different? Why is this so?

Understanding

The second phase of the listening process is understanding what you have heard. *Understanding* refers to the ability to decode a message by assigning a meaning to it. One way of distinguishing between hearing and understanding is to recall a time that someone spoke to you in a foreign language. For instance, if someone asks "Quelle heure est'il?" and you do not know French, you will hear and recognize all the *sounds*, but you will be unable to assign a meaning to them. You will not understand that the person is asking "what time is it?" A person does not have to be speaking a foreign language, however, for you to have difficulty understanding. In any language speakers sometimes talk quickly, shortcut sounds, and mispronounce words, so that you may have trouble decoding the message. For instance, as a result of the way ideas are expressed, listeners may "hear" the following: "These deserts are cultivated by irritation *[irrigation]*"; "The Bible is full of interesting caricatures *[characters]*"; "Julius Caesar extinguished *[distinguished]* himself on the battlefields of Gaul."

Vocabulary

Because word symbols constitute a primary building block of messages, the size of your vocabulary will affect how well you understand what is being said and how hard you have to work to understand it. Listening effectiveness and vocabulary are definitely related. In Chapter 6 we

The size of your vocabulary influences not only how well you express yourself but also how well you comprehend others. When a child hears a word she doesn't understand, she usually asks for an explanation. Adults are often afraid of appearing ignorant, but there's nothing wrong with asking a speaker to define an unfamiliar term. Once you know what the words mean, you can concentrate on understanding their message.

emphasized the importance of building vocabulary to increase the effectiveness of messages you send. Similarly, it stands to reason that if you know the meaning of all the words a person uses, you will understand messages more easily and can thus devote more energy to retaining those meanings. Some students who have average or above-average intelligence but who do not perform well in school are handicapped by a limited vocabulary. If your vocabulary is weak, you are likely to be spending so much time trying to figure out the meaning of an unfamiliar word in a sentence that you miss other parts of the message.

What do you do when a person uses a word you do not understand? For many people the answer is nothing. People are often shy or hesitant to admit that they do not know the meaning of a particular word for fear of appearing foolish. But isn't it equally foolish to respond to a person as if you understand when you really do not? If your professor tells you your term paper reached the "nadir," and you smile and say "Thank you" even though you don't know what he or she is talking about, *that* behavior would be foolish. *Nadir* means the low point—the "pits." Although you may feel embarrassed having to ask what a word means, you are likely to *behave* foolishly if you do not ask. Even people who have extensive vocabularies will encounter words with which they are unfamiliar. Therefore, to politely ask the speaker, "Gee, I'm not sure I understand the word *nadir*, could you define it for me?" does not brand you as deficient. It does, however, indicate that you are serious about trying to understand the message.

Active Listening

A key to understanding is to practice active listening. *Active listening* includes mentally questioning in order to anticipate meanings, paraphrasing the meanings you have understood, and distinguishing among governing ideas, main points, and details in order to understand the relative importance of complex ideas that have been communicated. Active listening requires you to consciously think about the meaning of messages. Let's consider in detail these three procedures of active listening that can improve your understanding of the messages you receive.

1. *Ask yourself questions to help you anticipate material.* Suppose your boss says, "There are four steps to coding data"; you might ask yourself, "What are the four steps?" As your boss goes on to tell you the steps, having posed the question may help you recognize the steps as they are described. If the boss doesn't proceed to discuss the steps, your anticipatory question will remind you to ask him. For instance, if a person says, "An activity that provides exercise for almost every muscle is swimming," active listeners might inwardly question "How?" and then pay attention to the supporting material offered or request this information if the speaker does not supply it.

2. *Silently paraphrase to help you understand.* A *paraphrase* is a statement in your own words of the meaning you have assigned to a message. When you have listened to a message, you should be able to summarize your understanding. For example, after a person has spent a few minutes explaining the relationship between ingredients and amounts, you can say to yourself, "In other words, how the mixture is put together may be more important than the ingredients used." A silent paraphrase also can be verbalized in order to provide feedback to the speaker about your understanding. In the next chapter we will provide an opportunity for you to study and practice verbal paraphrases as a means of ensuring shared meaning. But silent paraphrasing is equally useful for ensuring your own understanding. If you cannot paraphrase a message, either the message was not well encoded or you weren't listening carefully enough.

3. *Separate the governing idea (or purpose), key points, and details to help you understand a complex message.* Some people mistakenly think they have understood a message when they can feed back most of the words that comprised the message. Understanding goes beyond that, however. In any extended message the speaker will have an overall purpose and will include key ideas (or main points) and details. For instance, during a conversation with a friend Gloria brings up the subject of teenage crime. As Gloria talks, she mentions three apparent causes: poverty, permissiveness, and broken homes. She includes information she has read or heard that relates to each of these points. When Gloria finishes speaking, her friend will understand the message as Gloria's view of the causes of teenage crime *(her purpose)*, the three specific factors she sees as causes *(her main ideas)*, and the evidence she has provided to support each factor *(details)*.

Sometimes, people organize their messages in such a way that it is relatively easy to understand their purpose, key points, and details. At other times, however, you must supply the structure for yourself if you are to achieve understanding. You can sort out the purpose, key points, and details of a complex message, and thus increase your understanding of the message, by mentally outlining the message. Such questions as "What am I supposed to know/do because I listened to this?" and "What is the speaker really saying?" allow you to determine purpose. Answers to such questions as "Why is this an issue?" and "Why should I do/think this?" will enable you to identify key points. The parts of the message that support other ideas or offer evidence to support other statements are the details.

PRACTICE in Understanding

In Groups

Each member of the group in turn should talk for one to two minutes on a topic with which they are familiar and on which they have an opinion. The other members should listen actively. When the speaker is finished, the listeners should quickly outline what they have understood to be the purpose and the main points. These outlines should be shared, compared, and discussed to determine both similarities in and differences between the intended meaning and the received meaning.

Interpreting

The third phase of the listening process is interpreting. *Interpreting* goes beyond understanding the content meanings of the words used in a message to entail the process of assigning some deeper meaning to that message by focusing on nonverbal cues and by empathizing.

Focusing on Nonverbal Cues

From the chapter on nonverbal communication you learned that up to 90 percent of the meaning of a social message may be carried nonverbally. Thus, when Paul says, "Great catch, George" after George drops a lazy fly ball hit right to him, as a result of the *sound* of Paul's voice we are likely to interpret the message to mean just the opposite of what Paul said. Likewise, when Mary says "Go on, I'll just finish my homework," we have to interpret more than just the words to tell whether Mary *really* wants to be left alone, or whether she actually plans to do her homework. We interpret messages more accurately when we know the speaker and when we can observe the nonverbal behaviors that accompany the words. Material we discussed in the chapters on both perception and nonverbal communication are relevant to your ability to interpret. Ultimately, however, your skill in interpreting depends on your skillful use of empathy.

Empathizing

Empathy relates to determining the emotional state of another person and responding in an appropriate manner.[5]

Detecting and Identifying Feelings. The first aspect of this definition, detecting and identifying how a person is feeling, emphasizes that part of the skill is perceptual—you must notice the nonverbal cues of another and then, based on these observations, identify the emotional state of the individual. The ability to detect and identify (1) may be a result of your own experience in a similar situation, (2) may be your fantasized reaction to that situation, or (3) may be based on your experiences in observing this person in similar situations. In perceiving the emotional state of another, you will see a situation through the other person's eyes, thus, empathizing is "other" oriented rather than "I" oriented.

Let's look at an example. George says to Jerry, "Professor Jones said my speech this time was a lot better than last, but when I got my grade, it was a C, the same as I got on the last speech!" As George talks, Jerry "reads" the look on George's face and notes the cues provided by George's gestures, movements, and posture. As Jerry hears the words George speaks, he perceives the changes in vocal quality and pitch as well as the presence or absence of vocal interferences. Then, based on both George's verbal and nonverbal cues, he can interpret George's feelings as expressed in the message. If, from his observation of George's words and nonverbal cues, Jerry is able to identify with the disappointment George experienced in getting the C, Jerry is empathizing. Even if Jerry himself has never had the same experience but can imagine the disappointment, he would be empathizing.

Responding Appropriately. The second aspect of the definition of empathy focuses on responding in an appropriate manner. When George says, "but when I got my grade it was a C," Jerry could respond by saying, "That must have really jolted you," spoken in a way that suggests an understanding of the pain and surprise that George must have felt. Such a response would show George that (1) Jerry understands what happened, (2) Jerry shares in the emotions George is feeling—he knows what it is like to be suffering pain or surprise, and (3) Jerry is willing to allow George to talk about his feelings and to offer what comfort he can.

People sometimes confuse *empathy* with *sympathy*. Although empathy and sympathy have similar meanings and some dictionaries even consider them to be synonymous, more often than not, *sympathy* denotes (1) a duplication of the feeling or (2) a feeling of pity or compassion for another person's trouble.

Empathy has two clearly definable elements—the *recognition* of another's feeling, which is a perception skill, and the *response* to it, which is a communication skill. In the next chapter, we consider a variety of response types that may be appropriate to a specific situation. Now let's talk further about how to achieve an empathic state of mind.

Achieving an Empathic State. Saying to yourself, "I'm going to try to empathize" may help you achieve an empathic state, yet such a statement may be too general to do much good. So let's consider specific actions that you can use to increase your ability to empathize.

1. *Adopt an attitude of caring.* Whether you can empathize directly is related to how much you decide to *care* about a person. If you remind yourself that the *other* person needs to be acknowledged by you, you will be more likely to be able to interpret the emotional content of that person's message. Simply stated, if you care, you will find it easier to empathize.

By considering your own possible states of mind for a moment, you can see the importance of caring. No doubt you will feel better when the people you like and/or respect identify with your feelings of pain, fear, anger, joy, and amazement; similarly, other people want and need *the same* expression of empathy from you that you want and need from them.

Some of us are reluctant to show that we care about others for *fear of showing weakness.* We may have learned that emotions should not be shared or acknowledged. Keep in mind that everybody has feelings, and the willingness to share feelings through empathy is not unmanly or unwomanly or "un" anything. When you empathize with another person's pain, you should show it.

2. *Consciously observe nonverbal behaviors and speculate on the emotions that may have caused them.* When another person begins a conversation with you, develop the habit of silently posing at least two questions to yourself: "What state of mind do I believe the person is in right now?" and "What are the cues the person is giving that I am using to draw this conclusion?" Consciously raising these questions will help you focus your attention on the nonverbal aspects of messages. As you develop the habit of making these assessments, you will become more adept at sensing the moods, feelings, and attitudes of those with whom you are communicating.

The procedure for empathizing can be summarized as follows:

1. When listening to what a person is saying, concentrate on both the verbal and nonverbal messages.

2. Adopt an attitude of caring for the person.

3. Try to recall or imagine how you would feel in similar circumstances.

4. Using the behavioral cues supplied by the person, speculate on the emotional state of the person.

5. Say something that indicates your sensitivity to the feelings you have perceived (this communication skill will be discussed in the next chapter).

PRACTICE in Empathizing

By Yourself

Recall the last time you effectively empathized with another person. Write a short analysis of the episode. Be sure to cover the following: What type of relationship do you have with this person? How long have you known the person? What was the emotional state of the person? How did you know this? What were the nonverbal cues? Verbal cues? Did you identify with the person through remembering a similar situation you had experienced or did you fantasize how you would feel? What did you do that showed you were empathizing? What was the outcome of this communication episode? Be prepared to discuss this analysis with others in class.

In Groups

Each person in the group should relate a recent experience to which they have had an emotional response. After the speaker has related an episode, the group should discuss what emotional states they perceive the speaker to have experienced, as well as describing the verbal and nonverbal cues that led them to their conclusions. Then group members should indicate whether they were able to empathize based on previous experiences or based on fantasy. Finally, the group should solicit comments from the speaker concerning the accuracy of their perceptions.

Evaluating

The fourth phase of the listening process is evaluating. *Evaluating* consists of the process of critically analyzing what has been understood and interpreted in order to determine how truthful, authentic, or believable you judge the meaning you have received to be. This aspect of listening is also called *critical listening*. For instance, when a person explains the causes for the downturn in the economy or tries to convince you to vote for a particular candidate for office, you will want to listen critically to these messages to determine how much you agree with the speaker and how you wish to respond to the message. If you fail to listen critically to the messages you receive, you risk inadvertently agreeing with ideas or plans that may violate your own values, be counterproductive to achieving your goals, or be misleading to others (including the speakers) who value your judgment. In addition, ineffective critical listening can alter the nature of your relationship with the speaker, because, by unquestioningly accepting the meanings you understand without evaluating them, you accord to the speaker greater control of your relationship. Thus, over time, the other person may come to dominate the relationship, and you may become resentful of the influence the other person exerts over you. Therefore, it is important for you to sharpen your skillfulness in evaluating the meanings you have understood and interpreted. Critical listening requires you to separate facts from inferences and to judge the accuracy of the inferences that have been made.

Separating Fact from Inference

Critical listeners are able to separate fact from inference. A *fact* is a statement whose accuracy can be verified or proven; it is usually a statement about something that can be or has been directly observed. By contrast, an *inference* is a conclusion or generalization based on what has been observed. Separating fact from inference thus means being able to tell the difference between a verifiable observation and an opinion related to that observation. Let's clarify this distinction with an example. Ellen tells a friend that she saw a Bob's TV Repair truck in her neighbor's driveway for the fifth time in the last two weeks. Ellen is reporting only what she saw; she is relating a fact. If, however, Ellen adds, "That new TV they bought is really a lemon," she would be making an inference. Ellen would be concluding—without actually knowing—that the truck was at her neighbor's house because someone was trying to repair the new television set. But think of how many other interpretations, or inferences, could be drawn from that fact. The driver of the truck may be a friend of Ellen's neighbor, or perhaps a special video system is being installed, or an old TV may have broken. The presence of the truck is fact; the explanation for the presence of the truck is inference. As a critical listener you should recognize when a statement is an inference and when it is a fact. Although an inference may be true, it may also be false, and it is important for you

Critical listening means evaluating and analyzing what you understand. Such active assessment is crucial when you need to distinguish facts from inferences. Part of that task requires you to identify assumptions and assertions, so that you can determine the speaker's reasoning.

to base your opinions and responses to messages on facts or on inferences whose correctness you have evaluated.

Evaluating Inferences

Critical listeners are able to analyze and evaluate typical types of inferences in order to determine their validity or correctness.

Identifying Types of Inferential Statements. Your first step in analyzing inferences is to identify the types of statements that can be used in presenting inferences. These include the facts used, the assumptions made, the assertions stated, and the actual conclusion, or inference, drawn. We have already stated that a fact is a statement whose accuracy can be verified or proven. An *assumption* is an unvoiced "truth" that nevertheless guides the logic of an inference. An *assertion* is a voiced statement offered as though it were true but without any evidence or facts to support it. Let's look at an example that may help you understand these aspects of an inference. Joyce says, "Next year is going to be a lot easier than the past year *(inference)*. I got a $200-a-month raise *(fact)* and my husband's happy in his new job *(assertion)*." Note that Joyce is also making several assumptions, including an assumption the economy's inflation rate will continue to be low so that she will realize a constant-dollar financial benefit from a $200-a-month increase in wages.

Determining the Nature of the Inference. The second step is to determine the nature of the inference, that is, the general relationship or link between the facts, assumptions, and assertions and the conclusion. Because the reasoning link is more often implied than stated, you must learn to phrase it before you can proceed further with your evaluation of the inference. For instance, a speaker may say:

My point is that once a government agency begins uncontrolled gathering of information, abuses—serious invasions of privacy—are inevitable. According to *The Chronicle* the Army's efforts at gathering information have led to the following abuses: . . . According to a consumer rights group the FBI's efforts at gathering information have led to the following abuses: . . . According to Professor George Jones the Census Bureau's efforts at gathering information have led to these abuses: . . .

Because in this argument the conclusion or inference is clearly stated and the facts are well documented, you would want to determine the reasoning link so you could assess whether or not the conclusion really *followed* from the facts. In this example the speaker is reasoning that *if* abuses resulted from information-gathering efforts in each of three governmental agencies analyzed, *then* it is reasonable to conclude that similar abuses would follow from information-gathering efforts of any or all government agencies.

Assessing the Inference. Once you have determined the reasoning link, you can begin to evaluate it by applying the proper tests to that type of reasoning. Perhaps the best way to identify the reasoning link is to ask, "How could the relationship between facts and conclusion be stated so that the conclusion does follow from the facts?" Then, to begin testing the soundness of the link, you can ask, "What circumstances would need to be present to prevent the conclusion from coming about even if the evidence is true?"

Explaining every reasoning link that can be established is beyond the scope of this book. We will, however, present the most common forms that people use in reasoning. By studying these you should be able to evaluate most of what you hear.

1. *Inferring by generalization.* You are listening to reasoning by generalization when the conclusion states that what is true in some instances is true in all instances. Reasoning from generalization forms the basis for public opinion polls and other statistical predictions. Consider, for example, these facts: "Tom, Jack, and Bill studied six hours for the test and earned A's." Now consider the conclusion based on these facts: "Anyone who studies at least six hours will get an A." The reasoning link could be stated as "What is true in these three representative instances will be true in all instances." To evaluate a generalization link, you must ask yourself, "Were enough instances cited? Were the instances typical? Were the instances representative?" If the answer to any of these questions is "no," you may wish to question the validity or truth of the inference.

2. *Inferring by causation.* You are listening to an inference by causation when the evidence and facts presented to support a conclusion are based on a single circumstance or set of circumstances and when those facts occurred prior to the conclusion. Causation links are one of the most prevalent types of inferences you will discover. An example would be: *Fact:* "We've had a very dry spring"; *conclusion:* "The wheat crop will be lower than usual." The inference link could be stated as "The lack of sufficient rain *causes* a poor crop to result." To test the strength of causal links, you must ask, "Are the facts presented important enough to bring about the particular conclusion inferred? If the facts had not occurred, would the effect be eliminated?" If the answer to one of these questions is "no," then you should be skeptical of the validity of the inference and should ask, "Do some other data that accompany the cited data cause the effect?" If the answer to this question is "yes," then you should also be skeptical of the validity of the inference.

3. *Inferring by analogy.* You are listening to an inference by analogy when the conclusion reached results from comparing two unlike phenomena. Inferring by analogy is frequently used because it is an easy way to teach someone about something with which they are unfamiliar. To do so, you simply compare and contrast characteristics of the unfamiliar to those of something with which the person is very familiar. Unfortunately, this is a weak form of inference. The analogy link may be stated as "What is true or will work in one set of circumstances is true or will work in another, comparable set of circumstances." An example would be: *Fact:* "A state lottery has proved very effective in Ohio"; *conclusion:* "A state lottery will prove effective in Kentucky." The reasoning link could be stated as "If something works in Ohio, it will work in Kentucky, because Ohio and Kentucky are so similar." To test this kind of inference, you should ask, "Are the subjects really capable of being compared? Are the subjects being compared really similar in all important ways?" If the answer to these questions is "no," you may wish to question the reasonableness of the comparison being made. Thus, in our example we may question whether one can really compare the behavior of Ohio's residents with the behavior of Kentucky residents even though they are adjacent to each other.

4. *Inferring by definition.* You are listening to inference by definition when the inference statement constitutes a definition or a descriptive generalization that follows from agreed-upon criteria. An example would be: *Facts:* "She takes charge; she uses good judgment; her goals are in the best interests of the group"; *conclusion:* "She is a good leader." The inference link could be stated as "Taking charge, showing good judgment, and considering the best interests of the group are the characteristics most often associated with good leadership." For this kind of inference you should test the link by asking, "Are the characteristics *(facts)* mentioned the most important ones in determining the definition? Are those characteristics *(facts)* best labeled with the stated term?" If the answer to these questions is "no," you may question the inferences.

5. *Inferring by sign.* You are listening to inference by sign when the conclusion is based upon the presence of observable facts that usually or always accompany other unobservable facts. For example, lights seen shining from the stadium *(fact)* are usually or always associated with the Reds playing a night game *(inference).* Even though a person driving by the stadium cannot see whether a game is in progress, the person may still conclude that it is. Signs are often confused with causes, but signs are indications, not causes. Lights shining from the stadium are a sign of a game, but lights do not *cause* a game. To test this kind of inference, you would ask, "Do the facts cited always or usually indicate the conclusion drawn? Are sufficient signs *(facts)* present to indicate the conclusion?" If your answer to either of these question is "no," you may need to further evaluate the inference.

PRACTICE in Listening Critically

By Yourself

1. *Separating Fact from Inference.* Read the following story and evaluate each witness's statement as either F (fact) or I (inference).

Two people came hurrying out of a bank with several large bundles, hopped into a long black car, and sped away. Seconds later, a man rushed out of the bank, waving his arms and looking quite upset. You listen to two people discuss what they saw.

_____ **a.** "The bank's been robbed!"

_____ **b.** "Yes, indeed—I saw the robbers hurry out of the bank, hop into a car, and speed away."

_____ **c.** "It was a long black car."

_____ **d.** "The men were carrying several large bundles."

_____ **e.** "Seconds after they left, a man came out of the bank after them—but he was too late, they'd already escaped."

ANSWERS: a. I b. I c. F d. I (men?) e. I

2. *Identifying Inference Links.* For the following typical inferences, indicate which ones are based on C (causation), G (generalization), A (analogy), D (definition), or S (sign).

_____ **a.** The chess club held a raffle, and they made a lot of money. I think we should hold a raffle, too.

_____ **b.** Tom is aggressive, personable, and highly motivated—he ought to make a good salesman.

_____ **c.** Three of my students last year got A's on this test, five the year before, and three the year before that. There certainly will be some A's this year.

_____ **d.** I saw Sally in a maternity outfit—she must be pregnant.

_____ **e.** Listen, I like the way Mike thinks, Paul is an excellent mathematician, and Craig and Phil are two of my best students, and all four are Alpha Alpha's. As far as I'm concerned, the Alpha's are the group on campus with academic strength.

_____ **f.** If George hadn't come barging in, I never would have spilled my iced tea.

_____ **g.** Maybe that's the way you see it, but to me when high city officials are caught with their hands in the till and when police close their eyes to the actions of people with money, that's corruption.

_____ **h.** Barb wears her hair that way and guys fall all over her—I'm getting myself a hairdo like that.

ANSWERS: a. A, b. D, c. G, d. S, e. G, f. C, g. C, h. A

3. *Analyzing Your Listening Behaviors.* To find out what listening skills you may need to work on, complete the following analysis, answering each item honestly. For each item score 5 for "almost always," 4 for "usually," 3 for "occasionally," 2 for "seldom," and 1 for "almost never."

_____ **a.** I listen *differently* for enjoyment, understanding, and evaluation.

_____ **b.** I stop listening when what a person is saying isn't interesting to me.

_____ **c.** I consciously recognize the speaker's purpose.

_____ **d.** I pretend to listen to people when I'm really thinking about other things.

_____ **e.** When people talk, I differentiate between their main points and supporting details.

_____ **f.** When a person's manner of speaking annoys me (such as muttering, stammering, or talking in a monotone), I stop listening carefully.

_____ **g.** At various places in a conversation I paraphrase what the speaker has said to check my understanding.

_____ **h.** When I perceive the subject matter as very difficult, I stop listening carefully.

_____ **i.** When I am listening for information or to evaluate, I take good notes of major points and supporting details.

_____ **j.** When people use words that I find offensive, I stop listening and start preparing responses.

Add together your scores on all *even*-numbered items, which focus on negative listening behaviors. Then add together your scores on all *odd*-numbered items, which focus on positive listening behaviors. If your total score for the odd-numbered items is much higher than your total score for the even-numbered items (20 points or more to 10 points or less) you are relatively skilled at listening. If your two scores are about the same, you need to work on limiting negative behaviors and perfecting skills that will raise your level of positive behaviors. If your score for the even-numbered items is much higher than for the odd-numbered items (20 points or more to 10 points or less), you need to work a great deal on developing skills designed to improve your listening.

Remembering

The final phase of the listening process is remembering. Too often, people forget almost immediately what they've heard. To illustrate, ask yourself how many times you were unable to recall the name of a person to whom you were introduced just thirty seconds earlier! Yet, curiously enough, there are times when ideas and feelings imprint themselves so deeply on your memory that a lifetime of trying to forget them will not erase the images. For instance, a song lyric may rattle around in your mind for days, or a cutting remark made by a loved one may haunt you for years. Remembering requires conscious application of four techniques: repetition, recognition of patterns, regrouping material, and note-taking. Let's consider each of these techniques.

Repetition. By repetition we mean the act of mentally verbalizing the material immediately upon receiving it. Repeating it two, three, or even four times makes it far more likely that you will remember the material at a later date. So, when you are introduced to a stranger named Jack McNeil, if you mentally say, "Jack McNeil, Jack McNeil, Jack McNeil, Jack McNeil," you will probably remember his name. Likewise, when a person gives you the directions, "Go two blocks east, turn left, turn right at the next light, and it's in the next block," you should immediately repeat to yourself, "two blocks east, turn left, turn right at light, next block—that's two blocks east, turn left, turn right at light, next block."

Recognition of Patterns. If you can find or create some organizational pattern, you are far more likely to remember the material. One way of organizing information is to use mnemonic devices to remember lists of items. A *mnemonic device* is any artificial technique used as a memory aid. Some of the most common rules for forming mnemonics are taking the first letters of items that you are trying to remember and forming a word. For example, a very easy mnemonic for remembering the five great lakes is HOMES, (*H*uron, *O*ntario, *M*ichigan, *E*rie, *S*uperior). When you are trying to remember some items in sequence, you can form a sentence with the words themselves, or you can assign words using the first letters of the words in sequence and form some easy-to-remember statement. For instance, when you studied music the first time, you may have learned the notes of the scale in the following way. For the notes on the treble clef lines (EGBDF) you may have learned "*every good boy does fine.*" And for the notes on the treble clef spaces (FACE) you may have remembered the word *face*. A second way of organizing information is to see whether a chronological, spatial, or topical relationship exists among the ideas and then group them accordingly. Directions are best remembered chronologically, descriptions may be remembered spatially, and other kinds of material can be grouped topically.

Regrouping Material. If you can regroup long lists of items under two or three headings, you are far more likely to remember them. Many times, people will express their thoughts as a series of items of equal weight. For instance, when a person is trying to show you what you need to do to complete a woodworking project, the person might tell you to gather the materials, draw a pattern, trace the pattern on wood, cut out the pattern so that the tracing line can still be seen, file to the pattern line, sandpaper edges and surfaces, paint the object, sand lightly, apply a second coat of paint, and varnish. This list includes ten steps of apparently equal weight, and the chances of your remembering all ten steps in order are not very good. But if you analyze the ten steps, you will see that you can regroup them under three headings: (1) Plan the job (gather materials, draw a pattern, trace the pattern on wood), (2) cut out the pattern (saw so the tracing line can be seen, file to the pattern line, sand edges and surface), and (3) finish the object (paint, sand lightly, apply a second coat of paint, and varnish). The regrouping appears to add three more steps, but in reality, by turning ten separate steps of apparently equal weight into three steps with three, three, and four subdivisions, respectively, you are much more likely to remember the entire process.

This technique is effective because it takes into consideration the limitations of most people's abilities to process information. Psychologists who study human memory processes have discovered that most of us can hold a maximum of 4 to 7 bits of information in our active consciousness at one time.[6] Thus, the list of ten steps is too long for us to remember.

Instead, we "store" three main points and three to four subpoints, an amount of information that can easily be retained.

Note-Taking. Although note-taking would be inappropriate in most casual interpersonal encounters, it represents a powerful tool for increasing your recall of the information you have heard. Because note-taking is especially useful during classroom lectures, telephone conversations, briefing sessions, interviews, and business meetings, we will briefly discuss how to take notes. Repeating, asking questions, paraphrasing, and separating governing idea, key points, and details will all aid you in taking good notes.

What constitutes good notes will vary depending on the situation. Good notes may consist of a brief list of main points, key ideas, or governing points plus a few of the most significant details. Or good notes may be a short summary of the entire concept (a type of paraphrase) after the message is completed. For lengthy and rather detailed information, however, good notes likely will consist of a brief outline of what the speaker has said, including the overall idea, the main points of the message, and key developmental material. Good notes are not necessarily very long. In fact, many excellent lectures can be reduced to a short outline of notes.

Suppose you are listening to a supervisor instruct his or her staff about the importance of clear writing in their reports. In the instructions the supervisor discusses the need to test the readability of the report by computing a fog index. The supervisor might say:

The brass is really concerned with the quality of the report writing that is coming from the major divisions. The word is that reports just aren't as readable as they should be. In the future every report will be required to include its fog index, including a summary of the figures used for the computation.

A fog index is one of the most common tests of readability. It's an easy one to use and generally reliable. Like most readability tests it is based on computations of sentence length and word length. The theory is that the shorter the sentences and the words, the easier the reading.

Computing a fog index for a report involves six easy steps.

First, select five random sections of at least 100 words each. In a five-page report this would be one passage per page. Begin at the start of a paragraph and count off 100 words, and then continue to count until the end of that sentence. So your passage will have 100 words or more.

Second, compute the average sentence length of each passage. If a 116-word passage has five sentences, then the average sentence length of that passage would be 23.2 words.

Notes

Computing a Fog Index

I. Include a fog Index on future reports.
Fog Index, a readability test based on sentence and word length.
Short sentences and words, easier reading.
II. Computing involves six steps.
1. Select five random sections, at least 100 words each.
2. Compute the average sentence length of each.
3. Compute number of difficult words per hundred.
Count words three syllables or more.
Don't count proper names, verbs that become three syllables by adding es, ed, or ing.
Round off.
4. Add two figures.
5. Multiply answer by .4 to get a FI.
Number of years of schooling required to read the passage easily.
6. Compute the average for the five passages.
Write figure at the end of the report with computations.
III. Rewrite reports until FI is between 10 and 13.

Figure 7.1 Example of effective note-taking.

Third, compute the number of difficult words per hundred. The beauty of this test is that "difficult" words are easily identified as *any* word of more than two syllables except proper names and verbs that become three syllables by adding *-es*, *-ed*, or *-ing*. So, if that 116-word passage has 12 difficult words, you would divide 12 by 116. That passage then would have 10.3 difficult words per hundred. For both steps two and three, round off the figures to the nearest whole number.

Fourth, add the average sentence length to the number of difficult words per hundred. In the case of the example you would add 23 and 10.

Fifth, multiply the answer by .4. The result is the fog index. The resulting figure stands for the number of years of schooling required to read the passage *easily*.

Sixth, because you will have done five passages, you will then compute the average index for the five passages. Write that figure at the end of the report and include computations.

We have been instructed to rewrite reports until we achieve a fog index of between 10 and 13 for each.

This short passage includes a great deal of specific detail, much more than you will find in most instructions. Yet the 397 words of explanation can be outlined in just 134 words (see Figure 7.1). In good note-taking the number of words used may range from 10 percent of the original material to as high as 30 percent (the amount in our example). The point is not the number of words, however, but the accuracy of the notes in reflecting the sense of what the speaker said.

PRACTICE in Note-Taking

With a Friend

Have a friend assume the role of a fellow worker on your first day in an office job and read the following information to you once, at a normal rate of speech. As the friend reads the instructions, take notes. Then give yourself the test that follows, answering true or false, but *without* referring to your notes. Then repeat the quiz, but use your notes this time. How much does your score improve? Although the temptation is great to read this item to yourself, try not to. You will miss both the enjoyment and the value of the exercise if you do.

Since you are new to the job, I'd like to fill you in on a few details. The boss probably told you that typing and distribution of mail were your most important duties. Well, they may be, but let me tell you, answering the phone is going to take most of your time. Now about the typing. Goodwin will give the most, but much of what he gives you may have nothing to do with the department—I'd be careful about spending all my time doing his private work. Mason doesn't give much, but you'd better get it right—she's really a stickler. I've always asked to have tests at least two days in advance. Paulson is always dropping stuff on the desk at the last minute.

The mail situation sounds tricky, but you'll get used to it. Mail comes twice a day—at 10 A.M. and at 2 P.M. You've got to take the mail that's been left on the desk to Charles Hall for pickup. If you really have some rush stuff, take it right to the campus post office in Harper Hall. It's a little longer walk, but for really rush stuff, it's better. When you pick up at McDaniel Hall, sort it. You'll have to make sure that only mail for the people up here gets delivered here. If there is any that doesn't belong here, bundle it back up and mark it for return to the campus post office.

Now, about your breaks. You get ten minutes in the morning, forty minutes at noon, and fifteen minutes in the afternoon. If you're smart, you'll leave before the 10:30 classes let out. That's usually a pretty crush time. Three of the teachers are supposed to have office hours then, and if they don't keep them, the students will be on your back. If you take your lunch at 11:45, you'll be back before the main crew goes.

Oh, one more thing. You are supposed to call Jeno at 8:15 every morning to wake him. If you forget, he gets very upset. Well, good luck.

With Notes	Without Notes	
_____	_____	1. Mail that does not belong in this office should be taken to Harper Hall.
_____	_____	2. Mail comes twice a day.
_____	_____	3. You should be back from lunch by 12:30.
_____	_____	4. Paulson is good about dropping work off early.
_____	_____	5. Mason gives the most work.
_____	_____	6. Goodwin gives work that has little to do with the department.
_____	_____	7. Your main jobs, according to the boss, are typing and answering the telephone.
_____	_____	8. Mail should be taken to McDaniel Hall.
_____	_____	9. The post office is in Harper Hall.
_____	_____	10. You get a fifteen-minute morning break.
_____	_____	11. Call Jeno every morning at 8:45.
_____	_____	12. You don't have to type tests.

ANSWERS: 1. F 2. T 3. T 4. F 5. F 6. T 7. T 8. F 9. T 10. F 11. F 12. F

In Class

Each person in class should select a newspaper or a magazine article and prepare a two-minute reading of it. As each person reads, everyone in class should take notes. At the end of each reading members of class will compare notes and discuss why they chose to write what they did.

Summary

Listening means making sense out of what you hear. Improving your listening is essential to developing competence in your communication. Effective listening requires hearing, understanding, interpreting, evaluating, remembering, and responding.

Listening problems include totally missing the message, hearing the message but not understanding it, hearing the message but creating meaning not intended by the sender, listening accurately but changing the meaning over time, and listening accurately but forgetting the meaning.

Hearing is the process of receiving sound waves and perceiving or identifying them. Hearing effectiveness can be increased by (1) adopting a positive listening attitude, (2) preparing to listen, (3) adjusting your hearing to the types of situations, (4) making the shift from speaker to listener a complete one, (5) hearing a person out before you react, and (6) eliminating physical impediments to listening.

Understanding is the ability to decode a message by assigning meaning to it. The larger your vocabulary, the greater the likelihood that you will know the symbols being used and therefore will understand the verbal message. A key to understanding is to practice active listening: silently questioning, paraphrasing, and separating governing idea, key points, and details.

Interpreting is the process of attending to the nonverbal aspects of a message in order to ascertain the emotional meaning the speaker attaches to the verbal message. An effective listener empathizes with the speaker. You can increase empathy by caring about people and by concentrating on their nonverbal behaviors.

Evaluating is the process of separating fact from inference and judging the validity of main points and their support. A fact is a verifiable statement; an inference is a conclusion drawn from what was observed. Critical listeners recognize inferences based on generalization, causation, analogy, definition, and sign. Once the logic of the inference is identified, critical listeners evaluate the truthfulness of the inference conclusions.

Remembering is the process of storing the meanings that have been received so that they may be recalled later. Remembering is increased by repeating information, looking for and storing information by an organizational pattern, reorganizing information when there is too much to be remembered, and, when feasible, taking notes.

Notes

1. Rudolph Verderber and Ann Elder, "An Analysis of Student Communication Habits" (unpublished study, University of Cincinnati, 1976).

2. Ralph G. Nichols and Leonard A. Stevens, *Are You Listening?* (New York: McGraw-Hill, 1957), pp. 5–6.

3. Florence I. Wolff, Nadine C. Marsnik, William S. Tacey, and Ralph G. Nichols, *Perceptive Listening* (New York: Holt, Rinehart & Winston, 1983), pp. 113–115.

4. Arthur S. Freese, *You and Your Hearing* (New York: Charles Schribbner's Sons, 1979), p. 67.

5. Robert J. Campbell, Norman Kagan, and David R. Krathwohl, "The Development and Validation of a Scale to Measure Affective Sensitivity (Empathy), *Journal of Counseling Psychology* 18 (1971): 407.

6. George A. Miller, "The Magical Number Seven, Plus or Minus Two: Some Limits on Our Capacity for Processing Information," *Psychological Review* 63 (1956): 81–97.

Chapter 8

Empathic
Listening:
Response Skills

Objectives

After you have read this chapter, you should be able
to define and/or explain:

Questioning for information

Paraphrasing information that
you think you understand

Supporting positive and negative feelings

Giving alternate
interpretations

Praising people

Giving constructive criticism

Eliminating inappropriate
responses

Part of your role as an effective communicator involves responding empathically to the person or persons with whom you are conversing. In the previous chapter we defined *empathy* as the detection and identification of how a person is feeling, followed by an appropriate response. We discussed how empathizing stresses seeing a situation through the other person's eyes—empathizing is "you" oriented rather than "I" oriented. In this chapter we focus on the second part of that definition, responding in an appropriate manner. Various kinds of responses—remaining silent, asking questions, changing the subject, arguing, showing understanding, giving opinions—influence the interpersonal relationship that exists between you and others. And your verbal as well as your nonverbal responses can either strengthen or weaken the effectiveness of the communication.

When you are listening empathically, what are the responses that reflect a measure of communication competence? In this chapter we consider several specific appropriate responses and several inappropriate problem responses.

Clarifying Meaning

Perhaps the greatest barrier to effective communication is misunderstanding. *Misunderstanding* commonly results from erroneously assuming accuracy of meaning, from inattention to what is being said, and from the need to hurry. We misunderstand far more often than we realize. We can apply two skills to clarify meaning: questioning, a familiar skill that we use regularly; and paraphrasing.

Questioning

Your understanding of another's meaning often depends upon your having enough information to work with. When a person has not given you complete information, your most appropriate response would be a question phrased to solicit additional information.

Although you have been asking questions ever since you learned to talk, you may still find that the questions you ask either don't get the

You can reduce misunderstanding by asking for clarification. Asking questions is a skill you've had lots of practice with, but it's also a skill you can always improve. Before you ask, consider your reason for questioning and how to phrase your request to obtain the information you need.

information you want or irritate or fluster the other person. Such reactions may result from poorly phrased questions. Let's see how questions may be phrased to obtain the kind of information you want.

Phrasing Questions to Obtain Accurate Information. The following are some of the most common reasons for questions.

1. You can ask questions to get important details.

ANN: "Nell, would you stop at the store on the way home and buy me some more paper?"
NELL: "What kind of paper would you like me to get, and how much will you need?"

2. You can ask questions to clarify the use of a term.

MARTHA: "He's just so sanctimonious."
ADELLE: "Could you tell me what you mean by 'sanctimonious'?"

3. You can ask questions to bring out a person's feelings.

NORM: "Billy called, but he's not coming over."
KAY: "Are you disappointed that he is not coming?"

Phrasing Questions in a Nonthreatening Manner. Good questions are phrased so that people will perceive them as an honest effort to discover information, not as actual or veiled attacks. The following guidelines will help you phrase questions in a way that lessens the likelihood of arousing defensiveness.

1. Do you have a good reason for asking the question? If you need further information before you can respond appropriately, then you should ask the question. If you have some other reason, however, maybe a paraphrase or some other response is more appropriate. And if you are just curious (nosy?), perhaps you need to curb your urge to question.
2. What is it you need to know? Is it more details, how a word is used or defined, or how the person feels? Phrase the question so that it focuses on the information you need.
3. Phrase the questions in ways that do not seem abrupt. For instance, in response to the statement, "He's so sanctimonious," the ques-

tions "What?" or "What do you mean?" are likely to be perceived as too abrupt.

4. Use positive nonverbal cues. Speak with a tone of voice that is sincere—not a tone that could be interpreted as sarcastic, cutting, superior, dogmatic, or evaluative.

5. If there is any possibility that the person may perceive the question as an attack, put the burden of ignorance on your own shoulders. For instance, you may say, "Martha, I know *sanctimonious* is a common word, but I never can remember what it means. Can you tell me what you meant when you said, "He's so 'sanctimonious'?"

The following are examples of *empathic* questions, contrasted with examples of less-than-helpful or inappropriately phrased questions.

Fred comes out of the committee room and says, "They turned down my proposal again!" Art asks:

Empathic: "Did they tell you why?" (This question is a sincere request for additional information.)

Inappropriate: "Well, did you explain it the way you should have?" (This question is a veiled attack on Fred in question form.)

As Jack and Maude are driving home from a party, Maude says, "With all those executives there I really felt strange." Jack asks:

Empathic: "What is it about their presence that makes you feel strange?" (Here the question is designed to elicit information that may help Maude.)

Inappropriate: "When you're with our bosses, why do you always say such stupid things?" (With this question Jack is intentionally hurting Maude. He is making no effort to be sensitive to her feelings or really trying to understand them.)

Note how the empathic questions get the necessary information but with less probability of a defensive reply. The inappropriate questions, on the other hand, seem deliberately designed to undermine or attack the person being questioned. Thus, to be effective, questions must have an empathic base. Questioning represents a useful response when the information sought is relevant to the conversation and when the questions derive from a spirit of inquiry and support and not from a conscious or unconscious need to make the person look bad.

Paraphrasing

When you do not understand, you ask a question. Do you need any special response skill when you *think* you understand what a person means? *Yes*, because serious communication problems can occur even when you think—or for that matter even when you are *certain*—you understand the meaning. Frequently, what we think a person means is far different from what the person really means. When it is especially important for you to understand what was said, or when you are under a lot of stress, before you respond to what you think a person has said, paraphrase.

Paraphrasing means putting into words your understanding of the meaning you get from a person's statement. Paraphrasing is not mere repetition. If Charley says, "I'm really going to study this time," and George replies, "This time you're really going to study," George's repetition shows that he *heard* the response but not that he necessarily *understood* it. An effective paraphrase states the meaning received in the paraphraser's own words. In fact, George could have obtained any of several meanings from

"Okay, so I pass that big oak and go left at the fountain until I reach the first building—is that right?" Paraphrasing, another useful method to lessen misunderstanding, involves more than repeating what you heard. When you're making sure you understand directions, you'll focus on what the speaker *says*. In other situations, you may concentrate on clarifying how the speaker *feels* about the message. Whether paraphrasing for content or for feelings, state your understanding of the message.

Charley's statement. If George thinks Charley is talking about specific study skills, George's paraphrase might be, "I take it this time you're going to read and outline every chapter carefully?" George's question is an acceptable paraphrase because it tells Charley the meaning George perceived from the expression "really going to study." If George has understood correctly, Charley might say, "Right!" But if George has received a meaning different from what Charley intended, Charley has an opportunity to correct the meaning with a statement such as, "Well, I'm going to read the chapters more carefully, but I doubt I'll outline them."

Perhaps you're thinking, "If I were in this situation, I'd just ask Charley the question, 'What do you mean by *really study*?'" Certainly, a sincere, well-worded question is appropriate when you are looking for additional information. In this case, however, George thinks he knows what "really study" means. So George isn't actually looking for new information; he's checking to make sure that his understanding of "really study" is the same as Charley's.

Types of Paraphrases. When you put a statement into your own words, you may concentrate on either the content of the message or on the speaker's feelings about the content. Either or both are appropriate, depending on the situation. *Content* means the substance or the denotative meaning of the message; *feelings* are the emotions that a person is experiencing in reference to the content. Let's go back to Charley's statement, "I'm really going to study this time." A good content paraphrase would be, "So, you're going to read and outline each chapter carefully"; a good feelings paraphrase would be, "So you're pretty upset with your grade on the last test." Do you see the difference? Let's look at another example that contains a longer message.

"Five weeks ago I sent the revised manuscript of my textbook to the publisher. I was excited because I felt the changes I had made were excellent. You can imagine how I felt when I got the book back yesterday and one reviewer said he couldn't see that this draft was much different from the first."

Content paraphrase: "If I have this correct, you're saying that the person who reviewed the manuscript saw no difference, yet you think your draft was both different and better."

Feelings paraphrase: "You seem disappointed that the reviewer didn't recognize the changes you had made."

Of course, in real-life settings we don't usually distinguish clearly between content and feelings paraphrases. Rather, we tend to employ both techniques to clarify meaning. For instance, a typical paraphrase of the statement in our example might well be "If I have this right, you're saying that the editor who read your revision could see no real differences, yet you think your draft was not only much different but better. Moreover, I get the feeling that the editor's comments really irk you."

From the examples presented you probably realize that several paraphrases would be acceptable or appropriate for any given statement. Now let's see how well you can do. Suppose you were talking with your professor about his summer.

PROFESSOR JOHNSON: "I don't know how things went for you, but for me the summer really flew by. And I'm afraid I didn't get nearly as much done as I'd planned, but I guess I'm not surprised. I hardly ever accomplish as much as I plan. Anyway, I'm really looking forward to the new term. I look at it as getting a fresh start."
YOU: [Write a paraphrase here.]

As with most statements people make, Professor Johnson's includes several ideas. Moreover, what he said comprises only a small part of what he is thinking. Your paraphrase which represents *your* understanding of his message in *your* words, might resemble one of the following:

"I get the feeling that not getting everything done that you intended isn't nearly as important to you as the excitement of starting a new term."

"It sounds like you enjoyed the summer but you're really excited about getting back to school."

"If I understand correctly what you're saying, you always expect to get more done during the summer than what you accomplish, but it doesn't bother you because you're always so excited about starting a new term."

You may be thinking that if people stated their ideas and feelings accurately in the first place, you would not have to paraphrase. Accurate wording might help you understand better, but we hope that our study of language has shown you that people can seldom be sure they accurately understand what others say. Therefore, as a student of communication, you need to perfect your paraphrasing ability.

When to Paraphrase. Not only must you know *how* to paraphrase, you also need to consider *when* the paraphrase is most useful. Common sense suggests that you wouldn't paraphrase after every sentence. In fact, paraphrases often are unnecessary. Before you state your own ideas or feelings, you should paraphrase the ideas or feelings of the other person when:

1. You think you understand what a person has said or how a person feels about what was said, but you're not absolutely sure.

2. You need a better understanding of a message before you can respond appropriately.

3. You perceive that what the person has said is controversial or was said under some emotional strain.

4. You have some strong reaction to what the person has said or how the person has said it, which may have interfered with your interpretation of the message.

To summarize, the procedure for effective paraphrasing is as follows:

1. Listen carefully to the message.

2. Determine what the message means to you.

3. If you believe a paraphrase is necessary, restate the message using your own words to indicate the meaning you have received.

PRACTICE in Questioning and Paraphrasing

By Yourself

Try to clarify the following statements by providing an appropriate question or paraphrase. To get you started, we have completed the first conversation for you.

ART: "It's Sally's birthday, and I've planned a big evening. Sometimes, I think Sally wonders whether I take her for granted—well, I think after tonight she'll know I think she's something special!"

Question: "What are you planning to do?"

Content paraphrase: "I get the idea you've planned a night that's totally different from what Sally expects on her birthday."

Feelings paraphrase: "From the way you're talking, I get the feeling you're really excited about your plans for the evening."

ANGIE: "Brother! Another nothing class. I keep thinking one of these days he'll get excited about something. Professor Jones is a real bore!"

Question:

Content paraphrase:

Feelings paraphrase:

GUY: "Everyone seems to be talking about that movie on Channel 5 last night, but I didn't see it. You know, I don't watch much that's on the 'idiot box'."

Question:

Content paraphrase:

Feelings paraphrase:

SARAH: "I don't know if it's something to do with me or with Mom, but lately she and I just aren't getting along."

Question:

Content paraphrase:

Feelings paraphrase:

AILEEN: "I've got a report due at work and a paper due in Management class. On top of that, it's my sister's birthday, and so far I haven't even had time to get her anything. Tomorrow's going to be a disaster."

Question:

Content paraphrase:

Feelings paraphrase:

In Groups of Three

A and B will hold a conversation on a topic such as "Why I like the type of work I'm doing," "The advantages or disadvantages of early retirement," or "Dealing with drug and/or alcohol abuse on campus or in industry." C will observe the conversation. For this exercise speakers are not allowed to state their ideas until they paraphrase what the other person has just said. At the end of three to four minutes C (the observer) discusses the paraphrasing of the two participants. Then B and C converse for three to four minutes while A observes; for the final three to four minutes C and A converse while B observes. After completing the exercise, the participants should discuss how they felt about paraphrasing and how the paraphrasing affected the conversations.

Helping Responses

Helping responses show approval of a person's feelings or acknowledge the person's right to have feelings; at times, they may reward people or show them how to do something better. In this section we will consider supporting, interpreting, describing behavior, praise, and constructive criticism.[1]

Supporting

When people express their feelings to you, they often need some kind of supporting response. *Supporting* entails saying something that soothes, approves, reduces tension, or pacifies. Supporting shows that you empathize

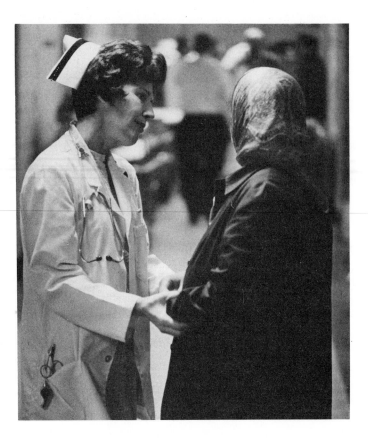

When you make a supporting statement you are empathizing with a person's feelings. Statements supporting positive feelings help a person to sustain those feelings; statements recognizing negative feelings may help a person work through those feelings without intensifying them.

with a person's *feelings*, both positive (joy, elation, pride, satisfaction) and negative (sadness, anger, sorrow, disappointment). Supporting statements are useful whether the feeling is mild or so intense that it almost short-circuits the thinking process. Whatever the direction or intensity of the feeling, the supporting statement indicates that you can empathize with that feeling, that you care about the person and what happens to him or her, and that you acknowledge the person's right to that feeling. Whether a person "should" be having the feeling is not the issue.

Supporting Positive Feelings. People like to treasure their good feelings; they don't want them dashed by inappropriate or insensitive words. When a person's feelings are positive, your supporting statement represents an attempt to share in the feelings and help sustain them.

JULIA *(hangs up the telephone and turns to Gloria):* "That was my boss. He said that he'd put my name in for promotion. I didn't realize he had ever really considered me promotable."
GLORIA: "Julia, that's great. I'm so happy for you. You really seem excited."

Gloria perceives that Julia is very happy with the news. The statement, "You really seem excited," shows that Gloria recognizes Julia's feelings; the statement, "I'm so happy for you," goes on to show that Gloria *cares* about what happens to Julia.

Supporting Negative Feelings. When a person's feelings are negative, your supporting statement represents an attempt to help the person work through the feeling without intensifying it or in some other way making the person more uncomfortable or unhappy. Your responsibility to make an appropriate response may be most difficult in situations of high emotion and stress. A person whose feelings are highly negative may need a few seconds, a few minutes, or even a few hours to calm down and think rationally. When a person expresses a highly negative emotion, you want to say something that will help defuse the emotion so the person can begin to return to normal.

JULIA *(slams down the phone):* "That was my boss—he called to tell me that they're letting me go at work, but he wouldn't even tell me why!"
GLORIA: "Oh Julia—that must hurt. Anything I can do to help?"

Gloria, empathizing with Julia, perceives her shock and anger. The statement, "Oh Julia—that must hurt," verbalizes her recognition of the feeling; the statement, "Anything I can do to help?" indicates that Gloria cares about what is happening to Julia and is ready to help her through this moment of disbelief.

Because negative feelings and negative situations are the most difficult to handle, let's look at two more examples that deal with negative situations.

JIM *(comes out of his history class clutching the paper he had been so sure he would receive a B or an A on):* "Jacobs gave me a D on the paper. I worked my tail off, did everything she asked, and she gave me a D."

AARON: "A D! As hard as you worked, I can see why you're so upset. That's a real blow."

Aaron's response is primarily an empathizing statement that shows an understanding of why Jim is so upset. By saying, "That's a real blow," Aaron also demonstrates that he is in tune with Jim's feelings. Perhaps at this point you might be inclined to say, "Jim, I can see why you feel so bad. You deserved an A!" Although such a statement would have supporting qualities, Aaron is in no position to judge whether the paper did in fact *deserve* an A. The support comes with Aaron showing an understanding of how hard Jim worked and, therefore, why Jim feels especially bad. You need to be very careful about making statements that either aren't true or that only tell people what they want to hear.

Sometimes, there's virtually nothing you can say that will be perceived as helpful. At these times perhaps the best way of showing your support is just by being there and listening. Consider this situation:

NANCY *(with a few seconds left in the basketball game and her team trailing by one point, Nancy steals the ball from her opponent, dribbles down the court for an uncontested layup, and misses. The gun sounds ending the game. Nancy runs to her coach with tears in her eyes.):* "I blew it! I lost us the game!"

A first reaction might be to say, "Don't feel bad, Nancy." But Nancy obviously does feel bad, and she has a right to those feelings. Another response might be, "It's OK, Nancy, you didn't lose us the game," but in fact Nancy's miss did affect the outcome. Perhaps the best thing the coach can do at that moment is to put her arm around Nancy to show that she understands. Later, she could say, "Nancy, I know you feel bad—but without your steal we wouldn't even have had a chance to win." Still, for the moment Nancy is going to be difficult to console.

Making supporting statements is not always easy, and a frequent temptation is to give advice instead. But if your goal is to soothe or to reduce tension, then simply acknowledging the feeling will most likely accomplish the purpose.

The procedure for phrasing helpful, appropriate supporting statements is as follows:

1. Listen closely to what the person is saying.

2. Try to empathize with those feelings. At least try to identify what you regard as the dominant emotion: disappointment? fear? anger? joy? guilt? satisfaction? resentment?

3. Phrase a reply that is in harmony with the feeling you have identified. Later in the conversation you may be able to say something that will help the person overcome the particular problem involved.

4. If it seems appropriate, you might indicate your willingness to be of service or to help if possible.

Interpreting

When a person sees only one possible explanation for a given event, your most helpful response may be providing an interpretation. *Interpreting* consists of attempting to point out an alternative or hidden view of an event to help a person see things from a different perspective. Many times people will say something about themselves or what they are thinking or feeling that shows a very limited view of a given event. People who are depressed for some reason often will read the worst into events and behaviors. Consider the following situation:

(After returning from his first date with Natalie, a woman he believes he might become very fond of, Ken is very upset. He had an excellent time, yet the end of the evening was very disappointing.)
KEN: "I take her to dinner and a great show, and when I get to her door she gives me a quick little kiss, says, "Thanks a lot," and rushes into the house. We didn't even have much time to talk about the play. I guess she really didn't like me."

Ken is interpreting Natalie's behavior negatively—he sees her action as a rejection of him as a person. Martin does not know what Natalie thinks, but he perceives that Ken is taking a very limited view of the events.

MARTIN: "I wonder whether she might not have been afraid that if she said or did any more, you'd get the wrong idea about what kind of girl she is?"

Whose interpretation is correct? We don't know. What we do know is that behavior can frequently be interpreted in more than one way. Too often, especially when we feel slighted, angry, or hurt, we interpret events negatively.

These two women appear to have much in common, but each has a unique point of view, which may give them two different interpretations of a situation. Interpreting—providing an alternative perspective—is a particularly useful response to comfort someone. Because people frequently misunderstand others, you may help clear up a problem by supplying another way of looking at it.

The following two examples will further illustrate how interpreting can work:

POLLY: "I just don't understand Bill. I say we've got to start saving money, and he just gets angry with me."
ANGIE: "I can understand why his behavior would concern you *(a supportive statement prefacing an interpretation)*. Perhaps he feels guilty

about not being able to save money or feels resentful that you seem to be putting all the blame on him."

GLEN: "I just don't seem to understand Aldrich. He says my work is top-notch, but I haven't got a pay raise in over a year."
SID: "I can see why you'd be frustrated, but maybe the company just doesn't have the money."

The procedure for interpreting may be summarized as follows:

1. Listen carefully to what a person is saying. If there are other reasonable ways to look at the event, presenting those potential alternatives may be a useful response.

2. Phrase an alternative to the person's own interpretation—one that is intended to help the person see that other interpretations are available.

3. When appropriate, preface the interpretive statement with a supportive one.

Remember, you are not a mind reader—you cannot know for sure why something was done or said. Your primary goal when interpreting is to help a person look at an event from a different point of view.

Praise

When people say or do things well, they deserve praise. Too often, however, the positive things people say and do are passed over with little comment. Yet, from our earlier discussion of self-concept, you'll remember that what we are, as well as how we behave, is often shaped by how others respond to us. When people have done something you appreciate, take the time to tell them.

When Gwenn makes an excellent tennis shot, you might say, "Gwenn, that ball was right into the corner. You've got a very good backhand."

When Marty offers to share his lunch with a student who forgot his lunch money that day, you might say, "Marty, that was nice of you to share your lunch with Pete. You're a very warm-hearted person."

When your mother prepares an excellent dessert, you might say, "Gee, Mom, I can't believe that after working all day you still had energy to make a pie. Thanks."

Praising doesn't take much time and it is almost always appreciated. The procedure for praising may be summarized as follows:

1. Make sure the context allows for praise.

2. Describe the behavior you are praising.

3. Focus on only one behavior.

4. Be specific.

5. Identify the positive feeling you experience as a result of the praiseworthy behavior.

Constructive Criticism

At times, people need help so they can perform better. A necessary, yet far too often misused response is constructive criticism. *Constructive criticism* is an evaluation of behavior—usually negative—given to help a person identify or correct a fault. To grow, to achieve our potential, we often need corrective help. Yet, because it is so easy to criticize, we are often too quick to criticize. Even though some people learn faster and better through praise of what is done well than through criticism of what is done poorly, there are still times when criticism is useful, especially when a person asks for criticism.

Because criticism is such an abused skill, we offer several guidelines that will help you compose criticism that is both constructive and beneficial.

1. *Make sure that the person is interested in hearing criticism.* The safest rule to follow is to withhold any criticism until it is asked for. Criticism will be of no value to a person who is not interested in hearing it. If a person has not asked for criticism, but you feel that criticism would be beneficial, you might ask the person whether he or she is interested in criticism. Remember, however, that even if the person says "yes," you must proceed carefully. Look for signs for receptiveness; watch for verbal or nonverbal cues indicating that some criticism would be welcomed. For instance, you might ask, "Are you interested in hearing any comments about the way you handled the meeting?"

2. *Before you criticize, make sure that you describe the person's behavior carefully and accurately.* *Describing behavior* means accurately recounting specific observable behavior without labeling the behavior good or bad, right or wrong. Because criticism alone does not inform, it may be met with defensive reactions. By first describing behavior, you lay an informative base on which good criticism may be built. Moreover, criticism that is prefaced by detailed description is less likely to provoke a defensive reaction. For example, if Paul asks, "What do you think of my forehand?" instead of blurting, "It's terrible," describe his behavior by saying, "You're bringing your arm back behind you at the start of your swing, and I think this is causing you to go off line with the swing and to lose much of your power." Based on this description Paul can then go about improving his forehand.

3. *Try to preface a negative statement with a positive one whenever possible.* When you are planning to criticize, it is a good idea to start with some praise. Of course, common sense suggests that superficial praise followed by crushing criticism will be seen for what it is. Thus, saying, "Betty, that's a pretty blouse you have on, but you did a perfectly miserable job of running the meeting" will be rightly perceived as patronizing. A better approach would be, "Betty, you did a good job of drawing Sam into the discussion. He usually sits through an entire meeting without saying a word. But you seem hesitant to use the same power to keep the meeting on track. You seem content to let anybody talk about anything, even if it is unrelated to the agenda." The praise here is significant; if you cannot give significant praise, then don't try. Prefacing criticism with empty comments made just to be "nice" is worthless.

4. *Be as specific as possible.* In the situation just discussed, it would not have been helpful to offer a generalized criticism such as, "You had some leadership problems." The more specific the criticism, the more effectively the person will be able to deal with the information. If the person wasn't in control, say so; if the person failed to get agreement on one item before moving on to another, say so.

5. *Make sure the criticism concerns recent behavior.* No one benefits from hearing about something the person did last week or last month. Criticism is best when it is fresh. If you have to spend time re-creating a situation and refreshing someone's memory, the criticism probably will be ineffective.

6. *Direct criticism at behavior the person can do something about.* It is pointless to remind someone of a shortcoming over which the person has no control. For instance, it may be true that Jack would find it easier to prepare arguments if he had taken a course in argumentation, but telling him so will not improve his reasoning. By contrast, telling him he needs to work on stating main points clearly and backing them up with good evidence is helpful because he can change these behaviors.

7. *Show the person you are criticizing what can be done to improve.* Don't limit your comments to what a person has done wrong. Tell the person how what was done could have been done better. If Gail, the chairperson of a committee, cannot get her members to agree on anything, you might suggest that she try phrasing her remarks to the committee differently; for example, "Gail, when you think discussion is ended, say something like, "It sounds as if we agree that our donation should be made to a single agency. Is that correct?"

PRACTICE in Helping Responses

By Yourself

1. Read each of the following situations and supply responses that are supportive and interpretive.

"The pie is all gone! I know there were at least two pieces left just a while ago. Kids! They can be so inconsiderate."

Supportive:

Interpretive:

"My boss was really on me today. I worked hard all day, but things just didn't jell for me. I don't know—maybe I've been spending too much time on some of the accounts."

Supportive:

Interpretive:

"I just got a call from my folks. My sister was in a car accident. They say she's OK, but the car was totaled. Apparently, she had her seat belt fastened when it happened. But I don't know whether she's really all right or whether they just don't want me to worry."

Supportive:

Interpretive:

2. Write out exactly what you said the last time you criticized someone's behavior. Which, if any, of the guidelines for constructive criticism did you follow or violate? If you were to offer the same criticism again, what would you say differently?

3. Consider the following two situations and work out an appropriate phrasing of criticism for each.

    a. You have been driving to school with a fellow student whose name you got from the transportation office at school. You have known him for only three weeks. Everything about the situation is great except that he drives too fast for you.

    b. A good friend says "you know" more than once every sentence. You like her very much, but you see that others are beginning to avoid her. She is a very sensitive girl who does not usually take criticism well.

In Groups

Share your phrasings of the criticisms in the previous two situations. Which of the wordings best meets the guidelines?

Problem Responses

Sometimes, even the best communicators respond in ways that create problems. Good communicators are aware of when they have made mistakes and try to repair them immediately and avoid them in the future. Responses create problems when they cause people to feel defensive, when they cause people to question their self-worth, and when they fail to achieve their goal.

We have already considered evaluation as a problem response. Four other problem responses are the irrelevant, the tangential, the incongruous, and the interrupting response.

Irrelevant Responses

An *irrelevant response* is one that bears no relation to what has been said. In effect, it ignores the speaker entirely.

BOB: "I'm concerned with the way Paul is handling arrangements for the benefit."
TOM: Hey, the Russian gymnasts are coming to town—I've got to get tickets for that."

When peoples' statements are totally ignored, the people not only question whether they were heard but also wonder about the worth of what they were thinking or saying, because anything important certainly will not be ignored. In the previous example Tom's irrelevant response causes Bob to wonder about the importance of what he was saying.

Tangential Responses

A *tangential response* is really an irrelevant response phrased in tactful language. Although the tangential response at least suggests acknowledgment of what a person was saying, the net result—changing the subject—is the same as with an irrelevant response.

BOB: I'm concerned with the way Paul is handling arrangements for the benefit."

TOM: "Well, you know Paul. I remember once when I was in charge of arrangements and forgot who I was supposed to contact."

Even though Tom has acknowledged Bob's statement, by shifting emphasis to his own experience Tom appears to be saying that the issue is not important enough to discuss. Again, such responses chip away at a person's feelings of self-worth. Bob thought that he was raising an issue of great importance. Either Tom fails to see the importance of Bob's statement or Bob places too much emphasis on Paul's behavior. The real problem is that Tom's response addresses neither possibility, and the subject of Paul's behavior is left unresolved. Tom's apparent withdrawal from discussing Paul's behavior thus creates a problem between Bob and Tom.

Incongruous Responses

In our discussion of nonverbal communication we indicated that problems occur when nonverbal messages appear to conflict with the verbal messages. An *incongruous response* is an example of this problem.

BOB: "Well, we got some things done today."
TOM *(in a sarcastic tone):* "Yeah, that was a great meeting."

On the surface Tom seems to be acknowledging and verifying Bob's statement, but his sarcastic tone causes Bob to wonder whether he is confirming Bob's ideas or making fun of them. Because nonverbal reactions are likely to override verbal meaning with most people, Bob will probably take Tom's words as sarcasm. If they are in fact sarcastic, Tom's insensitivity to Bob's honest statement of feelings will contribute to the creation of a barrier between them. And if Tom's words are sincere, Bob's confusion about Tom's meaning likewise will lead to a barrier between them.

Interrupting Responses

An *interrupting response* occurs when a person breaks in before the other person has finished a statement.

BOB: "I'm concerned with the way Paul . . ."
TOM: "I know—that Paul is something else, but I don't think there's any real problem."

People interrupt when they believe what they have to say is more important than what the other person is saying, when they believe they know what the other person is going to say and they want that person to know that they already know, or when they are not paying close attention. All of these factors leading to interrupting responses reflect either a lack of sensitivity or a superior attitude, or both. People need to be able to verbalize their ideas and feelings fully; constant interruptions are bound either to damage people's self-concepts or to make them hostile—and possibly both. Simply stated, whatever you have to say is seldom so important that it requires you to interrupt a person. When you do interrupt, you should realize that you are putting a person down and increasing chances for a defensive reaction. The more frequent the interruptions, the greater the potential harm.

Are you an interrupter? This behavior is so common that many of us don't even realize how often we do it. Do you like to be interrupted? Very few people can honestly say that they do. To check on your own interrupting behavior, for the rest of the day be very conscious of any time you interrupt—whatever the reason. And remember that the person you interrupt feels much the same as you do when you are interrupted.

Summary

How you respond to others is vital in determining the quality of the conversation.

Clarifying responses help ensure that people are sharing the same meanings. Questioning and paraphrasing are two skills that you can use to ensure understanding.

Helpful responses give people information about themselves or about what they have said. By supporting, interpreting, describing behavior, praising, and giving constructive criticism, you can provide helpful responses. There are several guidelines that must be followed to ensure beneficial criticism: make sure the context allows for evaluation, give the data upon which criticism is based, precede negative statements with positive ones if possible, focus on one behavior at a time, be specific, examine only recent behavior, and show what a person can do to correct a problem.

Inappropriate responses hinder communication by planting the seeds of discontent within people about themselves or about what they are thinking or feeling. Furthermore, inappropriate responses ignore or scuttle efforts at understanding meaning. Interruptions, irrelevant comments, tangential statements, incongruous replies, and unsolicited evaluations are some of the most common types of responses that should be avoided.

Notes

1. George Gazda et al., *Human Relations Development: A Manual for Educators*, 3rd ed. (Boston: Allyn & Bacon, 1984). This book focuses on developing helpful response skills and provides a good supplement to the material in this chapter.

Chapter 9

Interpersonal

Influence

Objectives

After you have read this chapter, you should be able
to define and/or explain:

Influence	Sources of credibility
Power and its sources	Emotional language
Power in relationships	Ethical standards
Persuasion	Assertiveness
Reasoning	

As Tom and Judy watch their newborn baby asleep in the crib, Tom says, "You know, when you really think about it, being a parent is an awesome responsibility. I hope that we can always be a good influence on her."

"Bart, would you talk to Jack?" Bart's mother says. "He's a good kid, but he's just not studying the way he should. I'm asking you because he really seems to respect you, and I think he'll pay attention to what you say."

"Debbie, we've got to figure out what we can say to them. We've read all about what can happen and we just have to convince them that this is the right way to respond. How can we put it so they'll understand?"

Each of these examples represents an interpersonal situation in which one person is in a position to influence others. The study of influence and how to achieve it are fundamental to effective interpersonal communication.

Influence consists of the ability to bring about changes in the attitudes and/or actions of others. Knowing that something you said or stood for has influenced (or seemed to influence) people to alter their thinking or behavior satisfies interpersonal control needs.

Influence can be unintentional as well as intentional—you often influence without being aware of it. For example, if you have a new hairstyle or are wearing a new outfit or have purchased a flashy new car, you may well influence someone else to try your hairstyle or to buy a similar outfit or car. Likewise, professors frequently exert unintentional influence on their students. For instance, students may observe their professor's style in answering difficult questions and adopt that style in their own interpersonal communication without even realizing that their style is patterned after their professor's. Parents and older brothers and sisters influence young children in a similar manner.

In this chapter, however, we will focus on *intentional influence*, which involves power, persuasion, and assertiveness. Because this book focuses on interpersonal competence in ongoing relationships, we will continually address *ethical* means of accomplishing intentional influence.

Power and Influence

A prerequisite to being able to influence is to be *perceived* as having some power. *Power* represents the potential to influence. Having the potential to change another's beliefs or actions, however, is not the same as deciding to do so and then acting on that decision. Yet without power effective influence is not possible.

Even though everyone has some power at some times and under some circumstances, most people, as a result of many interpersonal and environmental factors, occasionally will regard themselves as powerless. They may feel that, for one reason or another, they have no control over their own destinies, no power to influence any aspect of their own lives. Nothing is more frustrating than to know that change must occur yet lack the power to bring it about. This section explains what the different sources of power are and how power works within a relationship so that you can recognize and develop your power.

Sources of Power

The sources of power have been the subject of many studies. John French and Bertram Raven[1] identify five kinds of power: legitimate, reward, coercive, expert, and referent.

Legitimate Power. The first type of power, *legitimate power*, occurs when a person has the right to influence another because of the authority he or she has been granted by society. Authority may derive from election, from selection, or from the position a person holds. Thus, people submit to influence attempts because of the legitimate authority they believe people in certain positions have. For instance, the President of the United States and members of Congress gain legitimate power through the ballot. Your teachers, your boss, and police officers also wield legitimate power because of the roles they play in society. In families the father and mother as well as the oldest child may have legitimate power because of tradition or cultural norms.

Recognizing your legitimate power can be very important in building your potential to influence. Think about other people's perception of your potential legitimate influence. Perhaps you are a chairperson of an organization, a coach of a team, or a parent or guardian. In these cases the members of the organization, the members of the team, and/or your children are likely to accept your attempts at influencing them because they recognize your position of authority.

The extent to which you may succeed in influence attempts depends on whether the content of your attempt is thought to be within the *scope* of your legitimate authority. Thus, bosses may succeed in persuading their employees to work overtime on a project—that is one of their duties. If, however, they try to influence employees to frequent a particular restaurant or donate to a certain fund, their influence attempts probably will be rebuffed, because they have no "right" to exert influence in these areas.

Reward Power. The second type of power, *reward power*, exists when a person is capable of providing things for other people that they desire to have. Reward power derives from the ability or potential ability of one person to bestow monetary, physical, or psychological benefits on another person.

People generally will use rewards as a motivator for change in attitude, belief, or action. Children may be influenced to do household chores because they perceive that their parents may reward them with an increase in allowance or permission to include a friend on a family outing. Students may study hard for a test hoping to be rewarded for their effort with a good grade. Your boss may attempt to motivate you through influence attempts based on reward power, such as a year-end bonus.

The ability to reward forms a useful power base if (1) people see your reward as large enough or important enough compensation for the action called for and (2) they believe that you can deliver the promised reward. Let's illustrate these two qualifications. If you offer to reward your little brother with an ice cream cone for taking a bath, he may well decide that the treat is too small a reward for enduring the pain of such a cleanup. And if you offer him all the ice cream he can eat, he may well doubt your financial ability to provide the reward. Similarly, if your instructor offers to reward good work in the course with an A grade, but you believe that the time and effort involved are more than you care to expend, the A grade might not arouse enough motivation in you. Or, if you regard grades as unimportant, you won't make the effort to do the work. In these cases the reward is insufficient to produce the desired behavior.

Although reward power may constitute an effective base for exerting influence, care must be taken so that influence attempts from this base are not seen as bribes. If people are offered rewards for actions they believe to be undesirable, illegal, or unethical, they may reject the offer or seek to bring down the people or agency misusing the reward power base. By definition *bribery* is a reward offered for questionable motives to do questionable deeds. Most people who believe an offer to reward actually represents an attempt to bribe are likely to resent it.

Coercive Power. The third type of power, *coercive power*, occurs when a person is capable of punishing others, either physically or psychologically. As with other types of power, a person can have coercive power and yet never intentionally attempt to use it in influencing others. The old vaudeville routine, with the question, "Where does a gorilla sit when he comes into a room?" and the answer, "Anywhere he wants to," illustrates the unintentional influence that can arise from coercive power.

How do people use their coercive power to influence? Most often, influence attempts based on coercive power sources take the form of a threat. For example, you may attempt to coerce your little brother into taking his bath by threatening to hit him if he does not. Muggers attempt to coerce their victims to hand over money by threatening to harm them with a gun, a knife, or a club. Supervisors may attempt to influence employees by threatening to fire them or to give them undesirable assignments. Such influence attempts work when the people being coerced perceive the demanded action as less harmful to them than the threatened punishment. By contrast, coercive power fails as a means of exerting influence if the people perceive the demanded action as more painful than the threatened punishment. Jack Benny, who built his comic image on being a tightwad, brought about one of the longest sustained laughs in his show's history when he responded to the threat "Your money or your life" with a long pause, then, "Just a minute, I'm thinking." If your little brother decides that getting hit is less painful to him than taking a bath, he just may take the punishment—if he cannot run faster than you can.

Despite its potential to exert short-term influence, coercive power is usually ineffective as a base from which to exert long-term influence in most interpersonal relationships. If the sole criterion for effectiveness is obtaining the desired result in the short run, then coercion may be very effective. Because we are concerned with influence that will improve or at least not harm the interpersonal relationship, however, we recommend that intentional influence attempts based on coercion be avoided. Certainly, most people resent the threat of punishment. Indeed, some individuals become so resentful at the threat of even mild punishment that they will subject themselves to brutal hardships rather than submit even to an implied threat of force. And others who initially comply to influence attempts based on coercive power because of their distaste for the threatened punishment may resort to revenge behavior—that is, they may look for any way possible to strike back. Thus, if your goal is to achieve influence in a healthy, long-term relationship, coercive power is neither an effective nor an ethical source of interpersonal influence.

Expert Power. The fourth type of power, *expert power*, exists when a person has more information or skill in an area than do most other people. For example, your professors usually hold expert power in the classes they teach because they have knowledge and expertise that you need; coaches may hold expert power in the locker room because they have knowledge and expertise that their players seek. Likewise, you may have expert power in several areas, such as marketing, playing tennis, or repairing automobiles.

Because information can be learned, however, once people believe that they have received all the relevant information you possess, you may lose your power to influence them. Moreover, expert power must be real. That is, the person wielding the expert power must have the superior knowledge to back it up. For example, if one of your friends works as an auto mechanic in a dealer's garage, that person has the potential to influence your choice of sparkplugs. Suppose, on the basis of the mechanic's opinion that XYZ sparkplugs are superior, you purchase them for your car only to discover two months later that they have burned out. You are not likely to accept again your friend's advice on auto repair, which means that person will have lost all expert power as far as you are concerned.

Note, however, that expert power can help you influence others only within the limited area of expertise. A tennis coach who has expert power over members of the tennis team may influence them to change grips, but she is unlikely to successfully influence them on the subject of politics.

Referent Power. The final type of power, *referent power*, exists when a person has the potential to influence others because they respect the one attempting to influence. Many people wield this type of power because of personal qualities and characteristics that cause others to love and trust them. In other words they have credibility.

Referent power comprises a particularly effective base for influence attempts. Not only does it stand on its own as a potential for influence, but it also can increase the value of the other bases of power we have considered. Expert power, legitimate power, reward, and even coercion have greater potential for influence if the people possessing those powers are also perceived as having referent power. Conversely, if the referent power base is weak, people are less likely to be influenced by attempts based on the other types of power. In the section on persuasion we will look more closely at the characteristics of referent power.

Although we have considered each of these bases of power separately, in most cases people have more than one source of power available to them with which to influence others. In addition, other classifications of types of power have been suggested. For example, L. R. Wheeless, R. Barraclough, and R. Stewart have analyzed the typologies of French and Raven and others and have argued for three categories of power types: (1) preview expectations/consequences, (2) invoke relationships/identification, and (3) summon values/obligations.[2] In this classification scheme French and Raven's reward and coercive power would fall in the first category, expert and referent in the second, and legitimate in the third. Although such efforts to redefine categories have provided a better foundation for empirical research, none of them provides a clearer explanation of power in interpersonal relationships than do French and Raven.[3]

Power in Relationships

Our discussion of sources of power that you might possess as bases for your influence attempts implies that power exists within any given relationship. For example, whatever power Irene wields in her relationship with Ted does not extend to other individuals. Moreover, Irene's influence on Ted depends on how much power he allows her to have.

Richard Emerson argues that the power in a relationship is based on the dependency within that relationship.[4] Person A is dependent on person B if (1) person B has something that person A needs or wants and (2) person A is not likely to get it anywhere else. Thus, person B has power over person A to the extent that person A is dependent on person B to satisfy this want or need. This want or need can be either physical or psychological, perhaps information, a reward, avoidance of a punishment, or the need to meet social expectations. Thus, French and Raven's sources of power are in fact the sources of dependency! The power of B over A is equal to the dependency of A on B.

Let's look at an example to see how this theory works in practice. George and Susan have been married for eighteen years. During this time Susan (person A) has never worked outside the home. We could say that Susan is dependent on George (person B) for money, food, shelter, and clothing. Because Susan has never held a job, it would be difficult for her to get the money she needs and has been accustomed to. Thus, Susan is dependent on George, *and* George can influence Susan because of this dependence.

Susan is an excellent cook, however. Because George cannot even prepare canned soup, he is, to some extent, dependent on Susan for meals. Perhaps George's power over Susan is greater than Susan's power over George, but Susan nevertheless has some power over George. Thus, she may use George's dependence as a means of exerting influence.

A relationship in which power and dependency are equally distributed is likely to be more satisfying for both members because each person will influence the nature and direction of their interactions. In many relationships, however, one person dominates. Dominance exists when one person is significantly more dependent on the other. If George's income allows him to hire a cook or eat outside the home, the distribution of power in his relationship with Susan becomes more lopsided because Susan is still dependent upon him for income, but he is no longer dependent on her for food preparation.

If you find yourself in an unbalanced relationship in which you are more dependent—that is, you depend on another person for many things whereas the other person does not depend on you for much of anything— you may become uncomfortable. Although some people like to be totally dominated, most prefer balance. What can you do to balance the dependence and power in a relationship? There are four strategies that may help.

1. *Seek alternative ways to satisfy your needs.* If you have a need that only one person can satisfy, then you are bound to be dependent on that person. You can try to find a way to satisfy that need in some other way, thus reducing your dependency. For instance, Susan might begin a catering company in order to develop her own source of money. If she can earn some or all of her own money, she can reduce her dependence on George and thus his power potential to influence her.

2. *Alter your desire to have what the other person provides for you.* If you cease to want or need what the other person has, you are no longer dependent. Although reducing your desires is easier said than done, at times it may be your only option. George gives Susan money to meet her needs, so if Susan can reduce her material needs, she will no longer be as dependent on George's money. She will have to sacrifice, but she may decide that it is better in the long run than being dependent on George.

3. *Reduce the alternative sources available to the other person for meeting his or her needs.* Both parties in a relationship have needs. If you can somehow reduce the other person's ability to satisfy needs outside the relationship, you increase that person's dependence on you and thus balance the relationship. If George can be shown that the cook he has hired cannot cook all the dishes that Susan can or cannot cook them as well, George may decide that hiring a cook is not an alternative to Susan's cooking. Because the cook cannot meet his needs, George will become more dependent on Susan.

4. *Increase the other person's desire to have what it is that you can provide.* If you can demonstrate you are better at meeting a need than anyone else is, then you can create dependence. Susan might attend a special Indian gourmet cooking class and, on the cook's days off, prepare such a delicious and exotic meal that George decides to fire the cook.

Power exists between and among people in a multitude of relationships. In a successful and satisfying relationship people hope for a certain balance in the dependencies that yield power. But if a relationship is not in balance, if you see yourself becoming powerless, you have opportunities to try to bring the relationship back into a more desirable state.

PRACTICE in Identifying Types of Power

By Yourself

1. The following statements represent attempts to influence based on some type of power. Mark each statement as an example of R (reward power), C (coercive power), L (legitimate power), Rf (referent power), or E (expert power).

—— **a.** You will wear your hair the way I tell you to wear your hair because I'm your mother.

—— **b.** After studying the effects of radiation for eight years, I have concluded that . . .

—— **c.** As long as you do what I say, no one will get hurt.

—— **d.** Sara, I'd be so proud of you if you make the dean's list.

—— **e.** If you'll drop my books at the library, I'll clean the room.

—— **f.** Trust me—I can do it.

ANSWERS: a. L, b. E, c. C, d. Rf, e. R, f. Rf

2. Consider a relationship (with a parent, a brother or sister, a roommate, a boyfriend or girlfriend) in which you are dominant. What is the principal source of your power?

3. Consider a relationship in which you are in a position of dependency. What is the dominant person's primary source of power over you? What, if anything, are you doing to try to balance the power in the relationship?

Persuasion

Persuasion, one type of expression of power, represents your intentional verbal attempt to influence the attitudes or behaviors of others. That persuasion is central to interpersonal communication has been verified by

When you allow people a choice in accepting or rejecting your proposals, persuasion can be a positive way to try to influence them. Success in persuasion depends on your credibility and your ability to reason logically and affect the emotions of your listener. An appeal that combines the rational and emotional is usually the most compelling.

researchers.[5] Persuasion is an appropriate means of influencing people primarily because it allows freedom of choice. Dorwin Cartwright and Alvin Zander point out that because, in our democratic society, we value freedom of choice, persuasion becomes a positive means of exerting influence.[6] Thus, knowledge of means of persuasion is vital in maintaining what Paul Keller and Charles Brown describe as the *interpersonal ethic*, which requires that your influence attempts allow others freedom of choice in accepting them.[7]

Three legitimate means of influence attempts are persuasion through logical reasoning, persuasion through speaker credibility, and persuasion through emotional language.

Reasoning

You are more likely to persuade people when you can cite logical reasons for changing their attitudes or behaviors. Human beings pride themselves on being "rational"—that is, they seldom do anything without some real or imagined reason. Sometimes, the stated reasons for behavior are not clearly stated; sometimes, they are neither real nor very good; and sometimes, the reasons come *after* people do something rather than before. Nevertheless, whether the reasons are good or bad, whether they come before or after the fact, people seek reasons for their actions and beliefs.

Reasons are statements that answer the question "Why?" Think about one of your actions during the past couple of days. You probably can identify a reason or set of reasons that affected your action or that subsequently explained it. Did you watch television last night? Why? Because you needed a little relaxation? Because the program you watched is almost always good? Because a friend wanted to watch? Because you were bored and had nothing else to do? Each of these is a reason.

If you want to influence other people's beliefs or actions, you may present reasons why they should modify their beliefs or actions. Because interpersonal communication is purposeful, you usually will know when you plan to try to influence another person, which suggests that you have given yourself some time to think about your plan. A persuasive plan involves determining a number of possible reasons and choosing the ones that seem best for the particular situation.

How do you compile reasons? In most of your interpersonal settings reasons will become apparent if you just think about the problem at hand. For instance, a department head may want to convince a student to accept a position on the college curriculum committee. Why should a busy student take on such a responsibility? The student might be able to work in the best interests of the department, the student might obtain valuable experience, and/or the student might get to know faculty and administrators in the college.

Although creative thinking will supply reasons for most of your interpersonal settings, there will be times when you need to plan ahead and make sure that you can present the best argument possible. Suppose, for example, that you believed it would be in the best interests of your department to have a student newsletter published each term prior to preregistration. In this case your reasons probably will be a product of your own thinking plus any interviewing or reading that you might do. After talking with other students in the department and department heads at three similar schools, you might come up with the following list of reasons:

1. Students would like to have brief sketches of courses offered the next quarter.

2. Students are willing to bear the responsibility for publishing such a newsletter.

3. Similar schools that have such newsletters experience high student and faculty satisfaction.

4. Newsletters supply practical writing experience.

5. Student newsletters don't cost a lot of money to publish.

6. Students would like to have up-to-date news about faculty and students.

Finding and giving good reasons is the key to logical persuasion in interpersonal communication. When you make your argument, however, you will not want to use every reason you can think of or find. Why not? The effectiveness of your argument will depend on at least the following three criteria.

1. *The reason must genuinely support what you are proposing.* What superficially appears to be a valid reason in fact may not supply much support for your argument. The statement "Newsletters supply practical writing experience" is certainly true, but it's hardly a valid reason for establishing a department newsletter—students have many opportunities to gain writing experience.

2. *The reason must itself be supportable.* Some reasons are quite valid in themselves, but if they cannot be supported with facts, then they shouldn't be used. You cannot be sure that a reason is supportable until you have done some reading or until you have talked with someone who knows. For instance, "Similar schools that have newsletters experience high levels of student and faculty satisfaction" represents a good reason for establishing a newsletter—*if* you can find facts to support it. If, in your discussion with department heads at other schools, you cannot find any real support for the reason, then you shouldn't use it.

3. *The reason must have an impact on the person you are trying to persuade.* A reason will have impact on a person if that person is likely to

accept it. Although you cannot always be sure about the potential impact of a reason, if you know the person you are trying to persuade, you can make a reasonably good estimate of possible impact.[8] Suppose you are trying to convince your friend to eat at the Sternwheeler restaurant based on the accepted fact that the seafood at the Sternwheeler is excellent. Even though this is a good reason, your argument would be ineffective if your friend *did not like seafood*!

Credibility

You are more likely to persuade people when they like, trust, and/or have confidence in you. The Greeks had a word for this means of persuasion— *ethos.* Today, we speak of *credibility.* Almost all studies confirm that credibility (referent power) has a major effect on a person's beliefs and attitudes.[9]

Why are people willing to determine their behavior based on the word of someone else? Many times, people look for shortcuts in their decision making—they rely on the judgment of others. Their thinking often goes something like this: "Because I don't want to spend the time to learn about the tax proposal, when someone I trust tells me it's a good idea, I'll vote for it." Or, "Because I don't have the money to try every restaurant in town, when someone I trust tells me that The Haven is the best, I go there."

How do you determine whom you will rely on? Is it blind faith? No, the presence (or your *perception* of the presence) of certain qualities will make the possessor of such qualities a *high-credibility* source. Although the specific number of distinguishing characteristics of credibility differs somewhat in various analyses, most lists include the characteristics of competence, intention, character, and personality.

Competence refers to a person's knowledge and/or ability to perform. For example, a certain professor may influence you because you perceive her or him as competent. Although all professors are supposed to know what they are talking about, some are more convincing than others. They present accurate information, they give additional details when asked, and they can lead you to additional sources of information. Competence usually is important in interpersonal settings. If Alan sees his friend Gloria as a competent mathematician who understands mathematical principles and is able to apply them, Alan may be willing to rely on her to do his income taxes, to help him with calculus, or to manage the budget.

The second component of credibility is *intention*, which refers to a person's apparent motives. People's intentions or motives are particularly important in determining whether another person will like them, trust them, have respect for them, or believe them. For instance, you know that clothing salespersons are trying to sell you the garments they help you try on, so when they say to you, "This is perfect for you," you may well question their intentions. However, if a bystander looks over at you and exclaims, "Wow, you really look good in that!" you are likely to accept the statement at face value. The bystander has no reason to say anything, so you have no reason to doubt his or her intentions. The more positively you view the intentions of people, the more credible their words will seem to you.

The third component of credibility is *character*, which refers to a person's mental and ethical traits. People trust and believe in those who have a record of honesty, industry, trustworthiness, dependability, inner strength, fortitude, and ability to hold up under pressure. People will often overlook what are otherwise regarded as shortcomings if the person shows character.

The fourth component of credibility is *personality*, which refers to the personal impression an individual creates, to the total of a person's behavioral and emotional tendencies. Sometimes, you have a strong "gut reaction" to a person based solely on a first impression. Certain people may strike you as friendly, warm, enthusiastic, and positive. Because they have ready smiles and really seem to care, you cannot help liking them.

Building Your Credibility. Over time, you can build your credibility. To achieve credibility, you must first demonstrate competence. Competent people show that they know what they are doing and why they are doing it. By contrast, some people are perceived as being incompetent because they are careless, because they try to do too many tasks at one time, or because they do not double-check details.

Second, you can show that you care about the effects on others of what you say and do. Some people develop reputations as manipulators because, though their intentions are good, they fail to state why they behave as they do. Remember, people are not mind readers. When you don't explain your behavior, others may assume they know your intentions or may misread your behavior. Although you can't change your character or personality on the spur of the moment, you can make your actions reflect your character and personality. For instance, if you perceive yourself as hard working, you can give yourself totally to the jobs at hand. Likewise, if you are friendly or likable, you can smile when you meet strangers or offer to help people with their jobs. If people do not see you as a credible person, you may be able to change your image by improving your competence and sharing your intentions.

Third, and perhaps most important, you can build your credibility by behaving in ways that are ethical. *Ethics* are the standards of moral conduct that determine behavior; they relate both to how you act and to how you expect others to act. When you believe strongly in the rightness of your cause, you may well be tempted to say or do anything, ethical or not, to achieve your goals. Before you succumb to such temptation, think of all the people in the world who have ridden roughshod over any moral or ethical principles operating within society to achieve their goals. Simply stated, in interpersonal communications the ends do *not* justify the means.

How you handle ethical questions says a great deal about you as a person. What is your code of ethics? The following four behaviors are widely accepted as unethical.

1. *Lying.* Of all the attitudes about ethics, the one most universally held is that lying is unethical. When people know they are being lied to, they will usually reject the ideas of the person lying to them. If they discover the lie later, they often look for ways to take revenge on that person.

2. *Grossly exaggerating facts.* Although some people seem willing to accept a little exaggeration as human nature and may even use gross exaggeration for dramatic effect, most people regard the use of exaggeration in attempts to influence the same way they regard lying. Because the line between "some" exaggeration and "gross" exaggeration or distortion is often difficult to distinguish, many people view any exaggeration as unethical.

3. *Name-calling.* Again, there is almost universal agreement that name-calling, although common in interpersonal conversation, is unethical.

4. *Misrepresenting.* Misrepresenting entails giving an impression that is not supported by the facts. You can make something sound good or bad, better or worse by the phrasing you select, and if you do so consciously, it is unethical. Advertisers are particularly good at misrepresenting facts. For years, the advertisers of Anacin have said, "Two out of three doctors recommend the ingredients in Anacin." These advertisers no doubt are aware that some people will interpret this statement as meaning "Two out of three doctors recommend Anacin," or at least, "Two out of three doctors recommend ingredients that can be found only in Anacin." These advertisers may say, "We can't be responsible for how people interpret our message." What the sentence really says, however, is that two out of three doctors recommend aspirin for headaches and other minor problems. And aspirin is one of the ingredients in Anacin. The advertisers do not tell you that other brands such as Bayer, Excedrin, and St. Joseph's also contain aspirin as the major ingredient.

At one time or another everyone creates different impressions by the way they speak. "Hector," his mother asks, "why were you out until 3:00 A.M. this morning?" Hector replies indignantly, "I wasn't out anywhere near 3:00 A.M." (He got in at 2:20!) Marjorie says to Allison, "I want you to know that I was not the one who told your mother that you were smoking. I'd never do that!" What Marjorie fails to say is that she did tell Brenda and suggested to Brenda that perhaps she could tell Allison's mother! Such people often say to themselves, "I did not tell a lie," and then feel rather good about their characters. Yet such behavior is still unethical.

In interpersonal interactions where only two persons are involved, some people do not judge speaker responsibility in quite the same way as they do in public speeches. We believe, however, that any message source has the same responsibility, regardless of the setting in which statements are made, to ethical conduct. Thus, any attempt to influence others should follow some ethical guidelines. Justifying unethical behavior on the ground of informal setting is itself unethical and reprehensible.

Emotional Language

You are more likely to persuade people when you use language that affects their emotions. Although you may induce people to act on the basis of good reasons alone, people frequently *believe* they should do something but don't act upon that belief. For instance, Jonas may believe that he should give money to his church, but he may not do so. What motivates you to move from simply *believing* in something to *acting* on the belief often is the degree of your emotional involvement. Emotions are the driving force behind action, the instrument that prods or nudges you from passive to active.

Various researchers[10] have attempted to determine the effect of the use of emotional appeals in persuasion. So far, the results of the research have been inconclusive and at times contradictory. The effectiveness of emotional language seems to depend a great deal on such factors as the mood and attitude of the person you are persuading and the language itself. Our experience has been that emotion is best used to supplement or to highlight good reasons. Because effective persuasion is likely to be logical-emotional, reasoning and emotion ought to be inseparable elements of a persuasive message.

Suppose you are talking to your friend about the need for more humane treatment of the elderly in our society and you want to point out that present options for dealing with the elderly are ineffective. Saying, "Our present means are ineffective" provides little motivation for your listener to respond, let alone act, however *true* the statement may be. By making the statement more specific, however, you add some emotional power: "Our present means alienate the elderly from the society they worked so many years to support." "Alienate" and "worked so many years to support" are phrasings that may arouse guilt, sadness, or some other feeling.

In informal interpersonal communication, what can you do to create a mental state for yourself in which you can phrase statements that will have greater emotional impact—that will motivate?

1. *Identify your own feelings about the topic.* How do you really feel about your proposal? Are your feelings inspired by sadness? Happiness? Guilt? Anger? Caring? Grief? If you don't really have any strong feelings, then you probably will not be able to say anything that will trigger feelings on the part of the person you are talking with.

2. *Construct mental pictures that portray your feelings.* When you feel strongly about a particular subject, what images do your emotions cause you to see? If you feel sadness, anger, and grief when you think about the elderly and nursing homes, you might envision the looks of despair on the faces of those in wheelchairs, the blank looks on those huddled together in front of televisions.

3. *Describe your feelings to the other person.* The more you practice the skill of describing feelings, the better you will become at it in spontaneous settings. Your major means of motivating is through language that is adapted to the needs of the person you are talking with.

PRACTICE in Persuading

By Yourself

1. Try to frame a series of reasons for supporting each of the following: (1) welfare reform, (2) not smoking in the classroom, (3) registering to vote, (4) limiting nuclear experimentation.

2. Develop emotional appeals for each of the issues in question 1.

3. List ways that you could show your credibility for each issue.

In Groups

1. Your instructor will give you goal cards. One member of each group will pick a goal and then try to influence another member of the group

to support that goal. The other group members should observe the power bases the persuader works from and the means of persuasion that were used.

2. Try to define your ethical code. You might start by making a series of statements that begin, "It is wrong to _____; if someone does this, I am likely to react by _____." When you are finished, divide into groups of six and share as much as you feel comfortable in sharing. Notice the similarities in and differences between your code and others' codes.

Assertiveness

Many people who have power and understand the means of persuasion nevertheless are ineffective at exerting influence in their relationships because they are not assertive. *Assertiveness* means standing up for what you believe in and doing so in interpersonally effective ways.

Assertive Versus Passive or Aggressive Behavior

When people believe they are not being treated as they should be, they are likely to react with behavior that is either passive, aggressive, or assertive.

Passive Behavior. When people behave passively they do not attempt to influence the behavior of others. People who behave passively are reluctant to state their opinions, share feelings, or assume responsibility for their actions. Thus, they often submit to the demands of others, even when doing so is inconvenient or against their best interests. For example, when Bill uncrates the new color television set he purchased at a local department store, he notices a large, deep scratch on the left side of the cabinet. If Bill is angry about the scratch but nevertheless keeps the set and does nothing to influence the store clerk from whom he purchased it to replace it, he is behaving passively.

Aggressive Behavior. People who behave aggressively lash out at the source of their discontent with little regard for the situation or for the feelings

The difference between assertion and aggression is not how you feel but how you act on your feelings. And how you act will largely determine how others respond to you. Assertion is a forthright expression of your feelings without the exaggeration or belligerence common in the attack approach of aggression. Would you say these youths are behaving aggressively or assertively?

of those they are attacking. Unfortunately, too many people confuse aggressiveness with assertiveness. Unlike assertive behavior, aggressive behavior is judgmental, dogmatic, fault-finding, and coercive.

To illustrate the difference between agressive and assertive behavior, let's return to Bill's problem. If Bill behaved aggressively after discovering the scratch on the cabinet of his new television set, he might storm back to the store, loudly demand his money back, and accuse the clerk of intentionally selling him damaged merchandise. During his tirade he might threaten the store with a lawsuit. Such aggressive behavior might or might not get Bill a new television set; it would certainly damage the interpersonal relationships he had with those to whom he spoke.

Assertive Behavior. People who behave assertively state what they believe to be true for them, describe their feelings fully, give good reasons for their beliefs or feelings, suggest the behavior or attitude they think is fair, avoid exaggerating for dramatic effect, and take responsibility for their actions and feelings without personal attacks on others. If Bill behaved assertively, he would still be angry about bringing home a damaged set— the feeling of anger is common to each of the response behaviors. The difference between assertive behavior and passive or aggressive behavior is not the original feeling of anger but the way in which Bill reacts as a result of the feeling. If Bill responded assertively, he might call the store and ask to speak to the clerk from whom he had purchased the set. When the clerk answered, Bill would describe his feelings upon discovering a large scratch on the cabinet when he uncrated the set. He would then go on to say that he was calling to find out what to do to return the damaged set and get a new one. Whereas aggressive behavior also would achieve Bill's purpose of getting a new television set, the assertive behavior would achieve the same result at lower emotional costs to both Bill and those with whom he talked.

In order to highlight the contrast among the response styles, let's examine another situation, in which the issue is the quality of interpersonal relations. Betty works in an office that employs both men and women. Whenever the boss has an especially interesting and challenging job to be done, he assigns it to a male co-worker whose desk is next to Betty's. The boss has never said anything to Betty or to the male employee that would indicate he thinks less of Betty or her ability. Nevertheless, Betty is hurt by the boss's behavior.

If Betty behaved passively, she would say nothing to the boss. If Betty behaved aggressively, she would call her boss on his behavior by saying something like, "Why the hell do you always give Tom the plums and leave me the garbage? I'm every bit as good a worker and I'd like a little recognition!" If Betty behaved assertively, however, she would go to her boss and describe to him her perception of his behavior and her feelings about that behavior. She might say, "I don't know whether you are aware of it, but during the last three weeks, every time you had a really interesting job to be done, you gave the job to Tom. To the best of my knowledge, you believe that Tom and I are equally competent—you've never given me any evidence to suggest that you thought less of my work. But when you 'reward' Tom with jobs that I perceive as plums and continue to offer me routine jobs, it really hurts my feelings. Do you understand my feelings about this?"

If you were Betty's boss, which of her responses would be most likely to achieve her goal of getting better assignments? Probably the assertive behavior. Which of her responses would be most likely to get her fired? Probably the aggressive behavior. And which of her responses would be least likely to "rock the boat"? Undoubtedly the passive behavior—but then she would continue to get the boring job assignments.

Characteristics of Nonassertive People

Why are some people hesitant to assert themselves? Probably for one or several of the following reasons.

1. *They believe it's not worth the time or effort.* Some people are not assertive because they believe that it takes too much work to be assertive.

Sometimes, it does. If, however, you find yourself thinking or saying it's not worth the time or effort in most of the situations you are in, then you are giving an excuse for your behavior, not offering a reason.

Occasionally, you may find a champion, someone who will look out for your interests. Usually, however, you are the only one in a position to represent your position.

2. *They question their self-worth.* Some people do not assert themselves because they feel inferior. Perhaps because of problems in childhood or because of persistent failures as adults, they don't have confidence in their own thoughts and feelings. Let's consider two typical examples in which people don't assert themselves because they question their self-worth. First, suppose both Jim and Marsha have something they want to say and they begin talking at the same time. Jim stops talking and lets Marsha talk. Is this a matter of politeness? Perhaps, but it is also possible that Jim defers to Marsha because she is attractive, intelligent, and poised, qualities Jim feels he lacks. Second, suppose Mark receives a C on a term paper. As he reads his paper over, he's sure that what he said was worth more than a C. He thinks about going in to talk to his professor but says to himself, "He's not going to listen to me—I'm just a student." Is this a realistic appraisal? Maybe. It is also possible that Mark doubts his ability to argue for the worth of his paper even though he really believes it deserved a better grade than the professor gave it.

3. *They accept others' expectations.* A number of American women exhibit passive behavior because they accept the stereotype that society has taught them: Women are expected to be accepting, warm, loving, and deferential to men. Any signs of assertiveness thus are considered unfeminine. Fortunately, the stereotype that guides such passive behavior is no longer as influential as it once was, and many women who have spent the better portion of their lives being passive now recognize the value of learning to be assertive.

4. *They fear reprisal.* Some people do not assert themselves because they are afraid of the consequences. They fear that if they assert themselves, the person they are dealing with will punish them or withhold some reward. Is this fear real? Certainly, there will be times when you are penalized for being assertive—some people with power are very defensive and will react this way if they think you are threatening their security.

To illustrate the benefits as well as the risks of assertive behavior, let's return to the example of Betty. If Betty exhibits assertive behavior, her boss might become defensive and fire her. If being treated fairly is important to Betty, however, then she may risk such an outcome. Furthermore, the risk will be minimized if she develops her behavioral repertoire and selects the skills that are least likely to provoke a defensive response. If you can apply the skills presented in this text as tools for assertiveness (rather than for responding aggressively), you have a much better chance of influencing others and achieving your goals.

Still, you must recognize that being assertive may not achieve your goals. The skills we have discussed in this book are designed to increase the probability of achieving interpersonal effectiveness. Just as with self-disclosure and describing feelings, however, there are risks involved in being assertive. People who have difficulty asserting themselves do not realize that the potential benefits far outweigh the risks. Remember earlier we said that you teach people how to treat you. When you are passive—when you have taught people that they can push you around—they will. By contrast, when you are assertive, you are in a position to influence others to treat you as you would prefer to be treated.

Assertiveness, then, is a four-step process. You should:

1. Identify what you are thinking or feeling.

2. Analyze the cause of these feelings.

3. Choose the appropriate skills necessary to communicate these feelings, as well as any outcome you desire.

4. Communicate these feelings to the appropriate person.

PRACTICE in Being Assertive

By Yourself

1. Identify five situations in the past where you were nonassertive or aggressive. Try to write the dialogue for each situation. Then substitute an assertive response for the nonassertive or aggressive reactions you expressed in each case.

2. For each of the following situations write a passive or aggressive response and then contrast it with a more appropriate assertive response.

You come back to your dorm, apartment, or house to type a paper that is due tomorrow, only to find someone else is using your typewriter.
Passive or aggressive response:

Assertive response:

You're working at a store part-time. Just as your hours are up and you are ready to leave (you want to rush home because you have a big test tomorrow), your boss says to you, "I'd like you to work overtime if you would—Martin's supposed to replace you but he just called and can't get here for at least an hour."
Passive or aggressive response:

Assertive response:

During a phone call to your parents who live in another state, your mother says, "We're expecting you to go with us when we visit your uncle on Saturday." You were planning to spend Saturday working on your résumé for an interview next week.
Passive or aggressive response:

Assertive response:

You and your friend made a date to go dancing, an activity you really enjoy. When you meet, your friend says, "If it's all the same to you, I thought we'd go to a movie instead."
Passive or aggressive response:

Assertive response:

Summary

Influence is the ability to affect people's attitudes and/or behaviors. People can exert influence indirectly by not knowing that they have had any influence and without having any conscious intent to exert it. When a person engages in a conscious effort to influence another, it is accomplished through persuasion. Neither influence nor persuasion is possible without the presence of power.

Power is the potential ability to influence another person's attitude or behavior. Power derives from a legitimate base, the holding of an accepted position of power; from a coercive base, the threat of punishment; from a reward base, the ability to bestow gifts; from an expert base, the holding of needed information; or from a referent base having a charismatic effect. Power exists within dependency relationships. Person A has power over person B to the extent that person B is dependent on person A.

The verbal effort to influence is persuasion. Persuasion is the product of several elements that may be used alone or in concert. Persuasion can be a product of logical reasoning, of motivation through emotional language, and/or of speaker credibility. Effective interpersonal persuasion is always ethical persuasion—it does not depend upon lying, distortion of fact, or acting in the interests of the persuader at the expense of the one being persuaded.

Assertiveness is the skill of stating your ideas and feelings openly in interpersonally effective ways. Passive people are often unhappy as a result of not stating what they think and feel; aggressive people get their ideas and feelings heard but may create more problems for themselves because of their aggressiveness.

Notes

1. John R. P. French, Jr., and Bertram Raven, "The Bases of Social Power," reprinted in Dorwin Cartwright and Alvin Zander, eds., *Group Dynamics*, 3rd ed. (New York: Harper & Row, 1968), pp. 259–270.

2. L. R. Wheeless, R. Barraclough, and R. Stewart, "Compliance-Gaining and Power in Persuasion," in R. N. Bostrom, ed., *Communication Yearbook 7* (Beverly Hills, Calif.: Sage, 1983), pp. 105–145. Although we are not focusing on the tripart typology that Wheeler et al. suggest, their analysis is well worth the time for a serious student of interpersonal power.

3. Charles R. Berger, "Social Power and Interpersonal Communication," in Mark L. Knapp and Gerald R. Miller, eds., *Handbook of Interpersonal Communication* (Beverly Hills, Calif.: Sage, 1985), p. 444.

4. Richard M. Emerson, "Power-Dependence Relations," in Carl W. Backman and Paul F. Secord, eds., *Problems in Social Psychology* (New York: McGraw-Hill, 1966), pp. 193–202.

5. Gerald R. Miller, Franklin J. Boster, Michael E. Roloff, and David R. Seibold, "MBRS Rekindled: Some Thoughts on Compliance Gaining in Interpersonal Settings," in Michael E. Roloff and Gerald R. Miller, eds., *Interpersonal Processes: New Directions in Communication Research* (Beverly Hills, Calif., Sage, 1987), p. 89.

6. Cartwright and Zander, *Group Dynamics*, p. 221.

7. Paul W. Keller and Charles T. Brown, "An Interpersonal Ethic for Communication," *Journal of Communication* 18 (1968): 79.

8. For a more complete analysis of reasoning you may want to look at either of the following: Howard Kahane, *Logic and Contemporary Rhetoric*, 5th ed. (Belmont, Calif.: Wadsworth, 1988), pp. 3–17. An excellent analysis of forms of reasoning, with emphasis on detection of fallacies. Rudolph F. Verderber, *The Challenge of Effective Speaking*, 7th ed. (Belmont, Calif.: Wadsworth, 1988). Chapter 14 of this text provides a more detailed analysis of the reasoning process than is given in this book.

9. Kenneth E. Andersen and Theodore Clevenger, Jr., "A Summary of Experimental Research in Ethos," *Speech Monographs*, vol. 30 (1963): 59–78.

10. See Ronald L. Appelbaum and Karl W. Anatol, *Strategies for Persuasive Communication* (Columbus, Ohio: Charles E. Merrill, 1974), pp. 102–103, for a summary of conflicting research studies.

Chapter 10

Managing

Conflict

Objectives

After you have read this chapter, you should be able to define and/or explain:

Conflict

Kinds of conflict

Inappropriateness of withdrawal, surrender, and aggression

Role of discussion in managing conflict

Role of persuasion in managing conflict

Guidelines for managing conflict

Competitive versus cooperative approaches to conflict

Negotiation

Arbitration

Perhaps the ultimate test of your communication competence is how you react to conflict. Conflict management requires application of many of the skills we have considered thus far, as well as the use of new skills. This chapter will examine the nature of conflict and the skills that have proved most effective in conflict management.

Conflict is the clash of opposing attitudes, desires, interests, ideas, behaviors, goals, and needs. Many people view conflict as bad. To be sure, conflict situations are likely to make you anxious, uneasy, and at times extremely uncomfortable. And as much as you may wish that conflict did not exist, you seldom get through even one day without experiencing conflict. Conflict is not necessarily bad, however. As a result of conflict, people are forced to make choices and test the relative merits of their attitudes, behaviors, needs, and goals.

Conflict occurs because each person has unique ideas, feelings, motives, and ways of behaving. This chapter, therefore, will not discuss avoiding or suppressing conflict but rather will focus on managing conflict within interpersonal relationships.

Kinds of Conflict

If you are going to manage conflict, you have to understand what it is you are facing. All conflicts are not the same—some are easier to manage than others. Conflicts can be divided into four groups.

Pseudoconflict. A false conflict that appears to be real is known as a *pseudoconflict*. Pseudoconflict exists when people believe that two goals cannot be simultaneously achieved, although in fact they can be. If you are studying for tomorrow's geology exam and your boss calls to tell you that a report that you are working on must be submitted tomorrow, you may perceive these two actions as being in conflict. The tendency in a pseudoconflict is to put the choice between actions in an either-or framework—in this case *either* you study for the test *or* you finish the report. This might be a real conflict if it were truly impossible to do both within the prescribed time period. More often than not, however, you will set up a false set of choices, because it may be possible to do both.

Content Conflict. A conflict concerning message accuracy is known as *content conflict* and can take several forms.

1. *The conflict may be over a fact.* You may come in conflict with another person over whether the stock market rose or fell last year.

2. *The conflict may be over an interpretation of a fact or an inference drawn from a fact or series of facts.* You may disagree with another person over whether the rise in steel prices will trigger another round of inflation. The rise in steel prices may be documented as fact; what will result from that rise is a matter of opinion based on interpretation of the fact or on inference drawn from the fact.

3. *The conflict may be over a definition.* You may be drawn into a conflict with another person over whether the use of communication strategies to motivate people to buy a product constitutes unethical behavior or good salesmanship. In this type of conflict the antagonists agree on what is being done; the problem lies in how each person defines the behavior.

4. *The conflict may be over a choice among goals, actions, or means of arriving at goals.* You may disagree with a person on whether building a multilevel garage or using available space more efficiently is the better solution to the campus parking problem. In this type of conflict the opponents agree on the problem but disagree on the solution.

Value Conflict. Conflicts build and become more difficult to resolve as competing value systems are brought to bear on the issues. A *value conflict* represents a difference in views of life in general (or of an aspect of life) that is brought into focus on a particular issue. For example, you may argue with a friend about whether experience is more important than pay in an entry level position, a question that may result in a direct clash of values.

Values are the cluster of attitudes or beliefs—economic, esthetic, social, political, and religious—a person holds that serve as a guideline for measuring the worth of various aspects of life. For instance, if you value a trim, solid, healthy body, you may have strong beliefs about smoking, physical fitness, and other related topics. Note, however, that values can be both personal and societal. To illustrate, consider how most people in America believe that the individual is more important than the state, whereas other societies have differing values. So when the needs of government and the rights of the individual are in conflict, Americans are inclined to protect individual rights over governmental needs. Each individual also applies different personal values to individual events. For example, if Joan values educational opportunity more than she values personal wealth, she will be inclined to vote for a property tax increase to benefit the schools; Tony, whose personal values are the opposite of Joan's, will be inclined to vote against the tax increase.

A value, then, serves as a frame of reference to determine the relative worth of any object, situation, or behavior. And it is in the framework of people's individual value systems that value conflicts are likely to occur. Because of the deep-seated nature of values, conflicts over values are quite difficult to resolve.

Ego Conflict. *Ego conflict* occurs when the people in conflict view "winning" or "losing" the conflict as a measure of their expertise, personal worth, or image. In such situations the content of the conflict becomes less important than the egos of the people involved. Ego conflict represents the most difficult kind of conflict to manage.

Ego conflicts develop when discussion of content or values is undermined by personal or judgmental statements. When who you are, what you are, how competent you are, whom you have power over, and how much you know become an issue, then the conflict becomes ego conflict. The more competent you see yourself on a certain issue, the more likely you are to become ego-involved when your word is questioned. And once your ego becomes involved, your ability to remain rational often is lost. Before you realize it, emotions become involved in the conflict, words are said that cannot be taken back, and the conflict is blown out of proportion. For example, a simple disagreement over whether the stock market went up or down last year may escalate into an ego conflict when one or both parties see the issue as one of determining who is the economics expert. The eventual winner is master of economics; the loser becomes one who is ignorant about these vital matters.

Note that the various kinds of conflict are arranged in order of difficulty. The next section will consider broad-based personal styles and specific strategies for managing conflict.

PRACTICE in Identifying Types of Conflict

By Yourself

1. Identify the last three conflicts you had. Were they pseudoconflict? Content conflict? Value conflict? Or ego conflict? What was the outcome of each?

2. Label the following as P (pseudoconflict), C (content conflict), V (value conflict), or E (ego conflict).

_____ **a.** Joe wants to live with Mary, but Mary wants the two of them to get married.

_____ **b.** Stan believes that because he is an insurance salesman, Jerry should not dispute his position on annuities.

_____ **c.** George defends his failure to present an anniversary gift to Agnes by asserting that their anniversary is not today (May 8) but May 18.

_____ **d.** Martin calls to announce that he is bringing the boss home for dinner. His wife replies, "That will be impossible. The house is a mess and I need to go shopping."

_____ **e.** Jane says, "Harry, pick up your clothes—I'm not your maid!" Harry replies, "I thought we agreed that it's your job to take care of the house, I take care of the yard."

ANSWERS: a. V b. E c. C d. P e. C

Patterns of Managing Conflict

People engage in many behaviors, both positive and negative, to cope with or manage their conflicts. The various methods of coping and/or managing conflict may be grouped into five major patterns: withdrawal, surrender, aggression, discussion, and persuasion. Let's consider each.

Withdrawal

One of the most common, and certainly one of the easiest, ways to deal with conflict is to withdraw. *Withdrawal* entails physically or psychologically removing oneself from the situation.

Physical withdrawal is, of course, easiest to identify. Suppose Tom and Dorie get into a conversation about Tom's smoking. Dorie says, "Tom, I thought you told me that whether you stopped smoking completely or not, you weren't going to smoke around the house. Now here you are lighting up!" Tom may withdraw physically by saying, "I don't want to talk about it" and going to the basement to finish a project he was working on.

Psychological withdrawal may be less noticeable but is every bit as common. Using the same example, when Dorie begins to talk about Tom's smoking in the house, Tom may sit quietly in his chair looking at Dorie, but all the time she speaks he is thinking about the poker game he will be going to the next evening.

As well as being quite common, both of these behaviors are basically negative. Why? Because they neither eliminate nor attempt to manage the nature of the conflict. In the case of the physical withdrawal Dorie

Withdrawal is essentially a negative way of dealing with conflict because it avoids dealing with the problem and fails to resolve the issue. Occasionally, withdrawal works. Can you think of situations where it would be an appropriate response?

may follow Tom to the basement where the conflict will be resumed; if not, the conflict will undoubtedly surface later—and will probably be intensified—when Dorie and Tom try to resolve another, unrelated issue. In the case of psychological withdrawal Dorie may force Tom to address the smoking issue or she may go along with Tom's ignoring it but harbor a resentment that may negatively affect her relationship with Tom.

Nevertheless, conflicts do occasionally go away if left alone.[1] There appear to be two sets of circumstances in which withdrawal may work. First, when the withdrawal represents temporary disengagement for the purpose of letting the heat of the conflict subside, it may be an effective technique for managing conflict. For example: Bill and Margaret begin to argue over having Bill's mother-in-law for Thanksgiving dinner. During the conversation Margaret begins to get angry about what her mother-in-law had said to her recently about the way she and Bill were raising their daughter. Margaret says, "Hold it a minute, let me make a pot of coffee. We can both relax a bit and then we'll talk about this some more." A few minutes later, having calmed down, she returns, ready to approach the conflict more objectively. Margaret's action is not true withdrawal; it's not meant as a means of avoiding confrontation. Rather, it provides a cooling-off period that will probably benefit them both.

The second set of circumstances in which withdrawal may work is when a conflict occurs between people who communicate infrequently. Consider Jack and Fred, who work in the same office. At two office gatherings they have gotten into arguments about whether the company really cares about its employees. At the next office gathering Fred avoids sitting near Jack. Again, this form of withdrawal serves as a means of avoiding conflict rather than contributing to it. Withdrawal is a negative pattern only when it is a person's major way of managing conflict.

Surrender

The second method of managing conflict is to surrender. As you might suspect, *surrender* means giving in immediately to avoid conflict. Some people are so upset by the prospect of conflict that they will do anything to avoid it. For instance, Jeff and Marian are discussing their vacation plans. Jeff would like for just the two of them to go, but Marian has talked with two of their friends who will be vacationing the same week about going together. After Jeff mentions that he'd like for the two of them to go alone, Marian replies, "But I think it would be fun to go with another couple, don't you?" Jeff replies, "O.K., whatever you want." Even though Jeff really wants the two of them to go alone, rather than describe his feelings or give reasons for his position, he gives in to avoid conflict.

Surrender is a negative way of dealing with conflict for at least two reasons. First, decisions should be made on merits, not to avoid conflict. If one person gives in, there is no testing of the decision—no one knows what would really be best. Second, surrender can be infuriating to the other person. When Marian tells Jeff what she thinks, she probably wants Jeff to see her way as the best. But if Jeff simply surrenders, Marian might think not that Jeff dislikes her plan but that Jeff is playing the martyr. And his unwillingness to present his reasons could lead to even more conflict.

Aggression

The third method of dealing with conflict is through aggression. *Aggression* entails the use of physical or psychological coercion to get one's way. Through aggression people attempt to force others to accept their ideas, thereby emerging as "victors" in conflicts. Aggression seldom improves a relationship, however. Rather, aggression is an emotional reaction to conflict—thought is short-circuited, and the person lashes out physically or verbally. People who use aggression are not concerned with the merits of an issue but only with who is bigger, who can talk louder, or who can act nastier. With either physical or verbal aggression, conflict is escalated or obscured but not managed.

Persuasion

The fourth method of managing conflict is by persuasion. *Persuasion*, you will recall, is the attempt to change either the attitude or the behavior of another person. At times during the discussion of an issue, one party might try to persuade the other that a particular action is the right one. Suppose that at one point in their discussion about buying a car, Sheila says, "Don't we need a lot of room?" Kevin might reply, "Enough to get us into the car together, but I don't see why we need more than that." Sheila and Kevin are now approaching a conflict situation. At this point Sheila might say, "Kevin, remember the other day when you were cussing out our present car because it doesn't have much back-seat room? We carry a lot of stuff. I do food shopping, you're always carrying equipment for the guys at the lodge, and there are a lot of times when we invite another couple to go somewhere with us." Statements like this one represent an attempt at resolving the conflict through persuasion.

When persuasion is open and reasonable, it can be a positive means of resolving conflict; however, persuasion can also degenerate into manipulation. Although persuasive efforts may fuel a conflict, if that persuasion has a solid logical base, it is at least possible that the persuasion will resolve the conflict.

Discussion

The final method of dealing with conflict is through discussion. *Discussion* consists of a verbal weighing and considering of the pros and cons of the issues in conflict. Discussion is the most desirable means of dealing

The give and take of discussion is often the best—and most demanding—approach to managing conflict. Discussion requires cooperation—and a lack of cooperation is frequently part of the conflict.

with conflict in a relationship, but it is often difficult to accomplish because all parties involved must cooperate. Discussion requires the participants to be objective in their presentation of issues, honest in stating their feelings and beliefs, and open to the solution that proves to be most logical and in the best interests of those involved.

An effective discussion follows the same pattern as effective problem solving: define and analyze the problem, suggest possible solutions, select the solution that best fits the analysis, and work to implement the decision. (See Module D for more on problem solving.) In everyday situations all five steps are not always considered completely, nor are they necessarily considered in the order given. Discussion requires that when two people perceive a conflict emerging, they step back from that conflict and proceed systematically toward a solution. Does the process sound too idealized? Or impracticable? Well, discussion is difficult, but when two people commit themselves to trying, chances are they will benefit from it.

Guidelines for Managing Conflict

Now that we have considered the kinds of conflict and the major patterns for coping with them, let's consider guidelines you can follow in developing a constructive program of conflict management. A word of caution before we begin: Conflict can be an extremely complex process, and some conflicts may not be resolvable even through improved communication.[2]

Recognize the Signs of Conflict. Frequently, people slip into conflicts without even knowing it. When that happens, all too often one or both people start engaging in one of the negative means of coping with conflict without thinking about it. If, however, both parties are aware of a conflict, or if one says something like "I think we have a conflict here," then they can take steps to begin rational discussion.

Keep in mind that you need not fear conflict—the fear of conflict often brings about such negative responses as withdrawal and surrender. Conflicts are going to occur, but when conflict is approached properly, it can be a constructive force.

Focus on Specific Topics. We have already pointed out that conflicts often start on content levels. If you can keep the focus of the discussion on those content levels, the chances of the conflict growing out of proportion are lessened. For instance, if you find yourself in a conflict over a fact, try to disengage until a source for verifying the fact can be found or until some guidelines for selecting from among competing sources can be determined. Likewise, when the conflict centers on an interpretation of a fact, an inference drawn, or a definition, collect supporting material that is related closely to the issue. In short, confine the conflict to the issue at hand.

Some authorities refer to content conflict as "simple" conflict. Because facts can be looked up, inferences tested, definitions verified, and competing goals weighed and evaluated, the conflict can be confined to the specific issues and resolved rationally. Nevertheless, many conflicts will reveal competing value systems, which will confound conflict management.

Keep an Open Mind. Conflict can be lessened if participants remain open-minded rather than dogmatic in their view of new material. Open-mindedness refers to flexibility in the way a person processes information. Rather than seeing concepts in absolute terms, an open-minded person is willing to tolerate other views and examine other information. Dogmatism is just the opposite: A dogmatic person clutches tenaciously to his or her value system and judges every event on the basis of how it fits into that value system. Highly dogmatic people have a narrow perspective on the way the world operates, are rigid in their thinking, and believe *only* those people who are in positions of strong authority. By contrast, open-minded people may be committed to certain beliefs or attitudes that develop from their value systems, but they are aware of the common ground that exists between what they believe in and what they reject. For example, suppose a topic of conversation has religious ramifications. If the two people involved are, say, a Baptist and a Catholic, but both are open-minded, they can discuss the issues rationally and intelligently. In discussion they seek a middle ground between their positions in order to resolve the question. Participants who are dogmatic, however, focus on their differences. They view the controversy in terms of black and white and never see the gray areas that lie between their two positions. As a result, management is nearly impossible and conflict escalates.

Your goal in conflict management should be to open your mind as much as possible so that you can look for the common ground on which some agreement can be built. The open-minded or mildly dogmatic person compares and evaluates issues related to belief systems and accepts or rejects them according to merit, not values. In short, the open-minded person looks for evidence and draws conclusions on the basis of the weight of that evidence.

Test Criteria Used in Making Value Judgments. We recognize that differing individual values will create conflict. Under these circumstances it is necessary to seek an informative base for the evaluation rather than just rely on personal values. To illustrate, suppose that Don and Ann are talking about what they consider to be the best movie of the year. Without some structuring, consideration of the "best movie" becomes a matter of personal taste reflecting personal values. People need to identify criteria on which such a judgment may be based and establish a way of testing those criteria. In this case Don and Ann consider such criteria as story, message, music, acting, directing, popularity, and so forth.

Next, and probably most important to managing such conflicts, the criteria should be weighed to determine which are most important in making such judgments. But this weighing should be made according to some objective procedure. Otis Walter and Robert Scott suggest four questions that can be asked about each criterion: (1) Has the criterion produced desirable effects in the past? (2) Have authoritative figures accepted this criterion? (3) Does the criterion fit the needs of the people? and (4) Is the criterion justified by reasoning?[3] These tests will not eliminate value considerations, nor will they eliminate conflict. But they will lend structure to consideration of the issues, thereby allowing people to make a decision based on information, not personal values. For example, by asking the question "Have authorities accepted this criterion?" Don and Ann can read film authorities' comments to see whether the criteria of story, acting, directing, message and so forth are favored by the critics. If, for example, several critics cite "film message" as their major measure of film quality, Don and Ann can assign importance to that criterion in their evaluation of the year's movies.

Cooperate Rather Than Compete. When a conflict arises, the variable that first affects the outcome of the conflict is the participants' level of competitive or cooperative behavior. If the participants are competitive, their egos are likely to be involved. Conversely, if the participants are cooperative, they are willing to follow the steps of the problem-solving method: (1) identify the problem, (2) analyze the nature of the problem, (3) suggest possible solutions, and (4) select the solution that best meets the needs determined in problem analysis.

In some conflicts one person may initially look at the outcome competitively while the other has a cooperative outlook. In this situation the nature of the conflict will depend on whether the person looking at the conflict competitively draws the other person into the competition or whether the person looking at the outcome cooperatively influences the other person to cooperate.

If a person approaches the potential conflict competitively, how do you go about bringing the person into a cooperative state so the conflict can be considered rationally? First, do not talk about the issue at hand until you demonstrate to the other person that you wish to resolve the conflict in a mutually satisfactory way. Second, avoid any statements that would escalate the potential conflict or result in defensive behavior. Some of the following wordings may be useful in demonstrating your resolve to be cooperative and in preventing the conflict from escalating:

"I know you feel very strongly about what you believe is right. Before we consider whether your plan is the best one, perhaps we could consider what we want to accomplish with the plan."

"I know I sometimes get a little hotheaded in conflict situations, and I'm going to try to look at this problem as objectively as I can, but I may need all your help."

"You have good reasons for your belief, and I believe I have, too. Perhaps if we share our reasons and then consider the consequences of each of them, we can make a decision that we'll find satisfying."

Developing a cooperative atmosphere takes practice. You can, however, learn to recognize when you start to become ego-involved, at which time you can mentally step back, take a deep breath, and reapply yourself to seeking a workable solution. When you see someone else becoming competitive, you can paraphrase their feelings as well as the content of their message, perhaps with a statement such as "From the way you're making your point, I get the feeling that this particular approach is very important to you personally."

Remember, both your language and your nonverbal cues indicate your feelings not only about the conflict but also about the people with whom you are in conflict. If you approach others openly and respectfully, you should at least get a hearing; however, if you demean people's ideas or the people themselves by your words or actions, you will probably create defensiveness, cause hard feelings, and escalate the conflict.

Use Behaviors That Result in Positive Conflict Management. People are likely to have attitudes and feelings that determine the nature of their conversations. Positive behaviors help people integrate their resources toward a common task; negative behaviors foster a win–lose strategy between people—that is, if one person wins, it must be at the other person's expense. Conflicts that develop from these behaviors will certainly be difficult to resolve. The difference between positive and negative win–lose behaviors may be illustrated by comparing the behavior of people completing a jigsaw puzzle to that of people playing poker. In solving a jigsaw puzzle each person works with the other; in a poker game each individual works at the expense of the others. Let's look at five contrasting sets of positive and negative behaviors:

Behaviors That Will Reduce Conflict or Result in Positive or Useful Conflict	*Behaviors That Will Result in Negative Conflict*
1. Purposefully pursuing goals held in common	1. Purposefully pursuing your own goals
2. Maintaining openness	2. Maintaining secrecy

3. Accurately representing your own needs, plans, and goals

3. Disguising or misrepresenting your own needs, plans, and goals

4. Being predictable—using behavior consistent with past experience

4. Being unpredictable—using the element of surprise

5. Avoiding threats or bluffing

5. Threatening and bluffing

Suppose that Tom wants to make sure a meeting finishes by 3 P.M. so he can keep another appointment. If he doesn't reveal his intentions of trying to get the meeting over by 3 P.M., he is likely to engage in behaviors that will result in negative conflict. For instance, by being secretive instead of open, other members of the committee might get upset at any of his efforts to "rush" business. In his deliberate pursuit of the goal of getting the meeting over, he might interrupt people and short-circuit discussion that would lead to additional conflict. His need to get the meeting over with may be so overpowering that it alters his ordinary behavior—he may threaten or bluff to get his way. On the other hand, if at the beginning of the meeting Tom says, "I've got a meeting at 3 P.M.—let's try to finish by then. If we can't, either you can continue without me or we can meet at another time" he would be establishing a base for a cooperative approach. People would understand why he might be appearing to rush the process, and his efforts would be less likely to create conflict. Moreover, if his behavior did create conflict, members would have a better idea of how to cope with him.

Prearrange Conflict Management Procedures. Many of the difficulties of conflict management arise because people have not planned any procedure for coping with conflict. Just as people who have made plans for what they will do in case of a fire, a flood, or a tornado often weather the particular disaster better than those who have not made plans, so do people weather conflict better if they have a plan for conflict management.

The first step in this process is for someone to recognize when conflict is escalating. That person must then remind the other of the prearranged procedure. For instance, Gary and Gail have agreed to list the advantages and disadvantages of a particular action before the conflict heats up; then, when such a conflict occurs, the prearranged procedure will take precedence over any actions. Sometimes, the time spent going through the prearranged steps is enough to get people past that explosive moment when they are likely to say or do something they would like to take back later. Such prearrangement may not be practical at all times, but when people anticipate a great deal of conflict in a given issue, such prearrangements may be a necessity.

Negotiate literally means "to carry on business," and we tend to think of negotiation as something unions, governments, and corporations do. But it's also a valuable procedure in private life—This couple must work out an agreement on how to spend their money. Conflict over financial matters is a major problem in many marriages.

Many of the previously listed guidelines in this section can be put together into a package that will serve as a conflict management procedure. Following a plan allows rational analysis to take precedence over emotional outbursts. Fundamental to any plan is the possibility for *negotiation*, which means managing conflicts through trade-offs. Conflict often results when two actions are proposed but only one can be taken. You cannot go to a baseball game and a concert at the same time; you cannot eat at a Chinese and an Italian restaurant at the same time; if you can afford only one house payment, you can't buy a house and rent a house at the same time. Even after people have considered every aspect of the conflict rationally, they may still truly believe that their way is the best; perhaps then they should negotiate.

For some simple problems it is relatively easy to negotiate a solution. For example, in trying to resolve whether to go to the ballgame or the concert, a statement such as "I'll tell you what, Jill, I'll go to the concert with you tonight if you'll go to the ballgame with me this weekend" will probably achieve the desired results. Because this is not an either-or situation, both activities can be undertaken at different times.

For negotiation to work, the activities, goals, or ideas must be of fairly equal importance. Thus, in the conflict over whether to eat Chinese or Italian, if one of the participants says, "Joe, if you'll let me make the decision on where to eat tonight, I'll go along with you on whatever movie you want to see," chances are the conflict will be resolved. On the other hand, a statement such as "Alice, if you will let me decide on the kind of car to buy, I'll let you decide on where to eat" does not stand a chance unless Alice is an unusually passive person. Obviously, selecting a car is a far more important decision than picking a restaurant, a movie, or any other one-night activity. A person negotiating in this manner is not acting in good faith. Finding situations that are indeed parallel may be difficult, but when they can be found, they make an excellent base for negotiation.

If an issue is truly not negotiable—such as a conflict about whether to rent a house or buy one—and you and the other person cannot work out a decision cooperatively, you are not necessarily defeated. When negotiation fails, you may wish to seek arbitration. *Arbitration* requires the presence of an impartial person who, after hearing both sides, weighs and evaluates the alternatives and makes a binding decision for you. Labor unions and management sometimes use arbitration. It may work for you.

For interpersonal conflicts arbitration will work if you can agree on an arbitrator who in turn will agree to make the decision for you. The arbitrator must be a person whose judgment you both trust. The arbitrator also should be competent in some way to make a decision on the issue. Your lawyer may act as arbitrator for you over whether or not to sue about a car accident, but he or she is not qualified to help you resolve a conflict over whether to send your child to public or private school. Likewise, your financial counselor may arbitrate a conflict over whether to invest in a high-risk stock or a high-dividend stock, but not in a conflict over whether to live in the city or the country.

Too often people seek to pull in a close friend or a relative to arbitrate. Not only may these bystanders not have the expertise needed for the particular issue, but, more importantly, they are not independent, impartial agents. They may well be close to both parties or may have a vested interest in the outcome. Calling on such people puts them in a no-win situation (somebody may well be upset by their decision) or, at best, makes them feel very uncomfortable in the role.

If you do agree to arbitration, the verbal contract between you and the other person should include a clause stating that whatever decision is made, you will both willingly and happily comply. Remember, you will have gone to a third person because the two of you were unable to come to an agreement; if you are unwilling to abide by the decision, whichever way it goes, then you should not agree to arbitration in the first place.

In some circumstances the impartial third person will act as a *facilitator* rather than as an arbitrator. This person will not make the decision for you but rather will help the two of you (or you alone, in the case of an intrapersonal decision) apply the problem-solving method to your conflict. Psychologists, psychiatrists, marriage counselors, and other clinicians are skilled in facilitating decision making. A good facilitator not only sees to it that you are following the steps of problem solving but also helps you weigh and evaluate the variables. Even with a good plan, however, there are at least three additional important considerations.

1. *Don't be stubborn.* Interpersonal communication is not the place for "nonnegotiable" demands. If you go into a situation with a defensive attitude or a "this is the way we're going to do it or else" posture, you are more than likely going to heighten the conflict. If, after calm appraisal, it appears that your way is not the best, or at least not the only good way, you should try to avoid becoming so ego-involved that any modification of position will cause you to "lose face." Of course, willingness to back off from a position is easier said than done. By altering your stance on any issue, however, you pave the way for the other person to make some concessions. If you are in a long-term relationship, it is better to think in terms of improving the relationship in general rather than in terms of "winning" on a particular issue.

2. *"Win" and "lose" graciously.* This guideline follows logically from not being stubborn. Regardless of any advice we can give, you will sometimes feel very strongly about your position, and having to abandon it or even to modify it will be a tremendous blow to you. Yet the very worst thing you can do in such a situation is to punish the other person for "making" you give in. For instance, if your attitude (if not your actual behavior) goes something like this: "O.K., Laura, I'll go to your party, but you'll see, I'll be miserable the whole evening," you are not going to have much fun—and neither will Laura. Moreover, Laura will probably resent your attitude. When a decision is made through objective discussion, both parties are obliged to support the decision. Although your own defenses may not let you concede that the other person's plan is the better one for these circumstances, the continuation of the "war" during the implementation stages will only bring on new conflicts or heighten or regenerate older ones.

3. *Discuss conflict-resolution failures.* Ideally, you want to resolve every conflict as it comes up. (Never let the sun set on your anger.) There will be times, however, when no matter how hard both persons try, they will not be able to resolve the conflict. If the person is an intimate friend or relative—so that the relationship is especially important to you—after the heat of the conflict dies down, you should take steps to analyze the failure of the conflict resolution. You should consider such questions as "Where did things go wrong?" "Did one or more of us become competitive? Or defensive?" "Did we fail to implement the problem-solving method adequately?" "Were the vested interests in the outcome too great?" By seeing why conflict resolution failed, you put yourself in a better position to manage the next conflict more successfully.

PRACTICE in Analyzing Conflicts

By Yourself

1. Describe a conflict situation that arose between you and a friend.

2. Identify the kind of conflict it was.

3. Did you and your friend cope with the conflict through withdrawal, surrender, aggression, persuasion, or discussion?

4. What was the outcome of the conflict?

5. If the outcome was negative, sketch a method of coping with the conflict that would have been more productive for you.

Summary

When there is a clash of opposing ideas or feelings, conflict occurs. Although pseudoconflicts are not really conflicts at all, there are many sources of genuine conflict. They may be content conflicts over facts, interpretations of facts, definitions, or choices; they may be value conflicts over competing value systems that are brought to bear on the issues; or they may be ego conflicts that personalize the nature of the conflict. Conflicts become more complicated as they escalate to involve values and egos.

We cope with conflicts in a variety of ways. Negative behaviors include withdrawal, surrender, and aggression. Positive behaviors include discussion and persuasion. People who are able to manage conflict stick to the subject, keep an open mind, test the criteria for value judgments, cooperate rather than compete, and use behaviors that result in positive conflict management. Moreover, people in a relationship are likely to develop a plan for dealing with conflict that they can put into operation when conflicts arise.

Notes

1. Alan L. Sillars and Judith Weisberg, "Conflict as a Social Skill," in Michael E. Roloff and Gerald R. Miller, eds., *Interpersonal Processes: New Directions in Communication Research* (Beverly Hills, Calif.: Sage, 1987), p. 146.

2. Ibid., p. 143.

3. Otis M. Walter and Robert L. Scott, *Thinking and Speaking*, 3rd ed. (New York: Macmillan, 1973), p. 245.

Three

Applying

Interpersonal

Communication

Skills in

Contexts

Part Three applies communication skills in eight short modules or minichapters, each of which focuses on a single context or skill application. We examine the role of interpersonal communication in family relationships, male-female relationships, cross-cultural relationships, group situations, leadership contexts, information interviews, job interviews, and work relationships.

Module A

Family

Communication

Objectives

After you have read this module, you should be able to define and/or explain:

Three dimensions of family communication

Role of communication in family relationships

Means of overcoming family communication problems

Generally, our most important relationships occur in the family. What we are, how we behave toward ourself and others, and what we plan and hope for in the future are very much affected by our family communication. This module will discuss the nature of families, look at the importance of communication for the family members, and suggest specific strategies for improving family communication.

The Nature of Families

What do you think of when you hear the word *family?* Perhaps you think of the old stereotype of a group of people who are all related either biologically or through the institution of marriage. In its most dominant form the stereotypic or traditional family is composed of parents and their children, as portrayed in such television situation comedies as "The Cosby Show" and "Growing Pains." Although this definition has greatly influenced the way we think about our families, it is no longer descriptive of most families. New definitions of family have been developed to better capture the meaning underlying the relationships that people call family. For example, Charles Dramer defines a family as a basic social unit composed of people who have a past history, a present reality and a future expectation.[1] Kathleen Galvin and Bernard Brommel define the family as a system in which communication regulates cohesion and adaptability.[2] Taken together these definitions suggest that individuals in families have ongoing relationships with one another that have existed for some time and are expected to continue to exist. In addition, in these relationships it is through communication that intimacy is regulated and that relationships are able to change with time. To these insights we would add that membership in a family may result from biological relationships, marital relationships, or through voluntary psychological relationships with other members. In addition it is important to remember that the primary goal of the family unit is to meet the physical, safety, social, and esteem needs of its members.

Using these definitions, it is easy to see that families are of many different types: the traditional family with two parents and one or more children from the union of the two parents; single-parent families with one parent and one or more children; blended families with two adults and children, some or all of whom may not be from the union of *those* parents; as well as communal and other nontraditional families.

Families are unique social units: Each family develops its own ways of functioning, with family communication providing the means for dealing with major functions. David Olson and colleagues have developed a circumplex model with three dimensions—cohesion, adaptability, and communication—to explain specific aspects of the family functioning process.[3] For our purposes we view cohesion and adaptability as distinct processes—communication mediates between them. Let's consider the concepts of cohesion and adaptability.

Cohesion

Cohesion, of course, means "sticking together." What families do to help themselves stick together is an important function. And however diverse individual family members may be, a cohesive force usually unites the family and differentiates family members from outsiders. For instance, if you have brothers or sisters, you may recall "knock-down drag-out" conflicts with them over any number of issues. Tension between siblings can be tremendous. As soon as someone from outside the family made a crack about your brother or sister, however, you suddenly found yourself joining together to repel the attack from the outsider.

Throughout a family's history cohesion is subject to change, from both internal and external forces. Family members grow closer together and farther apart at various times. For example, a father may change from a daughter's best buddy to a virtual stranger seemingly overnight when that daughter experiences the onset of puberty. Or members of a family may develop more cohesive relationships as a result of fire that destroys many family possessions and records. Thus, a great deal of family energy is spent trying to develop or maintain cohesion.

Adaptability

Regardless of how cohesive a family may be, the family unit as well as individual members change constantly over time. A second important function of the family is adaptability—how the family responds to change. Families are called upon to change role relationships, power structures, and decision rules from year to year and sometimes from week to week. A family may appear remarkably stable for a long period of time but suddenly find that stability threatened by a change in schools for one or more of the children, a new job for one of the parents, a death in the family, or a mother returning to the work force.

Changes in families may bring them closer together or drive them farther apart. For instance, a death in the family may lead to a greater level of cohesiveness than the family has had in years, or it may create such chaos that the family takes months or even years to return to its former level of cohesiveness. If the family is unable to adapt to such changes, its cohesiveness may be irreparably damaged.

The Importance of Family Communication

Communication within the family unit serves at least three major purposes for individual family members: (1) Family communication affects self-concept formation in children; (2) family communication validates individual members' self-worth; and (3) family communication from members in positions of power serve as models of behavior for other family members.

Self-Concept Formation

In Chapter 2 we discussed the role of communication in formation of self-concept. Children's self-concepts that are well established by the time they are teenagers have been formed mostly by statements from other family members.

One major responsibility that family members have to one another is to talk (especially to the young children) in ways that will contribute to the development of strong self-concepts. Statements of praise ("Jim, you did really a nice job of cleaning your room" and " Betty, that's one of the best pictures you've painted"), statements of acceptance and support ("If you have good reasons to drop out of the Glee Club, we accept your decision" and "Andy doesn't see eye to eye with us, but he's welcome in our home because he's your friend, and we respect that"), and statements of love ("Bart, I know it hurts to play poorly in front of your family, but we love you and we'll be here again next game" and "We both love you very much, Tom") can do a great deal to enhance a child's self-concept.

Unfortunately, in many families parent-child communication is very damaging to developing self-concepts. Statements that *tease, blame,* and *evaluate* are particularly damaging to children. Teasing questions ("How are you today, clumsy?" and "Are you still going to be sucking your thumb when you're twenty-one?"), blaming statements ("You know, if I didn't have to raise you, I could be back at college" and "No, *you* didn't drop the plate, but your constant whining made me so nervous that I dropped it"), and evaluations ("Terry, why are you trying to make breakfast when you know you can't even boil water?" and "Marty, didn't you learn how to add? If what you want to do in life involves numbers, you'd better think of a different profession") are all too common. Statements like these are stored in a child's mind and may be played back over and over until the child believes them. An occasional negative statement like the ones quoted here may not have any lasting effect, but if the family's normal communication style is negative—teasing, blaming, and evaluating—damaged self-concepts are likely to result.

Validation

A second major responsibility of family members is to talk with each other in ways that will *validate*, or confirm the worth of, individual members. The importance of this responsibility cannot be overstated. Your family usually is made up of the people with whom you feel safest, and you often turn to them when you need praise, comfort, and reassurance. Yet in many families this important responsibility is forgotten in the rush of day-to-day living. For example, when Judy, the youngest daughter, comes home excited about the gold star she received for her spelling test, her mother and/or father need to take time to recognize the accomplishment regardless of how busy they are or what problems they may have faced this day. Validation is not, however, important only for children. Everyone, including the adults of the family, needs validation, confirmation, and support— they all need to be listened to. When people can't get validation from within the family, they go outside the family for it.

Models of Behavior

A third responsibility of family members is to talk in ways that serve as models of behavior for other family members. Parents, especially, serve as models, whether they want to or not. The saying, "Do as I say, not as I do" hardly represents a workable model of behavior, because it teaches only hypocrisy. If Julia sees her parents describing feelings and admitting mistakes, Julia will be more likely to describe her feelings openly and admit her mistakes. If, however, Julia sees family members acting secretively and bullying or bluffing their way through obvious mistakes, Julia will learn to behave similarly. How many times have we heard a parent say, "I don't understand Tim's or Betty's behavior," when that behavior strongly resembles the parent's?

Improving Family Communication

In outlining these three major family responsibilities, we have already made some suggestions for improving family communication. Now we turn to four specific behaviors that family members can use.

Opening the Lines of Communication. For any number of possible reasons lines of communication within a family are often scrambled or broken, which may cause family members to feel isolated. Excluding requests and orders from other family members ("Clean up your room," "Don't play the stereo so loudly"), many family members actually spend very few minutes each day really talking with one another. Rather, they devote far more time to conversing with people outside the home.

The first step in opening lines of communication is setting up a time specifically for communication, for getting together and talking. Each member of the family needs and should have the opportunity to talk about what happened to him or her that day. Perhaps the best time for families to converse together is during the evening meal, but the rush of busy lives and the ever-present television set—which competes for the attention of the family even when they are physically together—threaten such conversations. It may be difficult to have a family hour every day of the week, but some time should be set aside each week when everyone can share ideas and experiences.

The next step in opening lines of communication consists of establishing a pattern of communication that family members will follow in interacting with one another. The *network* of communication in a given family represents the dominant model or pattern of family communication (see Figure A.1). Some networks are *chains*, which means a low-ranking member of the family (let's say the youngest son) must talk to a higher-ranking member (perhaps the oldest daughter), who then relays messages to the mother or father. Some networks are *wheels*, with the mother or father at the center and all communication passing through him or her. The most desirable networks are *connected* or *all-channel*, which means each member talks with every other member on an *equal*

We first learn about interpersonal communication in our families, but just as individuals vary widely in their communication skills, so do families. Family members often take each other for granted, so it's important for a family to reserve some time together—daily if possible—simply to talk and share experiences.

status level to obtain advice, support, and friendship and to meet interpersonal needs.

Confronting the Effects of Power Imbalances. Members of a family are dependent upon one another for many things. For instance, children depend on their parents for food, shelter, clothing, and transportation as well as love. Children depend on one another for friendship and support. And parents depend on their children for companionship and love, to name but a few. Parents' dependence on their children is less obvious, but parents need their children's love and companionship, and in many cases parents need their children to behave in ways that validate the parents' self-concept. Because of the *nature* of these dependencies the distribution

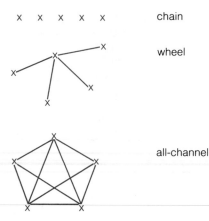

Figure A.1 Communication networks

of power within the family is unequal. Society gives parents legitimate power over their children, and because parents usually control the family budget and are physically stronger than their children, they wield considerable reward and coercive power. Older children often have great amounts of coercive and referent power over their younger brothers and sisters in addition to the legitimate power given them by the parents. Imbalances in referent power occur between two children when one of the children will go to almost any lengths to please the other (usually older) child. For instance, Todd, a younger child, may endure abusive treatment from his older brother, Mark, because Todd at least has the "privilege" of being with Mark. Within any family with children, then, some of the members will have more power than others. The younger child may be placed in the position of having to please three "parents"— mother, father, and an older brother or sister. If the demands of all three are in accord, few problems should arise. If, however, the older sibling begins to abuse the power relationship, the younger sibling may react by withdrawing or becoming hostile.

Family communication is often strongly influenced by these dependencies and the power distributions that derive from them. In many families children are not treated equally. The parents may realize that one of the children has certain gifts or talents that the others lack, so the parents allow this child privileges that the others do not enjoy. Occasionally, parents simply make a mistake and treat the children unequally because one child is more demanding or because the parents have forgotten how they treated the other children under similar circumstances.

If lines of communication within a family are open, it is possible to identify and confront the family power imbalances and the inequities they may be causing within relationships. Parents can then explain why they are behaving as they are rather than simply rely on their authority:

"Why should you be in by 10:30? Because I said so, that's why!" If parents level with their children and give them reasons for their behavior, then children will get into the habit of leveling with their parents. Children will feel free to ask why an older brother's rules are different from the parents' rules or why George got to drive the family car when he was sixteen but Matthew is denied such permission.

Recognizing and Adapting to Changes in Family Members. Members of a family know each other so well that they can often predict how a particular family member will think, feel, or act under many different circumstances. These predictions will not always be accurate, however. All people change with time—including family members—though such changes are likely to be gradual. For example, it isn't until Tanya returns from six weeks at summer camp that another member of the family is likely to recognize how she has changed.

Even as children grow and change, their brothers and sisters, and especially their parents, continue to see them as they once were, not as they are or are becoming. How often will a younger member of the family hear such statements as "Don't tell me you like asparagus—remember, I'm your brother, I know you" or "You're going to be a doctor? Come on, you faint at the sight of blood." The skill of dating generalizations, discussed in Chapter 3, is an important one for members of a family to master. It may well be true that Maggie didn't like asparagus or that Ginger used to faint at the sight of blood, but as the years go by, Maggie and Ginger change.

Recognizing and adapting to change appears to be especially difficult as children become teens and are striving to achieve independence at the very same time when their parents may be experiencing their own mid-life transition. Frequently parents who are occupied with their own adult life transition find it difficult to reexamine and change their relationship with the adolescent child to one that is better suited to the emerging needs of both of them. Thus parents continue to interact with the child in the habitual way and justify the behavior by asserting that the child must earn the right to be treated like a grown-up. Yet, a teenager who is treated like a child will probably act more childlike, whereas a teenager treated as an adult is likely to act more like an adult.

Recognizing change has another dimension as well. Family members need to be alert to the kinds of changes that may indicate stress or emotional distress in other members. Unfortunately, family members often are unable to notice gradual changes in behavior that serve as signals to problems until the family member is seriously troubled.

Respecting Individual Interests. Perhaps the most important recommendation for improving family communication is for family members to respect individual interests. Chapter 7 discussed the importance of listening, understanding, and empathizing, yet family communication can often be marked by indifference or apathy. Individual family members sometimes are overly concerned with what is important to themselves and fail to consider the feelings of others. When something nice happens to one member of the family, the first reaction of other family members should never be "Big deal." If other family members recognize what one person thinks is important, that person is likely to return the favor.

PRACTICE in Family Communication

By Yourself

1. Analyze the power relationships between you and (1) your mother or father, (2) your siblings, or (3) your children. How do these dependencies affect your communication?

2. Analyze the support systems in your family. Who listens? Who helps? Who can be counted on? Anyone?

3. Develop a plan for increasing the time your family spends communicating. Remember, you needn't try to schedule any one large block of time. Are there times for increasing communication with any member of the family that you have not considered?

4. Watch a television program that centers on family life such as "Family Ties," "Who's the Boss," "Growing Pains," or "The Cosby Show." Examine the role of communication in self-concept formation, validation, and behavioral models. What affect does the communication have on family cohesiveness and adaptability to change? On the basis of your analysis is the family communication portrayed as positive or negative? In what ways?

In Pairs

Select an actual problem you are having with a member of your family. Role-play this problem with a class member. Try to use confronting, dating generalizations, or caring as a means of attempting to resolve the problem.

Summary

The family is a basic social unit comprised of people who have a past history, a present reality, and a future expectation. The family represents the most important group you will belong to, because what happens during the years you live with your family is likely to profoundly affect the rest of your life.

The three dimensions of family communication are cohesion, adaptability, and communication. Cohesion involves what a family does to help it stay together. Adaptability is what a family does to help it meet the changing needs of its members. Communication mediates between cohesion and adaptability.

Family communication is important because (1) it affects self-concept formation in children, (2) it is the primary source for validating individual members' self-worth, and (3) it provides models of behavior from members in positions of power for other family members.

Family relationships are improved by opening lines of communication, by confronting the effects of power imbalances, by recognizing changes in family members, and by respecting individual interests.

Notes

1. Charles H. Dramer, *Becoming a Family Therapist* (New York: Human Sciences Press, 1980).

2. Kathleen M. Galvin and Bernard J. Brommel, *Family Communication: Cohesion and Change*, 2nd ed. (Glenview, Ill.: Scott, Foresman, 1986), p. 23.

3. David H. Olson, Candyce S. Russell, and Douglas H. Sprenkle, "Circumplex Model of Marital and Family Systems: Cohesion and Adaptability Dimensions, Family Types, and Clinical Applications," *Family Process* 18 (1979): 3–28. Also see Olson et al., "Circumplex Model of Marital and Family Systems: VI Theoretical Update," *Family Process* 22 (1983): 69–84.

Module B

Male-Female

Communication

Objectives

After you have read this module, you should be able
to define and/or explain:

Views on how sex-role differences develop

How socialization results in sex-role differences

What men and women are doing to cope with changes in sex roles

During the last several years people have become more aware of the potential communication problems stemming from differences between men and women. By far the greatest reason for communication problems between the sexes is the lack of understanding of each other's perspective. This module explores how sex and gender affect communication. We will discuss why male and female behavior differs, look at the role of socialization in male-female behavior, and examine how men and women are coping with changing sex roles.

Differences Between Male and Female Behavior

Theories that seek to explain the behavioral differences between men and women have focused on both biological and social factors.

Biological Differences

Obviously, males and females differ biologically. What's important to understand is how many of these differences affect male-female communication. One basic difference is in rate of physical maturation. In biological terms, at age two girls are as much as six months "older" than boys, and by the teen years girls may be as much as two years "older" than boys. Therefore, girls will often outshine boys all through the pre-college years because boys do not possess comparable physiological maturity to compete with girls on basic motor skills of finger movement, wrist movement, and manual dexterity.[1] Researchers have also suggested, though they have not proved conclusively, that other behavioral differences may be attributed to basic biological factors. For example, they theorize that both girls' superior verbal ability and boys' aggressive tendencies derive from their biological make-ups (nature) and not from social or cultural conditioning (nurture). In short, those who support biological difference theories view all differences in female and male behavior as genetically induced. Thus, for example, they would say that a woman's maternal behavior stems from an innate biological drive or instinct that men lack.

Socialization Differences

Although biological differences certainly explain some behavioral differences, many more of the differences can be attributed to psychological factors. Because the two sexes are treated differently from birth, they behave differently. To use a human example, research has shown that throughout their lifetime males tend to be more aggressive than females. Does this mean that all males are aggressive? Does it mean that all men are more aggressive than all women? Certainly not. In fact, in some cultures the women are notoriously more aggressive than the men. In American culture, if a little boy acts aggressively and is rewarded (or at least not punished!) for the aggressive behavior, then he is likely to incorporate into his behavior pattern what initially was just a tendency. If, however, the same little boy is punished for aggressive behavior, then the tendency will probably diminish as he learns what will and will not be accepted in a particular situation. Behavioral tendencies can be—and regularly are—modified by a person's family and society.

Social learning theory states that "boylike" and "girllike" behaviors are shaped early in a child's life. In order to appreciate these differences, let us briefly examine how the socialization process teaches people their appropriate sex-role behavior.

If you look into the nursery of any American hospital, you may be able to see firsthand the beginning of the sex-role socialization process. You may spot nurses picking up girls somewhat more gently than they do boys. At least one study shows that parents do just that, and that parents not only let their boy babies cry longer before picking them up but speak to them differently as well. Very young babies are often surrounded by toys that their parents believe are right for a child of that sex. A new father may buy his son a football, even though it will be many years before that child can begin to use it. Early on, a child's behavior is guided by what the parents, as part of the larger social structure, think is appropriate to the child's sex.

As a result of this continued social indoctrination, a little girl eventually learns that society expects her to be demure, quiet, passive, neat, caring, nurturing, and emotional. Likewise, a little boy comes to realize that society expects him to be strong, dominant, assertive, manually dextrous, persuasive, athletic, and in control of his softer emotions.

Cognitive development theory claims that a child's idea of what is "boylike" or "girllike" develops in stages. By about age five or six a child recognizes sex roles as stable variables that remain constant even in the face of changes in external characteristics such as clothing or hairstyle.[2]

How accurately do sex-role stereotypes reflect real differences in male or female behavior? Only four primary differences seem to be supported by data: (1) Girls have greater verbal ability than boys, (2) boys excel in visual-spatial development; (3) boys excel in mathematics, and (4) boys are more aggressive.[3] While research does support sex differences in these four areas, it is still unclear as to whether these are caused by biological differences and/or socialization experiences.

Although evidence does support other potential differences, none appear to be statistically significant. Then where do these ideas about biologically based behavior differences come from? Basically from sex-role stereotyping.

Even though traditional sex roles are changing, it is unlikely that you have fully escaped sex-role indoctrination. Yet the changes in sex roles do create a different set of problems for male-female relationships.

Coping with Changes in Sex Roles

Neither men nor women can develop their communication skills to the fullest to maximize their male-female relationships as long as they are prisoners of these stereotypes. Because effective communication entails shared meaning, both men and women need to be able to step outside the stereotypes, acquire each other's traditional skills, and become well-rounded communicators. Men need to develop those skills that help to nurture others and deal with emotions; women need to develop skills enabling them to present their own point of view clearly and firmly. There are many things that men and women can do to help this process and thereby improve their relationships.

Acknowledging Effects of Conditioning

The first step to improving male-female relationships is for men and women to acknowledge the effects of their early conditioning on their interpersonal communication. For example, Matt has trouble describing his feelings. Yet describing feelings, as you have learned, is one of the most important communication skills. Unless Matt is willing to probe his upbringing to find out why he is having difficulty developing this skill (perhaps he has been conditioned that "big boys don't cry"), he may never integrate this particular skill into his behavior. Similarly, unless Mary understands

Sex-role differentiation means that many women and men lack common experiences, which makes empathy difficult. Whether this woman has ever participated in a team sport or made a game-saving play, she knows that everyone appreciates praise for a job well done.

that the socialization process has encouraged her to be passive (perhaps she has been conditioned that "nice girls don't talk back"), she will find it difficult, if not impossible, to learn to be assertive and stand up for herself.

Let's examine the effect of these sex roles on relationships. Unfortunately, sex-role differentiation ensures that women and men have all too few common experiences upon which to build empathy. For example, if Marge believes that any form of aggressiveness is unfeminine and therefore undesirable, she will probably have trouble being assertive when returning damaged merchandise to a store. Yet Bob, her husband, may not be able to empathize with Marge's discomfort at all. Likewise, many women complain that their boyfriends, lovers, or husbands don't verbalize their affections. A woman frequently feels unloved or unwanted because the man is unwilling to say, "I love you," often enough. Although he may in fact not love her, it is more likely that he's simply adhering to the traditional male sex role that discourages men from expressing their feelings. Because the female sex role encourages expressing feelings, women may not be able to empathize with silent men.

Examining Dependency Relationships

The second step to improving male-female relationships is for men and women to examine the dependency relationships that result from sex-role stereotypes. Because society values traditionally masculine behaviors more highly than it does feminine behaviors, men have a power advantage.[4] Under these circumstances, as you can imagine, a climate of equality in communication between women and men is difficult to establish. A man who adopts a superior attitude toward a woman undermines the effectiveness of their communication.

The fact that society values masculine over feminine behaviors has ramifications for same-sex relationships as well. In our society, for example, Amy will probably cancel her plans to go shopping with Beth if Joe calls to say he'd like to stop by for lunch. Yet if Joe has plans to go out with his friend Tom, he probably will not cancel them to spend the evening with Amy—even if she really wants to see him. Simply stated, a man's company is more valued than a woman's. Women sometimes will even jeopardize their relationships with other women to advance what they believe to be a more socially desirable relationship with a man. Because masculine behavior is more valued, however, men don't often risk same-sex friendships in this way.

Confronting Sexist Attitudes and Behaviors

The third step to improving male-female relationships is for men and women to become aware of and confront sexist attitudes and behaviors. *Sexist behavior*, or sexism, is any behavior, however insignificant, that limits both women and men to rigid, stereotypic roles based solely on differences in sex. Note, however, that sexist attitudes and behaviors are not confined to men's behavior toward women, although sexism comes under heaviest attack as it limits the economic and social opportunities of women in a society where men have more power. The attitudes that men have about how other men should behave, the attitudes women have about men, the attitudes women have about other women, as well as the accompanying behaviors, also may be sexist. For example, many women never think of paying their own way on a date. That is sexist. Similarly, many women believe that *all* women should stay home with small children. That is sexist. And many men believe women have no place in the executive suites of corporate America unless they have memo pads or vacuum cleaners in their hands. That is sexist. Some men think that a man (but not a woman) who cries is weak. That, too, is sexist.

Very few people manage to completely avoid behaving or thinking in a sexist manner. By becoming aware of your own sexist attitudes and behaviors, you can guard against inhibiting communication by automatically assuming that other people feel and act the same way you do. You can also guard against saying or doing things that offend other people and perpetuate outdated sex-role stereotypes.

The language we use often reflects sexist attitudes. A man who refers to his fifty-year-old female office assistant as "my girl" is guilty of sexist language. Although language reflects reality, you should remember from the discussion of the Sapir-Whorf Hypothesis in Chapter 3 that language also *affects* reality. Those who wish to avoid sexism in language use champion the development of nonsex-based terminology: *chair* or *chairperson* or *presiding officer* for *chairman*, *mail carrier* or *letter carrier* for *mailman*, *firefighter* for *fireman*, *police officer* for *policeman*.

Some common expressions as well as individual words can be offensive. For example: "You're acting like a little old lady" or "Well, what can you expect; he's a man, isn't he?" These familiar expressions are based not on information about any one person but rather on generalizations about all women or all men—in other words, stereotypes. As such, they are detrimental to accurate and meaningful communication.

Is all this concern with sexist language important? We believe it is. Because the language you use affects the way you think, your use of sex-neutral terms and expressions will reflect the changes in male and female roles and will also enable you to discuss ideas and issues without fear of offending anyone.

Monitoring Sex-Role-Based Tendencies

The final step to improving male-female relationships is for men and women to monitor sex-role-based tendencies toward communication dominance or passiveness. If, as a normal part of your sex role, you tend to assume either an obviously dominant or an obviously passive communication role, then you are likely to create defensiveness in your communication partners. Remember, a good communication climate results in part from equality, which is impossible to achieve if one person is dominant.

A climate of equality makes people more willing to accept nontraditional sex-role behaviors. Even though more and more women hold nontraditional jobs, many people still have trouble acknowledging their right to do so. And men who pursue nontraditional jobs may have even more trouble being accepted. *Householder* is all too often a term of ridicule. It does not matter whether you personally wish to lead a nontraditional life. What does matter is this: If you desire successful interpersonal communication, you must be willing to accept behavior that is different from your own.

PRACTICE in Confronting Sex-Role Stereotypes

By Yourself

Select a weekly situation television comedy such as "Kate and Allie," "Newhart," "Designing Women," or "Cheers." Analyze the show on the basis of sexist attitudes and behaviors. What kinds of stereotypic behavior is portrayed, if any? How is this used to heighten the comedic effect of the show? Indicate any examples of effective male-female communication. Under what circumstances, if any, do these occur?

In Groups

1. Have one person begin, "Girls should be—" and someone else in the group finish the sentence. Repeat the process until the first person cannot think of any more endings, then go on to the next person in the group. When everyone has had a chance to say what girls should be, start over with "Boys should be—." Afterwards, the group should discuss individual reactions to the exercise.

2. Brainstorm a list of "famous old sayings" on sex roles (example: "Big boys don't cry"). Take a poll to determine which of the sayings seemed to be the most commonly heard. Discuss your reactions to them when you first heard them and your reactions now. Any differences?

Summary

Women and men often have trouble communicating because of the sex-role differences between them. Behavioral differences between men and women have been attributed to biological differences and socialization differences. Sex-role differentiation results in a lack of the behavioral flexibility necessary for healthy communication.

Male-female relationships can be improved by acknowledging the effects of conditioning on communication, by examining dependency relationships, by confronting sexist attitudes and behavior, and by monitoring the tendency toward dominance or passiveness.

Notes

1. B. Simmons and E. Whitfield, "Are Boys Victims of Sex-Role Stereotyping?" *Childhood Education* 56(2) (1979): 75–79.

2. D. N. Ruble, T. Balaban, and J. Cooper, "Gender Constancy and the Effects of Sex-Typed Television Toy Commercials," *Child Development* 52 (1981): 667–673.

3. E. E. Maccoby and C. N. Jacklin, *The Psychology of Sex Differences* (Stanford, Calif.: Stanford University Press, 1974).

4. A research study of college students showed that both women and men saw more of the typically masculine traits as desirable. See Paul S. Rosenkantz et al., "Sex Role Stereotypes and Self-Concept in College Students," *Journal of Consulting and Clinical Psychology* 32 (1968): 287–295.

Module C

Cross-Cultural

Communication

Objectives

After you have read this module, you should be able
to define and/or explain:

Culture

Problems affecting cross-
cultural relationships

How to improve cross-cultural
communication

Perhaps the greatest communication problem is communicating with people from different cultures. People who are confronted with strangers from different cultures tend to see cultural differences as barriers to communication. These differences in people represent unknown quantities. The more one person differs from another, the less either person is able to predict the behavior of the other. When people do not believe they know

If these students know anything about Indian history, they shouldn't be surprised that this woman, a new U.S. citizen, speaks flawless English with a British accent. But speaking the same language does not necessarily make cross-cultural communication easier. It's a mistake to assume that someone who shares your language also shares your meanings and beliefs.

how another person will behave, fear is a probable result. Some people express their fear by withdrawing or becoming compliant, while others mask their fear with aggressive behavior. Clearly, none of these behaviors improves communication.

In this module we will examine the concept of culture, look at some of the problems that arise in relationships between people from different cultures, and discuss some strategies for strengthening these relationships.

The Concept of Culture

A *culture* is a system of shared beliefs, values, symbols, and behaviors that characterizes a group. Every nation in the world contains cultures that differ from our own. The cultures of some nations, such as Canada and England, are very similar to the dominant white American culture. By contrast, the cultures of the Middle East, black Africa, the Far East, and even Mexico differ so much from our own that communication can be difficult. Furthermore, you don't have to cross national borders to encounter different cultures. Every dominant culture contains subcultures—groups both large and small that maintain their individual cultural identities. The United States has been called a melting pot of people and cultures, but because *melting pot* implies a total assimilation, our nation in reality is anything but a melting pot. This country is more accurately described as one with a large, dominant white American culture within which exist major subcultures, including black American, Mexican-American, Hispanic-American, Asian-American, native American, Appalachian, and others.

Influences on Cross-Cultural Communication

In this section we want to consider some of the major problems that make it difficult for people from different cultures to communicate. Communication across cultures can be helped by recognizing when one of the problems exists or is likely to exist and by consciously attempting to overcome the problem.

Stereotyping and Prejudice

We link these two problems because one follows from the other. As we noted in Chapter 2 and again in Module B, when you characterize people on the basis of the category or group to which they belong, you are stereotyping them. For instance, when Laura discovers that a man she has just met is a Muslim, Laura would be stereotyping the person if she viewed him solely in terms of his religious beliefs rather than in terms of his individual behavior. Moreover, Laura would be guilty of prejudice. *Prejudice* is an unjustified attitude toward a person or group. A prejudiced person is likely to continue to maintain his or her prejudices even in light of evidence that disproves them. Suppose that Roy, a black man, stereotypes all whites as racist. When Roy meets Phil, a white man, Roy will believe that Phil is racist. Later, if Roy is confronted with evidence showing that Phil's behavior is not racist, Roy may refuse to acknowledge the evidence or may reject the source of the evidence. Then we would say that Roy is prejudiced.

Stereotyping represents a shortcut in thinking. By developing an attitude or belief about an entire group and then applying that attitude to every member of the group, a person no longer has to consider the potential for individual differences—the stereotypic view applies to all persons in the group. It provides some people with a certain comfort to believe that blacks are lazy, that Italians are naturally hot-headed, that Arabs are so emotional they're incapable of reasoning, and that white Americans are racist. When the person meets a black, an Italian, an Arab, or a white American, the person already "knows" how to treat the new acquaintance.

One form of stereotyping that causes major problems in developing relationships is racism. *Racism* is any behavior, however insignificant it may seem, that results solely from racial stereotyping. Do you believe anything or behave in any way that is racist? Remember, the behavior may seem insignificant. For instance, leaving more space between you and another person on a bus, on a plane, in a lounge, or at a counter in a restaurant—a space wider than the space you would leave if the person you were sitting next to were of your race—is racist behavior. Telling jokes, listening to jokes, or encouraging repetition of jokes that demean people of other races is racist behavior. Ignoring the presence of another person when that person is of another race is racist behavior. You may say, "But I didn't *mean* anything by what I did"; however, your behavior is perceived as racist (resulting from racial stereotyping) and it will seriously harm your attempts to communicate.

Stereotyping, prejudice, and racism are hard to overcome because (1) people can always find someone who will conform with their preconceived attitudes and (2) people are likely to ignore any information or discount the source of any information that is counter to their attitudes. Still, the only way to fight these attitudes is with accurate information. If people are confronted with enough information over a long enough period of time, their attitudes can be changed.

Differences in Role Expectations

When we communicate with people from other cultures, we tend to expect that they will view the various roles in our culture and their interrelationships the same way we do, but roles differ between and among cultures. If someone is identified as a professor, minister, or doctor, people from other cultures may have expectations about how people who occupy those roles should think and behave based on what those roles symbolize in their particular cultures. *Before* making any assumptions, people should determine whether their preconceived notions are in fact valid.

To illustrate, note the conflict in American society over the roles of mothers and fathers in raising children. How can you expect people from another culture to understand your viewpoint on child-rearing when there are so many differing opinions on this issue in this country? Thus, before getting too deeply involved in discussions with people from another culture on the issue of child-rearing, you should have some understanding of what the father's or mother's role within that culture is with respect to raising children. And if you don't know, ask.

Language

Language can be an obvious barrier to communicating across cultures. For instance, people from Western cultures favor precision in language, whereas people from Eastern cultures favor ambiguities.[1] Asians are comfortable talking for hours without clearly expressing an opinion. Likewise, Asians can be suspicious of direct verbal expressions of love and respect.

Surprisingly, people who speak different languages expect to have some problem communicating and thus seem to take extra care to keep that barrier from becoming insurmountable. Language becomes a greater barrier for two people from different cultures who are speaking the same language, because they tend to believe they mean the same things when they use the same words. For example, if a person says that the government wants what is best for the nation, it would seem that others should have no difficulty understanding what is meant. Yet *best for the nation* can and does mean many different things to different people, depending on their politics, priorities, and so on. When people from another culture use a word and you perceive that word as particularly important to understanding, you should ask for examples so that you can be sure of what they mean.

Nonverbal Elements

Time, space, facial expression, gesture, and posture may be used quite differently in one culture than in another. Because nonverbal communication is not coded to the extent that verbal communication is, the meanings we think we get may be very different from the meaning intended, if in fact *any* meaning was intended.

One nonverbal element that can cause problems is time. For example, white Americans view time designations differently than do Hispanics, Japanese, and black Americans. And Americans in general view time *monochronically*, emphasizing schedules and promptness; in the Middle East people tend to view time *polychronically*—being late is common, and a schedule may be meaningless.[2] Edward Hall has done extensive research to show the link between views of time and culture.[3] The point is that there is no "right" way of viewing time designations. There are, however, different ways of doing so.

Space also reflects differences in cultures. People around the world have different attitudes about what constitutes appropriate distances between people for various interactions. For example, recall that Americans consider the space of up to a foot or eighteen inches from their bodies as personal or intimate space, and they do not expect people to violate that space. In the Middle East, however, men seek to move much closer to other men when they are talking. Thus, when an Arab talks with an American, one of the two is likely to be uncomfortable. Either the American will experience a sense of territorial invasion or the Arab will feel himself too far removed for serious conversation. The cultural differences in the meanings assigned to gestures, movements, and facial expression are too numerous and complex to discuss in detail, but gestures can assume completely different meanings, and the size and frequency of illustrators and so on vary from culture to culture. Affect displays also vary since members of some cultures have been socialized to deintensify emotional behavior cues while members of other cultures have been socialized to amplify their displays of emotions. In some Eastern cultures people are taught to mask their nonverbal cues. The cultural differences that are related to affect displays are often reflected in the interpretation that can be given to facial expressions.[4]

Because of all these nonverbal differences between various cultures, description of behavior and perception checking should precede any assignment of meaning to the nonverbal communication of people from different cultures. As we pointed out earlier, these behaviors should become an important part of your communication style with people from your own culture as well!

Improving Communication in Cross-Cultural Relationships

To make headway with your communication in cross-cultural relationships, you will need to take the following steps:

1. *Be personally committed.* If you care, if you understand the potential for problems in cross-cultural relationships, you will increase your chances for success.

2. *Be willing to work.* Improving communication across cultures takes time and energy. You must be open to ideas different from your own, and you must be willing to listen. And you certainly must not expect immediate results. Especially in situations in which communication may be hindered by years of distrust, it will take a relatively long time to build the necessary base for trust out of which a relationship can develop.

3. *Use all available skills.* Throughout this book we have been trying to help you develop both interpersonal communication competence and behavioral flexibility. Overcoming cross-cultural differences will test your abilities to use these behaviors. It is especially important for you to practice indexing statements. Remember that indexing is a verbal device for taking individual cases into account. You are going to find people of other cultures who are despicable, mean, racist, unsavory, untrustworthy, lazy, and every other negative quality imaginable. But as long as you can deal with them as individuals and not as proof of general cultural behavior, you will be well on your way toward improving your intercultural communication.

4. *Be willing to fail.* Not all your attempts to improve cross-cultural relationships will succeed. Sometimes, you will have difficulty because your skills are not yet sufficiently developed. And sometimes you will fail because someone is trying to sabotage your efforts. The person you are trying to communicate with must try, too. As you attempt to communicate, however, you will gain needed experience and also learn to identify others who are willing to try.

5. *Widen your perspectives.* You widen your perspective with information. The more you learn about people from other cultures, the more likely you are to succeed in developing relationships with them. You may also find it valuable to list your beliefs about that culture and its people and attempt to test them. By confronting some of your stereotypes and prejudices, you can widen your perspectives.

PRACTICE in Cross-Cultural Communication

By Yourself

1. List all the racial and cultural stereotypes you have heard. Now think of people you know who are in these groups. Do they fit the stereotype?

2. Make a special effort to talk with and find out about a person from another culture. What effect does your conversation have on your perception of the person?

Summary

Some of the major problems in cross-cultural communication derive from stereotyping and prejudice, from erroneous perceptions of cultural roles, from language barriers, and from different uses of nonverbal elements, such as time, space, gestures, facial expressions, and postures.

You can learn to improve your communication relationships across cultures if you are personally committed, willing to work, able to use all available skills, willing to accept failure, and willing to widen your perspectives.

Notes

1. William B. Gudykunst and Young Un Kim, *Communicating with Strangers: An Approach to Intercultural Communication* (Reading, Mass.: Addison-Wesley, 1984), p. 142.

2. Larry Samovar, Richard E. Porter, and Nemi C. Jain, *Understanding Intercultural Communication* (Belmont, Calif.: Wadsworth, 1981), p. 183.

3. Edward Hall, *The Silent Language* (Garden City, N.Y.: Doubleday, 1959).

4. J. R. Davitz, *The Communication of Emotional Meaning* (New York: McGraw-Hill, 1964), p. 14.

Module D

Interpersonal

Communication

In Groups

Objectives

After you have read this module, you should be able to define and/or explain:

Questions of fact, value, and policy

Solving a problem using the problem-solving method

Task roles

Maintenance roles

Negative roles

$\mathbf{M}$ost of us are members of some fraternal, governmental, religious, or work-related committee. A *committee* is a type of *work group*, a small unit whose members interact face-to-face and who strive toward a common goal. The size recommended for an effective group varies, but many researchers consider five to seven members as ideal. The types of goals for which groups strive may differ, but for any group to succeed, its members must not only use the interpersonal skills we have discussed so far, they must also be able to understand and use the problem-solving method and be able to fulfill necessary roles. In this module we focus on applying interpersonal communication skills to group settings.

Preparation for Problem-Solving Group Work

If a group is to succeed, it must be able to use the problem-solving method. Recall that problem solving includes stating the problem, analyzing the problem, suggesting solutions, and selecting the best solution.

Stating the Problem

In many groups much wheel spinning takes place during the early stages of group discussion, mainly due to members' questions about the function, purpose, or goal of the group. As soon as possible, the group should decide exactly what it will be doing, assuming that the person, agency, or parent group that created the particular work group has not assigned the group a specific task. For example, a group may be formed for the purpose of "determining the nature of the curriculum" or "preparing a guideline for hiring at a new plant." If, however, the group's responsibility is not stated in such clear terms, it is up to the group leader or representative to find out exactly why the group was formed and what its goals are. If stating the problem is up to the group, then the group should move immediately to get that problem down on paper; until everyone agrees on what they have to do, they will never agree on how to do it.

Groups can pinpoint the problem to be addressed by asking three types of questions: questions of fact, questions of value, and questions of policy.

Questions of Fact. These questions consider what *is*. Implied in such questions is the possibility of determining the facts by way of direct observed, spoken, or recorded evidence. For instance, "How much rain fell today?" is a question of fact because rainfall can be measured and recorded. "Is Smith guilty of robbing the warehouse?" is also a question of fact—Smith either did or did not commit the crime.

Questions of Value. These questions consider relative goodness and badness and are characterized by the inclusion of evaluative words such as *good, reliable, effective,* and *worthy*. The purpose of questions of value is to compare a subject with one or more members of the same class. "What was the best movie last year?" is a question of value. Although you can set up criteria for "best" and measure your choice against those criteria, there is no way of verifying your findings. The answer is still a matter of judgment, not a matter of fact. Thus "Is socialism superior to capitalism?" and "Is a small-college education better than a large-college education?" are also questions of value.

Questions of Policy. These questions judge whether a future action should be taken. The question is phrased so that the answer will represent a solution or will suggest a tentative solution to a problem or a felt need. "What should we do to lower the crime rate?" seeks a solution that would best solve the problem of the increase in crime. "Should the university give equal amounts of money to men's and women's athletics?" provides a tentative solution to the problem of how we can achieve equity in the financial support of athletics. The inclusion of the word *should* in all questions of policy makes them both the easiest to recognize and the easiest to phrase of all discussion questions.

Analyzing the Problem

Once the group agrees about the exact nature of the problem, it should move on to the next step, analyzing the problem. *Analysis* means determining the nature of the problem: its size, its causes, the forces that create or sustain it, and the criteria for evaluating solutions.[1] Sometimes, analysis takes only a few minutes; at other times it requires more time. Both in preparation for problem solving and in the discussion itself, however, analysis is too often ignored because most groups want to move directly to possible solutions. For instance, if your discussion topic is to determine what should be done to solve the problem of thefts of library books, you may be inclined to start by listing possible solutions. A solution or a plan,

The first step in solving a problem is to define it. The next step involves exploring the problem, then considering solutions and choosing the best one. Whether your role is to provide or request information, group work will call on all your interpersonal communication skills.

however, can work only if it solves the problem at hand. Before you can shape a plan, you must determine what obstacles the solution must overcome and what obstacles the solution must eliminate, as well as whom your plan has to satisfy.

Suggesting Possible Solutions

Most problems have many possible solutions. Although you need not identify every one of the possibilities, you should not be content with your work until you have considered a wide variety of solutions. If you are considering a problem that requires only a "yes" or "no" solution, your procedure may be simple. For example, the question "Should financial support for women's sports be increased?" has only two possible answers.

How do you come up with solutions? One way is to *brainstorm* for ideas. *Brainstorming* is a free-association procedure involving the stating of ideas as they come to you until you have compiled a long list. In a good ten- to fifteen-minute brainstorming session you may think of several solutions by yourself. Depending on the nature of the topic, a group may come up with a list of ten, twenty, or more possibilities in a relatively short time. Other possible solutions will come from your reading, your interviews with authorities, and your observation.

Selecting the Best Solution

If the group has analyzed the problem carefully and suggested enough possible solutions, then the final step involves simply measuring each proposed solution against the preestablished criteria. For instance, if you have determined that hiring more patrols, putting in closed-circuit television, and locking outside doors after 9:00 P.M. are three possible solutions to the problem of reducing crime in dorms, then you begin to measure each option against the criteria. The solution that meets the most criteria, or the one that meets several criteria most effectively, would then be selected.

Outlining the Problem-Solving Steps

Now let's list all the problem-solving steps in a sample (and somewhat abbreviated) outline that would help the group proceed logically. The group is being convened to discuss "Meeting the needs of women on campus."

1. State the problem—suggested wordings:
What should be done to improve the status of women on campus?
What should be done to increase opportunities for women on campus?
What should be done to equalize social, athletic, and political opportunities for women on campus? (The remainder of this outline assumes that the group has agreed upon this wording. In an actual situation you should probably not attempt to go very far in your analysis until the group has made such a decision.)

   2. Analyze the problem of meeting the needs of women:
   I. What is the size and scope of the problem?
      A. What is the ratio of females to males on campus?
      B. What opportunities are currently available to women?
         1. What is the ratio of women to men in social organizations?
         2. What is the ratio of women to men in political organizations?
         3. What is the ratio of women to men in athletics?
   II. What are the causes of the problem?
      A. Do societal norms inhibit women's participation?
      B. Do individual groups discriminate against women?
   III. What criteria should be used to test solutions?
      A. Will women favor the solution?
      B. Will it cope with discrimination if discrimination does exist?
      C. Will it be enforceable?
      D. Will it comply with Title IX?

   3. State possible solutions:
(This list can only be started at this point; other possible solutions will be revealed as the discussion progresses.)
A women's center should be initiated?
A special-interest seat on all major committees should be given to women?
Women's and men's athletic teams should be combined?
(Others to be added.)

   4. Determine best solution:
(To be completed during discussion.)

PRACTICE in Problem-Solving Group Work

By Yourself

1. Label the following questions F (fact), V (value), or P (policy).

_____ **a.** Is Ohio State the largest single-campus university in the United States?

_____ **b.** Should the United States support any government that seeks to remain free of communism?

_____ **c.** Which microcomputer costs the least to own and operate?

_____ **d.** Is Sparky Anderson the best manager in the American League?

_____ **e.** Should tuition be increased at Miller University next year?

ANSWERS: a. F b. P c. F d. V e. P

2. Take one of the questions just listed. Outline the problem-solving method you would use to deal with this question.

3. Think of the last group with which you worked. Did the group follow the problem-solving method? If not, what steps were left out? What effect did leaving out steps have on the discussion? On the quality of the solution?

Roles of Group Members

In productive groups individual members will serve in both task and maintenance roles. *Task roles* involve the work a group must do to accomplish its goal; *maintenance roles* involve the group behaviors that keep the group working together smoothly. As we proceed, you will notice that many of the roles correlate to interpersonal skills that we discussed earlier in this book. Of course, not all roles played in a group are positive. By accident, or occasionally by design, people say and do things that hurt the group's ability to work together.

Task Roles

In most discussion groups several major tasks roles can be identified: information or opinion giver, information seeker, expediter, and analyzer. Let's examine the function of each.

Information or Opinion Giver. The information or opinion giver provides content for the discussion. Giving information actually constitutes about 50 percent of what is done in a group, because without information (and well-considered opinions) the group will not have the necessary material from which to draw its conclusions. Chances are everyone in the group will fill this role during the discussion.

Playing the information-giving role well requires solid preparation and objective presentation. The more material you have studied, the more valuable your contributions will be. As information giver you will want to draw material from several different sources, and you will usually bring your sources with you to the discussion.

During the discussion you must present material objectively. Let's focus on two recommendations for ensuring objectivity of approach. First, report data; don't associate yourself with it. An excellent way of presenting data with a degree of disassociation is illustrated by the following statement: "According to *U.S. News & World Report*, crime has risen 33 percent in the past five years. That seems like a startling statistic. I wonder whether anyone else found either any substantiating or contradictory data?" Presenting data in this way tells the group that you want discussion of the data and that, whether it is substantiated or disproven, you have no personal relationship with it. Contrast that disassociative approach with the following statement: "I think crime is going up at a fantastic rate. Why, I found that crime has gone up 33 percent in the past five years, and we just can't put up with that kind of thing." This speaker is using data to take a position. Because anyone who questions the data or the conclusions will have to contend with the speaker, there's a good chance that any ensuing discussion will not be very objective.

A second recommendation for ensuring objectivity is to solicit all viewpoints on every major issue. Suppose that after doing your research on the question "Should financial support of women's sports be increased?" you decide that it should be. Although there is nothing wrong with formulating tentative opinions based on your research, in discussion you should present material objectively, whether it supports or opposes your tentative claims. If during the discussion you spoke only to support your position and took issue with every bit of contrary material, you would not be responding objectively. If the group's final conclusion corresponded to your tentative conclusion, fine. At least group members would have had the opportunity to present opposing material. If the group came to a different conclusion, you would not be put in a defensive position. Furthermore, by remaining objective, you may find that during the discussion your views will change many times. If the best answer to the topic question could be found without discussion, the discussion would not be necessary.

Information givers make such statements as: "Well, when Jones Corporation considered this problem, they found . . ." "That's a good point you made—just the other day I ran across these figures that substantiate your point." "According to Professor Smith, it doesn't necessarily work that way. He says . . ."

Information Seeker. The information seeker asks for more information when it is needed. Frequently, groups try to draw conclusions before they have enough information. The information seeker asks the kinds of questions that stimulate members to share more of their information on the topic. Again, in most groups more than one person assumes the role of information seeker during the discussion, and one or more members often are especially perceptive in noticing when more information is needed.

Information seekers ask such questions as: "What did we say the base numbers were?" "Have we decided how many people this really affects?" "Well, what functions does this person serve?" "Have we got anything to give us some background on this subject?"

Expediter. The expediter keeps the group on track. Whether the group is meeting once or is an ongoing group, almost invariably some remarks will tend to sidetrack the group from the central point or issue. Sometimes, apparent digressions are necessary to establish the background of the problem, enlarge its scope, or even give people an opportunity to air their feelings. Yet in a group these momentary digressions may lead the group off on tangents that have little to do with the assignment. Because tangents are sometimes more fun than the task itself, a tangent often is not realized for what it is and the group discusses it as if it were important to the group decision. Expediters are the people who help the group stick to its agenda. When the group has strayed, expediters lead it back on track with such statements as: "Say, I'm enjoying this, but I can't quite see what it has to do with whether permissiveness is really a cause." "Let's see, aren't we still trying to find out whether these are the only criteria that we should be considering?" "I've got the feeling that this is important to the point we're on now, but I can't quite get hold of the relationship—am I off base?" "Say, time is getting away from us and we've only considered two possible solutions. Aren't there some more?"

Analyzer. The analyzer probes group content and reasoning. Analyzers know the problem-solving method inside out. The analyzer knows when the group has skipped a point, has passed over a point too lightly, or has not considered relevant material. More than just *expediting*, analyzers help the group penetrate to the core of the problem they are working on.

First, the analyzer probes the contributions of group members. As information is presented, all members of the group are obliged to determine whether that information is accurate, typical, consistent, and otherwise valid. Suppose that a person reports that according to *U.S. News & World Report* crime has risen 33 percent in the past five years. As an analyzer you should ask such questions as "What was the specific source of the data? On what was the information based? What years are being referred to? Is this consistent with other material? Is any countermaterial available?" The purpose of such questions is to test the data. If data are partly true, questionable, or relevant only to certain aspects of the issue, a different conclusion or set of conclusions would be appropriate.

Second, analyzers examine the reasoning of various participants. The analyzer makes such statements as: "Tom, you're generalizing from only one instance. Can you give us some others?" "Wait a minute, after symptoms, we have to take a look at causes." "I think we're passing over Jones too lightly. There are still criteria we haven't used to measure him."

Maintenance Roles

In most discussion groups at least three major maintenance roles help preserve good working relationships: supporter, harmonizer, and gatekeeper. Let's consider the functions of each.

Supporter. The supporter responds nonverbally or verbally whenever a good point is made. People participating in groups are likely to feel better about their participation when their thoughts and feelings are recognized. Although we expect that nearly everyone will be supportive, people sometimes get so wrapped up in their own ideas that they may neglect to acknowledge the positive comments that are made.

The supporter responds verbally, or at least nonverbally, whenever a good point is made. Supporters give such nonverbal cues as a smile, a nod, or a vigorous head shake and make such statements as: "Good point, Mel." "I really like that idea, Susan." "It's obvious you've really done your homework, Peg." "That's one of the best ideas we've had today, Al."

Harmonizer. The harmonizer brings the group together. It is a rare group that can expect to accomplish its task without some minor if not major conflict. Even when people get along well, they are likely to become angry over some inconsequential point in a heated discussion. Most groups experience some classic interpersonal conflicts caused by different personality types. Harmonizers are responsible for reducing tensions and for straightening out misunderstanding, disagreements, and conflicts. They soothe ruffled feathers, encourage objectivity, and mediate between hostile, aggressively competing sides. A group cannot avoid some conflict, but if there is no one present to harmonize, participation can become an uncomfortable experience. Harmonizers make such statements as: "Bill, I don't think you're giving Mary a chance to make her point." "Tom, Jack, hold it a second. I know you're on opposite sides of this, but let's see where you might have some agreement." "Lynne, I get the feeling that something Todd said really bugged you, is that right?" "Hold it, everybody, we're really coming up with some good stuff; let's not lose our momentum by getting into a name-calling thing."

Gatekeeper. The gatekeeper helps to keep communication channels open. If a group has seven people in it, the assumption is that all seven have something to contribute. If all seven are to feel comfortable in contributing, however, those who tend to dominate need to be held in check and those who tend to be reticent need to be encouraged to speak. The gatekeeper is the person who sees that Mary is on the edge of her chair, ready to talk, but just cannot seem to get a word in; or that Don is rambling a bit and needs to be directed; or that Tom's need to talk so frequently is making Cesar withdraw from the conversation; or that Betty has just lost the thread of discussion. As we said earlier, a characteristic of good group work is interaction. Gatekeepers assume the responsibility for helping interaction by making such statements as: "Joan, I see you've got something to say here." "You've made a really good point, Todd; I wonder whether we could get some reaction on it." "Bill and Marge, it sounds like you're getting into a dialogue here; let's see what other ideas we have."

Negative Roles

In most discussion groups four common negative roles should be avoided: aggressor, joker, withdrawer, and monopolizer. All of these roles can have an adverse affect on the group problem-solving process. Let's consider each role.

Aggressors. Aggressors are the people who seek to enhance their own status by criticizing almost everything or blaming others when things get rough. Aggressors' main purpose seems to be to deflate the egos or statuses of others. One way of dealing with aggressors is to confront them by asking them whether they are aware of what they are doing and of the effect it is having on the group.

Jokers. Jokers' behavior is characterized by clowning, mimicking, or generally disrupting by making a joke of everything. Jokers, too, are usually trying to call attention to themselves—they must be the center of attention. However, a little bit of joking goes a long way. If the group cannot get the jokers to consider the problem seriously, their antics will be a constant irritant to other members. One way to deal with jokers is to encourage them when tensions need to be reduced but to ignore them when there is serious work to be done.

Withdrawers. Withdrawers refuse to be a part of the group. Simply stated, withdrawers are mental dropouts. Sometimes, they are withdrawing from something that was said; sometimes, they are just showing their indifference. There are several ways of dealing with withdrawers. One is to try to draw them out with questions; another is to find out what they are especially good at and rely on them when their skill is required. Sometimes, compliments will draw them out of their shell.

Monopolizers. Monopolizers need to talk all the time. Usually, they are trying to impress the group with how well read and knowledgeable they are and with how valuable they are to the group. They should, of course, be encouraged when their comments are helpful. When they are talking too much or when their comments are not helpful, however, the leader needs to interrupt them or draw others into the discussion.

PRACTICE in Group Communication

In Groups

1. Each group has ten to fifteen minutes to arrive at a solution to the following dilemma: Five people are boating: the father, a fifty-five-year-old heart specialist reputed to be the best in the state; his thirty-six-year-old wife, a dermatologist; their eight-year-old child; their neighbor, a forty-three-year-old industrial salesman for a major corporation; and his wife, a thirty-five-year-old former model who appears in television commercials. If the boat started to sink and only one of the five could be saved, who should it be? One observer will be appointed for each group. The observer should use the decision analysis in Figure D.1.

2. After the discussions the group should determine (1) what roles were operating in the groups during the discussions, (2) who was performing those roles, and (3) what factors helped or hindered the problem-solving process.

Decision Analysis

1. Did the group arrive at a decision?

2. What action is taken as a result of the discussion?

3. Was the group consensus a good one?

4. Comments?

Figure D.1

Summary

As an effective group participant, you have many responsibilities. The first is to be prepared. Whether you need only to think about the problem or whether you need to do some research, you should have some solid material to take into the discussion with you.

In preparing for the actual problem-solving group work, you should state the problem by determining the kind of questions you are discussing, analyze the size and scope of the problem by determining the criteria you will need to apply to tentative solutions to the problem, and outline some possible solutions to the problem. In the discussion itself you will weigh and evaluate to determine the best solution.

The measure of your value in the group discussion will be in your participation. You may perform one or more of the task roles of giving and seeking information, expediting, and analyzing. You may perform one or more of the maintenance roles of supporting, harmonizing, or gatekeeping. You will want to avoid the negative roles of aggressor, joker, withdrawer, or monopolizer.

Notes

1. For further information on analysis see Rudolph Verderber, *Communicate!* 5th ed. (Belmont, Calif.: Wadsworth, 1987), pp. 219–222.

Module E

Leadership

in Group Communication

Objectives

After you have read this module, you should be able
to define and/or explain:

Characteristics of leadership

Differences between task and
maintenance leadership

Preparation for leadership

Seven leadership
responsibilities

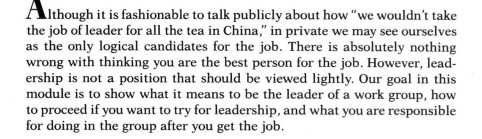

$\mathbf{A}$lthough it is fashionable to talk publicly about how "we wouldn't take the job of leader for all the tea in China," in private we may see ourselves as the only logical candidates for the job. There is absolutely nothing wrong with thinking you are the best person for the job. However, leadership is not a position that should be viewed lightly. Our goal in this module is to show what it means to be the leader of a work group, how to proceed if you want to try for leadership, and what you are responsible for doing in the group after you get the job.

Leadership Defined

The definition of leadership differs from source to source, yet most definitions include some mention of influence and accomplishment. *Leadership* means exerting influence that results in some goal being attained. Let's explore these two ideas.

1. *Leadership means exerting influence. Influence* is the ability to bring about changes in the attitudes and actions of others. Influence can be indirect (and unconscious) or direct (and purposeful). As we discussed in Chapter 9, people often exert influence without being aware of it. If you have a new hairstyle, or are wearing a new outfit, or have purchased a flashy new car, you may well influence someone to try your hairstyle or to buy a similar outfit or car. In this section, however, we will focus on the potential for direct, purposeful influence by examining what you can do consciously to help guide your group through the decision-making process.

2. *Leadership results in attaining a goal.* In the context of task or problem-solving discussions this means accomplishing the task or arriving at the solution that tests out to be the best solution available at that time.

Who will make the best leader may depend on an individual's leadership traits and leadership style.

Leadership Traits

There have been numerous research efforts devoted to identifying those particular leadership traits that would enable us to predict leadership ability and account for leadership success. Although researchers have, at times, downplayed the presence of verifiable leadership traits, during the last decade substantial research on leadership traits has been done.[1] Paul J. Patinka[2] is but one researcher who has substantiated Marvin Shaw's claim that enough consistency among individual traits and leadership measures exists to make some generalizations.[3]

What conclusions have been drawn? In group studies leaders have displayed traits related to ability, sociability, motivation, and communication skills to a greater degree than do nonleaders. With regard to ability leaders exceed average group members in intelligence, scholarship, insight, and verbal facility. In terms of sociability leaders exceed group members in dependability, activity, cooperativeness, and popularity. In the area of motivation leaders exceed group members in initiative, persistence, and enthusiasm. And of particular interest here, leaders exceed average group members in the various communication skills we focus on in this text. The results of these studies do not mean that people who have superior intelligence, who are most liked, who show the greatest enthusiasm, or who communicate best will necessarily be the leaders. They do suggest, however, that people are unlikely to be leaders if they do not exhibit at least some of these traits to a greater degree than do those they are attempting to lead. If you see these traits in yourself, then you are a potential leader.

Leadership Styles

The collection of a person's behaviors is called *style*. A casual examination of groups you are familiar with should reveal a variety of leadership styles. Some leaders give orders directly; others look to the group to decide what to do. Some leaders appear to play no part in what happens in the group; others seem to be in control of every move. Some leaders constantly seek the opinions of group members; others do not seem to care what individuals think. Each leader will tend to direct a group with a style that reflects his or her own personality and needs. Although people have a right to be themselves, an analysis of group dynamics shows that how well groups function and how they feel about the work they have done depends upon the style of leadership.

What are the major leadership styles? Most recent studies classify leadership styles as either task-oriented (sometimes called authoritarian) or person-oriented (sometimes called democratic).

Task Leadership and Maintenance Leadership. The task leader exercises more direct control over the group. Task leaders will determine the phrasing of the question, analyze the procedure, and state how the group will arrive at the decision. Task leaders are likely to outline specific tasks for each group member and suggest the roles they desire members to play.

The maintenance leader may *suggest* phrasings of the question, *suggest* procedure, and *suggest* tasks and/or roles for individuals. Yet in every facet of the discussion maintenance leaders encourage group participation to determine what actually will be done. Everyone feels free to offer ideas to modify the leader's suggestions, because maintenance leaders will listen, encourage, facilitate, clarify, and support. In the final analysis it is the *group* that decides.

Which leadership style is best? If we accept the definition of leadership as exerting influence to reach a goal, we can see that an effective style is one in which the leader takes some active role in the discussion in order to influence its outcome. If that's the case, then isn't the task style the ultimate form of leadership? Not necessarily. Although in some situations task leadership may in fact be most effective, in other situations maintenance leadership works better.

Contingency Model of Leadership. A third model of leadership styles is Fred Fiedler's *contingency model* of leadership effectiveness.[4] Fiedler's work benefits the study of leadership behavior in at least two important ways. First, it clarifies the variables that interact in a given leadership situation, and second, it provides guidance in determining whether a task (or structuring) or a maintenance style is most likely to be effective. Fiedler sees effective leadership as fulfilling either the task or the maintenance function within a group.

To understand Fiedler's viewpoint, let's first consider the variables that interact in a group: leader-member relations, task structure, and position power. Through these three dimensions we can determine the favorableness of the leadership situation. *Leader-member relations* are the interpersonal relations the leader has with members of the group. Specifically, leader-member relations center on such issues as trust, loyalty, and friendship. *Task structure* can be viewed in terms of four dimensions: (1) goal clarity (how sharply the goal is defined), (2) goal-path multiplicity (the extent to which there are other ways to accomplish the task), (3) decision verifiability (the extent to which accomplishments can be evaluated by objective, logical, or feedback means), and (4) decision specificity (whether the task has only one correct outcome or several equally good outcomes). Thus, the clearer the goal, the fewer ways in which there are to accomplish the task. The more objectively the task accomplishment can be verified and the greater the extent to which one outcome can be judged to be correct, the more favorable the task structure is to the leader. *Position power* may be analyzed along the lines of social power, which we considered in our discussion of influence in Chapter 9. The leader can be judged to be in a low-power or a high-power position. The higher the power position, the more favorable the situation is to the leader.

This leads us to the second benefit of Fiedler's work: guidance in determining when a given leadership style is most appropriate. Fiedler suggests that whether a task-oriented leader or a maintenance-oriented leader will be more effective is contingent on the interaction among leader-member relations, task structure, and position power. Fiedler's observations also imply, however, that a person's leadership style is predetermined and somewhat inflexible; thus, instead of a leader changing styles for different situations, Fiedler suggests changing leaders.

Now let's see how Fiedler puts these variables together. Figure E.1 summarizes his framework. In situations 1 through 3 conditions are such that a task-oriented style is likely to be quite effective. Notice that in situations 1 through 3 good leader-member relations exist. The task is structured in two of the three, and in the remaining unstructured task, the leader is in a high-power position. In situations 5 through 7 leader-member relations are relatively poor. In situation 4 leader-member relations are good, the task is unstructured and leader position power is weak. In the situations that are relatively unfavorable to the leader, a mainte-

Situation	Leader–member relations	Task structure	Position power	Appropriate leader style	Favorableness of situation to leader
1	Good	High	Strong	Task	Favorable
2	Good	High	Weak	Task	Favorable
3	Good	Low	Strong	Task	Favorable
4	Good	Low	Weak	Maintenance	Less favorable
5	Fair to poor	High	Strong	Maintenance	Less favorable
6	Fair to poor	High	Weak	Maintenance	Less favorable
7	Fair to poor	Low	Strong	Maintenance	Less favorable
8	Fair to poor	Low	Weak	Task	Unfavorable

Adapted from Fred E. Fiedler, *A Theory of Leadership Effectiveness* (New York: McGraw-Hill, 1967), p. 34. By permission.

Figure E.1 Summary of Fiedler's contingency model

nance-style leader will have greater opportunity for success. Yet in situation 8, the situation that is least favorable to the leader, a task leader is likely to have the greatest success even though everything points toward failure. It seems that in this case everything is so bad that only a task-style leader could possibly achieve success.

Keep in mind that the model does not take into account the potential for a leader to be both task-oriented and maintenance-oriented. Regardless of your basic orientation, you can learn to adapt to either approach. You can then use the Fiedler model to help determine when you should approach a situation from a strong task orientation and when you should adopt a strong maintenance orientation.

The question ultimately is not which style is best, but rather, which style will work best under the circumstances. As Fiedler and others' research suggest, one style will not work under all circumstances. Thus, you should examine your own style very closely. What is your natural inclination? How has it worked in the past? What can you do that will allow you to work in a situation that requires a different style?

PRACTICE in Analyzing Leadership Style

By Yourself

1. What traits do you have that would make you a good leader?

2. What is your leadership style? What are the strengths and weaknesses of that style?

Responsibilities of the Leader

To lead a group effectively, a leader must shoulder several responsibilities, including establishing a climate, planning the agenda, directing the flow of the discussion, and maintaining control of the group. Let's examine each responsibility.

All leaders have a unique style but share some fundamental traits, including an exceptional ability to communicate. Leaders often get the glory, but they also bear the most responsibility for seeing that a group meets its objective.

Establishing a Climate

As leader your first job is to set up a comfortable physical setting that will encourage interaction. You are in charge of such physical matters as heat, light, and seating, so make sure that the room is at a comfortable temperature, that there is enough lighting, and, most important, that the seating arrangements will stimulate spirited interaction.

Many times, seating is either too formal or too informal for discussion to flow easily. A too-formal arrangement is the board-of-directors style. Imagine the long, polished oak table with the chairperson at the head, leading lieutenants at right and left, and the rest of the people down the line. Because seating may be an indication of status, how the seating is arranged can help or hinder real interaction. In the board-of-directors style a boss-and-subordinates pattern emerges, and people are unlikely to speak until they are asked to do so. Moreover, no one has a really good view of all the people present. An excessively informal seating, however, may also inhibit interaction—especially if people sit together in small groups or behind one another.

The ideal seating arrangement is the circle. Everyone can see everyone else. At least physically, everyone has equal status. If the meeting place does not have a round table, you may be better off with either no table at all or an arrangement of tables that approximates the circle pattern.

Planning the Agenda

A second responsibility of the leader is to plan the agenda. You can do this alone or in consultation with the group. When possible, the agenda should be in the hands of the group several days before the meeting. How much preparation any individual member will make is based on many factors, but unless an agenda is established beforehand, group members will not have an opportunity for careful preparation. Too often, when no agenda is planned, the discussion progresses haphazardly, frustrating members and leading to unsatisfying results.

What goes into the agenda? Usually a sketch of some of the things that need to be accomplished. In a problem-solving discussion the agenda should include a suggested procedure for handling the problem. In essence, the agenda comprises an outline form of the steps of problem solving discussed earlier in this chapter. Suppose you are leading a group concerned with integrating the campus commuter into the social, political, and extracurricular aspects of student life. The following would be a satisfactory agenda:

1. How many students commute?

2. Why aren't commuters involved in social, political, and extracurricular activities?

3. What criteria should be used to test possible solutions to the problem?

4. What are some of the possible solutions to the problem?

5. What one solution or combination of solutions will work best to solve the problem?

Directing the Flow of Discussion

The leader is responsible for directing the discussion. It is in this area that leadership skill is most tested. Let's examine carefully four of the most important elements of this responsibility.

Give Everyone an Equal Opportunity to Speak. Decisions are valid only when they represent the thinking of the entire group. In discussions, however, some people are more likely or more willing to express themselves than are others. At the beginning of a discussion you must assume that every member of the group has something to contribute. To ensure opportunity for equal participation, you must restrain somewhat those who tend to dominate and bring into the discussion those who are content to observe.

Accomplishing this ideal balance represents a real test of leadership. If ordinarily reluctant talkers are embarrassed by a member of the group, they may become even less willing to participate. Likewise, if talkative yet valuable members of the group are constantly restrained, they may lose enthusiasm, thereby detracting from the effectiveness of the discussion.

Often, apparently reluctant speakers want to talk but cannot get the floor. As leader you may solve this problem by clearing the road for them. For instance, Mary may give visual and verbal clues of her desire to speak: She may move to the edge of her seat, look as if she wants to talk, or even start to say something. Because reluctant speakers may often relinquish the opportunity if other, more aggressive persons compete to be heard, you can help considerably with a comment such as "Just a second, Jim, I think Mary has something she wants to say here." Of course, if Mary is sitting back in her chair with a somewhat vacant look, such a statement would be inappropriate.

A second method of drawing out reluctant speakers is to phrase a question requiring an opinion that is sure to elicit some answer and then perhaps some discussion. For instance, a question such as "Mary, what do you think of the validity of this approach to combating crime?" is much better than "Mary, do you have anything to say here?" Not only is it specific, but it also requires more than a "yes" or "no" answer. Furthermore, such an opinion question will not embarrass Mary if she has no factual material to contribute. Such tactful handling of shy or reluctant persons can pay big dividends. You may elicit some information that could not have been brought out in any other way. Moreover, when Mary contributes a few times, it builds up her confidence, which in turn makes it easier for her to respond later when she has more to say.

As leader you must also use tact with overzealous speakers. Remember that Jim, the talkative person, may be talkative because he has done his homework—he may have more information than any other member of the group. If you turn him off, the group may suffer immensely. After he has finished talking, try statements such as "Jim, that's a very valuable bit of material; let's see whether we can get some reactions from other members of the group on this issue." Notice that a statement of this kind does not stop Jim; it merely suggests that he should hold off for a while.

There are three common patterns of group communication. In Figure E.2 the various lines represent the flow of discussion among the eight participants. Panel a depicts a leader-dominated group, in which the lack of interaction often leads to a rigid, formal, and usually poor discussion. Panel b depicts a more spontaneous group; however, because three people dominate and a few are not heard, conclusions will not fully reflect group thinking. Panel c depicts something close to the ideal pattern. It illustrates a great deal of spontaneity, a total group representation, and—at least theoretically—the greatest possibility for reliable conclusions.

Ask Appropriate Questions. Perhaps one of the most effective tools of leadership is the ability to question appropriately. This skill requires knowing both when to ask questions and what kinds of questions to ask.

By and large, the leader should refrain from questions that can be answered with a simple "yes" or "no." To ask group members whether they are satisfied with a point that was just made will not lead very far, because after they answer affirmatively or negatively, you must either ask another question to draw them out or change the subject. The two most effective types of questions are those that call for supporting information and those that are completely open-ended, giving members complete freedom of response. For instance, rather than asking John whether he has

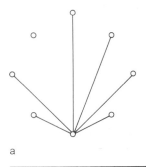

a

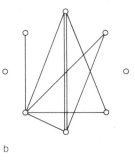

b

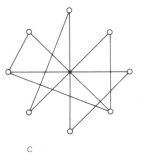

c

Figure E.2 Patterns of group communication

had any professors who were particularly good lecturers, you could ask, "John, what are some of the characteristics that made your favorite lecturers particularly effective?"

Knowing when to ask questions is particularly important. Although we could list fifteen to twenty such circumstances, let's focus on four purposes of questioning.

1. *To focus discussion.* Individual statements usually have a point; the statements themselves relate to a larger point being made; and the general discussion relates to an issue or to an agenda item. You can use questions to determine speakers' points or to determine the relationship of the points to the issue or agenda item. For example: "Are you saying that the instances of marijuana leading to hard-drug use don't indicate a direct causal relationship?" Or, to what has just been said, "How does that information relate to the point that Mary just made?" Or, to ask about an issue or an agenda item, "In what way does this information relate to whether or not marijuana is a health hazard?"

2. *To probe for information.* Many statements need to be developed, supported, or in some way dealt with. Yet members of a group often apparently ignore or accept a point without probing it. When the point seems important, the leader should do something with it. For instance, on a question of source you can say, "Where did you get that information, Jack?" Or, to develop a point, "That seems pretty important; what do we have that corroborates the point?" Or, to test the strength of a point, "Does that statement represent the thinking of the group?" Or, to generate discussion, "That point sounds rather controversial—should we accept the point as stated?"

3. *To initiate discussion.* During a discussion there are times when lines of development are apparently ignored, when the group seems ready to agree before sufficient testing has taken place. At these times it is up to the leader to suggest a starting point for further discussion. For instance: "O.K., we seem to have a pretty good grasp of the nature of the problem, but we haven't looked at any causes yet. What are some of the causes?"

4. *To deal with interpersonal problems that develop.* Sometimes, the leader can help members vent very personal feelings. For instance: "Ted, I've heard you make some strong statements on this point. Would you care to share them with us?" At times, a group may attack a person instead of the information that is being presented. Then you can say, "I know Charley presented the point, but let's look at the merits of the information presented. Do we have any information that goes counter to this point?"

Note, however, that questions by themselves are not going to make a discussion. In fact, some questions can hurt the discussion that is taking place. Thus, the effective leader uses questions sparingly but decisively.

Summarize Frequently. Often, group members talk for a considerable period, then take a vote on how they feel about the subject. A good problem-solving discussion group should proceed in an orderly manner toward intermediate conclusions represented by summary statements seeking group consensus. For instance, on the question "What should be done to lower the crime rate on campus?" the group would have to reach consensus on each of the following questions:

1. What is the problem?

2. What are the symptoms of the problem? (Draw intermediate conclusions; ask whether the group agrees.)

3. What are the causes? (Draw intermediate conclusions on each cause separately or after all causes have been considered; ask whether group agrees.)

4. What criteria should be used to test the solutions?

5. What is one criterion? (Draw conclusions about each criterion.)

6. What are some of the possible conclusions? (Determine whether all possible solutions have been brought up.)

7. What is the best solution?

8. How does each of the solutions meet the criteria? (Discuss each solution and draw conclusions about each; ask whether group agrees.)

9. Which solution best meets the criteria? (The conclusion to this final question concludes the discussion; ask whether all agree.)

During the discussion the group might draw six, eight, ten, or even fifteen conclusions before it is able to arrive at the answer to the topic question. The point is that the group should not arrive at the final conclusion until each of the subordinate questions is answered to the satisfaction of the entire group.

As leader you must point out these conclusions by summarizing what has been said and seeking consensus on a conclusion. Everyone in the group should realize when the group has really arrived at some decision. Left to its own devices, a group will tend to discuss a point for a while, then move on to another before a conclusion is drawn. You must sense when enough has been said to reach a consensus. Then phrase the conclusion, subject it to testing, and move on to another area. You should become familiar with phrases that can be used during the discussion.

"I think most of us are stating the same points. Are we really in agreement that . . ." (State the conclusion.)

"We've been discussing this for a while and I think I sense an agreement. Let me state it, and then we'll see whether it does summarize group feeling." (State the conclusion.)

"Now we're getting into another area. Let's make sure that we are really agreed on the point we've just discussed." (State the conclusion.)

"Are we ready to summarize our feelings on this point?" (State the conclusion.)

Maintain Necessary Control. A leader must maintain control of the discussion. Remember, absence of leadership leads to chaos. Group members need to feel that someone is in charge. If the group has a set of formal rules, be sure that the rules are followed (at times, bending of the rules is necessary, but totally breaking them does not help the group). You are in charge. You are responsible. You have authority. You will need to exercise it on occasion for the benefit of the group. If Jim is about to talk for what seems like the fortieth time, it is up to you to harness him. If Jack and Monica are constantly sparring with each other, it is up to you to reestablish harmony. If something internal or external threatens the work of the group, it is up to you to deal with it. Also, when the group has solved its problem, end the discussion smoothly. Just because you are scheduled to meet for an hour does not mean that you cannot stop in forty-five minutes if the job is completed.

PRACTICE in Analyzing Leadership

In Groups

Each group should be given or should select a task that requires some research. In class each group should then discuss their topic for approximately thirty to forty minutes. While group A holds its discussion, members of group B should observe and, after the discussion, analyze the proceedings. Leadership can be analyzed by using Figure E.3. In the next class period group B should discuss and group A should observe and critique. Some sample questions for discussion are: "What should

Leadership Analysis					
For each of the following questions, rate the leadership on a 1 to 5 basis: 1, high; 2, good; 3 average; 4, fair; 5, poor.					
Leadership Traits:	1	2	3	4	5
Has sufficient understanding?					
Stimulates group?					
Has the respect of the group?					
Leadership Methods:	1	2	3	4	5
Establishes a good working climate?					
Has an agenda?					
Promotes systematic problem solving?					
Directs the flow of discussion?					
Encourages balanced participation?					
Asks good questions?					
Clarifies and crystallizes ideas?					
Summarizes frequently?					
Maintains necessary control?					
Brings the discussion to a satisfactory close?					

Analysis: Write a short profile of this person's leadership based on the above checklist. Consider the person's relative effectiveness in helping the group achieve its goal.

Figure E.3

be done to improve parking (advising, registration) on campus?" "What should be done to increase the participation of minorities in college or university teaching (governance, administration)?"

Summary

Leadership entails exerting influence to accomplish a goal. Although leaders may show greater degrees of ability, sociability, motivation, and communication than others in the group, the presence of such traits does not guarantee effective leadership.

How well you lead may depend on your style and how you put it into operation. Some leaders adopt the task style, focusing on what needs to be done and how to do it; others adopt the maintenance style, focusing on interpersonal relationships of group members. As Fiedler's work has shown, how a leader performs is contingent on the interaction of task structure, leader-member relations, and position power. Through Fiedler's work we can better understand the variables involved in the decision whether to adopt a task or a maintenance approach to leadership.

Once you hold a position of leadership, you must establish a good working climate, plan an agenda, be able to direct the flow of discussion, summarize when necessary, and maintain the necessary control to keep the discussion from getting out of hand.

Notes

1. John F. Cragan and David W. Wright, "Small Group Research of the 1970s: A Synthesis and Critique," *Central States Speech Journal* 31 (Fall 1980): 202.

2. Paul J. Patinka, "One More Time: Are Leaders Born or Made?" in James G. Hunt and Lars L. Larson, eds., *Crosscurrents in Leadership* (Carbondale, Ill.: Southern Illinois University Press, 1979), pp. 36–37.

3. Marvin E. Shaw, *Group Dynamics: The Psychology of Small Group Behavior*, 3rd ed. (New York: McGraw-Hill, 1981), p. 325.

4. Fred E. Fiedler, *A Theory of Leadership Effectiveness* (New York: McGraw-Hill, 1967).

Module F

Interviewing

for Information

Objectives

After you have read this module, you should be able
to define and/or explain:

The methods of interviewing

Open and closed, primary and
secondary, and neutral and
leading questions

Procedures for conducting an
informative interview

Interviewing is a form of interaction based primarily on the asking and answering of questions. Unlike most of your interpersonal communication, interviewing can be planned ahead.

An interview may be for appraisal (making value judgments that may lead to hiring, promotion, reward, or firing), for counseling (helping people to examine and perhaps solve their problems), for persuasion (influencing people to buy a product), or for gaining information and job interviewing. In this module we consider the phrasing of questions and informative interviews; in the next module we consider procedures for job interviews.

Questions in Interviewing

An interview differs from other forms of interpersonal communication in its reliance on the asking and answering of questions. Although we deal here specifically with questions in the interview situation, a knowledge of good question construction can be applied to any interpersonal encounter. Questions may be phrased as open or closed, neutral or leading, primary or secondary.

Open Versus Closed Questions

Open questions are broad-based questions that ask the interviewee to provide whatever information he or she wishes to answer the questions. Open questions range from those with virtually no restrictions, such as "What can you tell me about yourself?" to those that give some direction, such as "What do you believe has prepared you for this job?" Why do interviewers ask open questions? Mostly to encourage the person to talk, allowing the interviewer an opportunity to listen and to observe. Through the open question the interviewer finds out about the person's perspectives, values, and goals. Keep in mind, however, that open questions take time to answer, which means interviewers can lose sight of their original purpose if they are not careful.

By contrast, *closed questions* are narrow-focus questions that require very brief answers. Closed questions range from those that can be answered "yes" or "no," such as "Have you had a course in marketing?" to those that require only a short answer, such as "How many restaurants have you worked in?" By asking closed questions, interviewers can control the interview; moreover, they can obtain large amounts of information in a short time. On the other hand, the closed question seldom enables the interviewer to know *why* a person gave a certain response, nor is the closed question likely to yield much voluntary information.

Which type of question should you use? The answer depends upon what kinds of material you are seeking and how much time you have for the interview. Both kinds of questions are used in most information and employment interviews.[1]

Neutral Versus Leading Questions

Neutral questions are those questions for which the person is free to give an answer without direction from the interviewer. An example of a neutral question would be "How do you like your new job?" There is nothing about the wording of the question that gives the respondent any indication of how the question should be answered. Except in very rare instances your questions in information-seeking and employment interviews should be neutral.

By contrast, *leading questions* are questions phrased in a way that suggests the interviewer has a preferred answer. For instance, "You don't like the new job, do you?" is a leading question. In the majority of the interviewing situations leading questions are inappropriate, because they try to force the person in one direction and tend to make the person defensive.

Primary Versus Secondary Questions

Primary questions are those questions you plan ahead of time. Primary questions serve as the main points for your interview outline. They may be open or closed, depending on the kind of information you want; in addition, they may be neutral or leading. As you plan your interview, be sure to include enough primary questions that you will obtain all the information you want.

Secondary questions follow up on the answers given to primary questions. Secondary questions may be planned ahead if you can anticipate possible interviewee answers. More often than not, however, secondary questions are composed as the interview goes along. To come up with good secondary questions, you must therefore pay close attention to what the interviewee is saying. Some secondary questions encourage the person to continue ("And then?" "Is there more?"); some probe into what the person has said ("What does 'frequently' mean?" "What were you thinking at the time?"); and some plumb the feelings of the person ("How did it feel to get the prize?" "Were you worried when you didn't find her?").

The major purpose of secondary questions is to motivate a person to enlarge upon an answer that appears inadequate. Such follow-up questions are often necessary because the interviewees may be purposely trying to be evasive, because their answers may be incomplete or vague, or because they may not really understand how much detail you are looking for.

Your effectiveness with follow-up questions may well depend upon your interpersonal skill in asking them. Because probing questions can alienate the interviewee (especially when the questions are perceived as threatening), such in-depth probes work best after you have gained the confidence of the interviewee and when the questions are asked within the atmosphere of a positive interpersonal climate.

PRACTICE in Identifying and Phrasing Questions

By Yourself

1. Indicate which of the following are O (open questions) and which are C (closed questions). If the question is open, write a closed question seeking similar information; if the question is closed, write an open question (make sure that all your write-in questions are neutral rather than leading).

_____ **a.** What makes you think that Parker will be appointed?

_____ **b.** How many steps are there in getting a book into print?

_____ **c.** Will you try out for cheerleaders?

_____ **d.** What is your opinion about guidelines for promotion?

_____ **e.** How do you think the school should make its budgetary decisions?

ANSWERS: a. O b. C c. C d. O e. O

2. Change the following leading questions to neutral questions:

   a. Doesn't it depress you to see so many patients who never get well?

   b. After what Angeline did, I bet you are really out to get her, aren't you?

   c. Wouldn't you be upset about going to Toronto if you were traded?

d. Aren't you really excited about your promotion?

e. After the way he acted, I'll bet you're really going to chew him out the next time you see him, aren't you?

3. You are interviewing your professor for an article for the school paper. To the question "What motivated you to choose college teaching as a career?" the professor answers, "It seemed to me like a really good job." Write three well-phrased follow-up questions you would be likely to ask.

a.

b.

c.

Interviewing for Information

Interviewing can be a valuable method for obtaining information on nearly any topic. Students interview outside sources to obtain information for papers; lawyers interview witnesses to establish facts on which to build their cases; doctors interview patients to obtain medical histories before making diagnoses; and reporters interview sources to get facts for their stories.[2] A good interviewing plan involves clearly defining the purpose of the interview, selecting the best person to interview, determining a procedure, and conducting the interview.

Defining the Purpose of the Interview

Too often, interviewers go into an informative interview without a clearly identified purpose. A clear purpose is a specific goal that can be summarized in one sentence. Without such a statement of purpose your list of questions more than likely will have no direction, and you will come out of the interview with information that does not fit together well.

Suppose you wish to obtain information about the food service in your dormitory. Possible specific purposes would be:

1. To find out about the person responsible for planning meals

2. To determine the major elements a dietitian must take into account in order to plan dormitory meals

3. To determine how a dietitian can run a cost-efficient program that provides good nutrition at a reasonable price

Selecting the Best Person to Interview

Somewhere on campus or in the larger community there are people who have or who can direct you to the information you want. How do you find out whom you should interview? If you are pursuing the second purpose, "To determine the major elements a dietitian must take into account in order to plan dormitory meals," one of the kitchen employees can tell you who is in charge of the dining hall. Or you could phone your student center and inquire about who is in charge of food service. When you have decided whom you should interview, make an appointment—you cannot walk into an office and expect the prospective interviewee to drop everything just to talk to you.

Before going into the interview, research the topic. If, for instance, you plan to interview the dietitian who creates menus and orders food, you should learn something about a dietitian's job and the problems of ordering and preparing institutional food. Interviewees are more likely to talk with you if you appear informed; moreover, familiarity with the subject will enable you to ask better questions. If for some reason you go into an interview uninformed, then at least approach the interviewee with enthusiasm for and apparent interest in the subject. You should also be forthright in your reasons for scheduling the interview. Whether your interview is for a class project, for a newspaper article on campus food, or for some other purpose, say so.

Planning the Interview

Good interviewing results from careful planning. A good plan begins with good questions. Write down all the questions you can think of, revise them until you have worded them clearly and concisely, and put them in the order that seems most appropriate. Your questions should be a mix of open and closed questions and should be neutral rather than leading. Moreover, you will need to be alert to the need for follow-up questions.

When you list your questions, leave enough space between them to fill in answers as completely as possible. It is just as important to leave enough space for answers to the secondary questions you decide to ask during the course of the interview. Some interviewers try to conduct the entire interview spontaneously. Even the most skilled interviewer, however, requires some preplanned questions to ensure coverage of important areas. The order and type of questions you need depend somewhat upon what you are hoping to achieve in the interview. How many primary questions should you have planned? The answer, of course, depends on how much time you have for the interview. If, for example, you have thirty minutes, about ten questions would be a reasonable number. Why ten? In a thirty-minute interview that would leave about three minutes per question. Remember, for some of your questions you will need one or more follow-up questions to get the information you want. If most of your questions are closed, then you can ask more than ten; if nearly all of your questions are open, maybe you'd want fewer. Keep in mind that you never know how a person will respond. Some people are so talkative and informative that in response to your first question they answer every question you were planning to ask in great detail; other people will answer each question with just a few words.

In the opening stage of the interview you should plan to ask some questions that can be answered easily and that will show your respect for the person you are interviewing. In an interview with the head dietitian, you might start with such questions as "How did you get interested in nutrition?" or "I imagine working out menus can be a very challenging job in these times of high food costs—is that so?" If the person nods or says "yes," you can then ask about some of the biggest challenges he or she faces. The goal is to get the interviewee to feel at ease and to talk freely. Because the most important consideration in this initial stage is to create a positive communication climate, keep the questions simple, nonthreatening, and encouraging.

The body of the interview includes the major questions you have prepared. A good plan is to group questions so that the easy-to-answer questions come first and the hard-hitting questions that require careful thinking come later. For instance, the question "What do you do to try to resolve student complaints?" should come near the end of the interview. You may not ask all the questions you planned to, but you don't want to end the interview until you have the important information you intended to get.

The following is an example of a question schedule you might construct if you were planning to interview the head dietitian:

Background:

What kind of background and training do you need for the job?

How did you get interested in nutrition?

Have you worked as a dietitian for long?

Have you held any other food-related positions?

Responsibilities:

What are the responsibilities of your job besides meal planning?

How far in advance are meals planned?

What factors are taken into account when you are planning the meals for a given period?

Do you have a free hand or are there constraints placed upon you?

Procedures:

Is there any set ratio for the number of times you put a particular item on the menu?

Do you take individual preferences into account?

How do you determine whether you will give choices for the entree?

What do you do to try to answer student complaints?

How do your prices compare with meals at a commercial cafeteria?

Conducting the Interview

By applying the interpersonal skills we have discussed in this book, you'll find that you can turn your careful planning into an excellent interview.

First, of course, you will want to be courteous during the interview. You should start by thanking the person for taking the time to talk to you. Remember, that person has nothing to gain from the interview. Try to develop a good rapport with the interviewee, and be patient at all times. And encourage the person to speak freely. Most of all, respect what the person says regardless of what you may think of the answers.

Second, listen very carefully. At key places in the interview you should paraphrase what the person has said. Remember that a *paraphrase* is a sentence that states in your own words what you perceive the idea and or feeling the person has communicated to be.

Third, keep the interview moving. You do not want to rush the person, but when the allotted time is ending, you should call attention to that fact and be prepared to conclude.

Fourth, make sure that your nonverbal reactions—facial expressions and your gestures—are in keeping with the tone you want to communicate. Maintain good eye contact with the person. Nod to show understanding. And smile occasionally to maintain the friendliness of the interview. How you look and act is likely to determine whether the person will warm up to you and give you a good interview.

Finally, if you are going to publish the substance of the interview, be prepared to offer to let the person see a copy of the article (or at least tell the person exactly when it will be published); this is a courtesy. Under some circumstances you may want to show the person a draft of your report of the interview before it goes into print. If a person does wish to see what you are planning to write before it is published, you must send a draft well before deadline to give him or her the opportunity to read it and to provide yourself with an opportunity to deal with any suggestions. Although this practice is not followed by many interviewers, it may help to build and maintain your own credibility.

PRACTICE in Interviewing

By Yourself

Conduct an interview outside of class and submit a written report or deliver a speech based upon the interview.

In Pairs

Conduct an in-class interview with a classmate on a subject of her or his expertise.

In Groups

Each group should determine a topic on which they might wish to conduct an information-seeking interview and identify whom they would interview. Then they should devise a list of questions for this interview according to the following guidelines. Ask open as well as closed questions. Check to make sure most questions are neutral rather than leading. Group the questions under major headings. Make sure some questions are appropriate for opening the interview. Write the finished product on paper for posting. Then the entire class should compare the various interview plans.

Summary

You are most likely to use interviewing as a means of obtaining information from an expert for a paper, an article, or a speech.

The key skill of interviewing is using questions effectively. Open questions allow for flexible responses; closed questions require very brief answers. Primary questions stimulate response; secondary questions follow up the primary questions. Neutral questions allow the respondent free choice; leading questions require the person to answer in a particular way.

When you are interviewing for information, you will want to define the purpose, select the best person to interview, determine a framework for the interview, and conduct the interview according to the framework.

Notes

1. For more information on asking questions see Charles J. Stewart and William B. Cash, *Interviewing: Principles and Practices*, 4th ed. (Dubuque, Iowa: Wm C. Brown, 1985).

2. An excellent source for information interviewing is Shirley Biagi, *Interviews That Work: A Practical Guide for Journalists* (Belmont, Calif.: Wadsworth, 1986).

Module G

Job Interviewing

Objectives

After you have read this module, you should be able
to define and/or explain:

Procedures used by job
interviewers

How to participate in a job
interview

Writing a résumé

Although there is some question about whether the interview constitutes a valid tool for personnel selection, applicants for nearly every position in nearly any field will go through an interview. At its worst an interview can be a waste of time for everyone; at its best an interview can reveal vital information about an applicant. A skillfully conducted interview can help interviewers determine the applicants' specific abilities, ambitions, energy, ability to communicate, knowledge and intelligence, and integrity. Moreover, it can help the interviewees show their strengths in these same areas.

Assuming the validity of the interview in the selection process, let's consider some of the procedures and methods that an interviewer uses in conducting an interview and that an interviewee uses in taking part in one.

Responsibilities of the Interviewer

As an interviewer you represent the link between a job applicant and the company. Much of the applicant's impression of the company will depend on her or his impression of you. You should be able to provide answers to questions applicants may have about your company. In addition to the obvious desire for salary information, applicants may also seek information about opportunities for advancement, influences of personal ideas on company policy, company attitudes toward personal life and life-style, and so forth. Moreover, you are primarily responsible for determining whether this person will be considered for the position available and whether this person will be kept in the running for possible future company employment.

Determining the Procedure

The most satisfactory employment interview is probably a highly to moderately structured one. In the unstructured interview the interviewer tends to talk more and to make decisions based on less valid data than in the structured interview.[1] Especially if you are screening a large number of applicants, you want to make sure that all have been asked the same questions and that the questions cover a variety of subjects.

Before the interview starts, you should be familiar with all available data about the applicant: application form, résumé, letters of recommendation, test scores if available. Such written data will help determine some of the questions you will want to ask.

Conducting the Interview

Like a good speech, an interview has an opening, a body, and a conclusion.

The Opening. Open the interview by greeting the applicant warmly by name, and introduce yourself so that he or she can use your name. A firm handshake can also be a good start. Be open with applicants. If you plan either to take notes or to record the interview, let the applicants know why you are doing so.

A major concern is whether you should begin with "warm-up" questions to help establish rapport or whether you should move right into the question schedule. A good interviewer senses the nature of the situation and tries to use a method that is most likely to encourage applicants to talk and provide adequate answers. Although warm-up questions may be helpful, most applicants are ready to get down to business immediately, in which case warm-up questions may be misinterpreted. Applicants may wonder about the motivation for such questions, and the questions may make them even more nervous. Unless you have good reason for proceeding differently, it seems advisable to move into the question schedule right away in as warm and friendly a manner as possible.

The Body. The body of the interview consists of the questions you are planning to ask. Let's begin with some guidelines for presenting yourself and your questions.

1. *Be careful of your own presentation.* Talk loudly enough to be heard. Try to be spontaneous. The interviewees are not going to respond well to obviously memorized questions fired in machine-gun fashion. Be sensitive to your own nonverbal communication. The interviewees are going to be looking for signs of disapproval—any inadvertent looks or unusual changes in quality or rhythm of your speech may give a false impression. Remember, too, that you can load a question by expressing it in a particular tone of voice.

2. *Do not waste time.* You have available a wide variety of information about the candidates from their résumés, application forms, and so on. Ask questions about things you already know only if you have some special reason for doing so. For instance, if an applicant indicates employment with a particular organization but does not give any detailed account of responsibilities, questions relating to that employment period would be appropriate.

3. *Avoid trick or loaded questions.* Applicants are always leery of questions that may be designed to make them look bad. Moreover, if candidates believe that you are trying to trick them, the suspicion may provoke a competitive rather than a positive atmosphere. Anything that serves to limit the applicant's responsiveness will harm the interview.

4. *Avoid questions that violate fair employment practice legislation.* In 1964 Congress created the Equal Employment Opportunity Commission (EEOC). In subsequent years EEOC has written detailed guidelines that spell out the kinds of questions that are lawful and those that are unlawful. Questions directed to a woman about her plans for marriage or, if she is married, about her plans to have children are not only irrelevant but illegal. Actually, any questions about marital status, family, physical characteristics, age, education, arrests, or social security are illegal if this information is not deemed to be a bona fide occupational qualification. By and large, the interview should focus on what the applicant has done in the past and what the applicant has learned from it.

5. *Give the applicant an opportunity to ask questions.* Usually, near the end of the interview, you should take the time to see whether the applicant has any questions.

Now let's look at some of the specific questions that interviewers usually ask. The following list was compiled from a variety of sources and is only representative, not exhaustive. It sets no limitations on your own creativity but is intended to suggest the kinds of questions you may wish to ask. You might use this as a starter list or as a checklist for your own wording of questions. Notice that some questions are open-ended and some are closed, but none is a "yes" or "no" question.

School:

How did you select the school you attended?

How did you determine your major?

What extracurricular activities did you engage in at school?

In what ways does your transcript reflect your ability?

How were you able to help with your college expenses?

Personal:

What are your hobbies?

How do you work under pressure?

At what age did you begin supporting yourself?

What causes you to lose your temper?

What are your major strengths? weaknesses?

What do you do to stay in good physical condition?

What kind of reading do you like to do?

Who has had the greatest influence on your life?

What have you done that shows your creativity?

Position:

What kind of position are you looking for?

What do you know about the company?

Under what conditions will you be willing to relocate?

Why do you think you would like to work for us?

What do you hope to accomplish?

What qualifications do you have that make you feel you would be beneficial to us?

How do you feel about traveling?

What part of the country would you like to settle in?

With what kind of people do you enjoy interacting?

What do you regard as an equitable salary for a person with your qualifications?

What new skills would you like to learn?

What are your professional goals?

How would you proceed if you were in charge of hiring?

What are your most important criteria for determining whether you will accept a position?

The Closing. Toward the end of the interview you should always tell the applicants what will happen next. Explain the procedures for making the decision. Answer any questions about who has the authority, when the decision will be made, and how applicants will be notified. Then close the interview in a courteous, neutral manner. You should neither build false hopes nor seem to discourage the applicants.

Responsibilities of the Job Applicant

Interviews are part—and an important part—of the process of seeking employment. Even for part-time and temporary jobs you will benefit if you approach the interviewing process seriously and systematically. There is no point in applying for positions that are obviously outside your area of expertise. It may seem a good idea to get interviewing experience, but you are wasting your time and the interviewer's if you apply for a position you have no intention of taking or a position for which you are not qualified.

When you are granted an employment interview, remember that all you have to sell is yourself and your qualifications. You want to show yourself in the best possible light. You should be concerned about your appearance; if you want a particular job, you should dress in a way that is acceptable to the person or organization that may—or may not—hire you. You should be fully prepared for the interview. Two important tasks you must complete before the interview itself are writing the cover letter and the résumé.

Cover Letter

The *cover letter* is a short, well-written letter expressing your interest in a particular position. You should always address the letter to the person with the authority to hire you. Because you are trying to stimulate the reader's interest in you, the applicant, your cover letter should not read like a form letter. The cover letter should include the following elements: where you found out about the position, your main qualifications (summary of a few key points), how you fit the requirements for the job, items of special interest about you that would relate to your potential for the job, and a request for an interview. You should also include a résumé.

Résumé

Although there is no universal format for résumé writing, there is some agreement on what should be included.[2] In writing your résumé you should consider including information about yourself, your professional objectives, your education, your experience, your activities and interests, and your background, as well as references. In addition, you should consider what format your résumé will follow—how wide your margins will be, how elements will be spaced and indented, and so on. Also, be honest with your appraisals. The résumé should be no more than three pages, preferably one or two. Figure G.1 shows a sample résumé of a person who has just graduated from college.

Some of the information you should include on the résumé is mandatory; that is, it is the kind of material that recruiters in the nation's largest corporations look for.[3] These items are starred in the following list. The remainder of the items are optional, which means that some, but not most, personnel directors are interested in such information.

Personal:

*Address(es), temporary and permanent

*Telephone number(s)

 Height

 Weight

 Marital status

 Military status

 Security clearance

 Dependents

 Health

 Citizenship

 Religion

Professional:

*Immediate objective

Education (reverse chronological order):

*Name of school

*Location

*Degree and date

*Major

*Honors

*Scholarships

 Other strengths

 Leadership roles

 Class standing

 Grade point average

<u>Joyce M. Turner</u>

Temporary Address: Permanent Address:

2326 Tower Ave.   914 Market
Cincinnati, Ohio 45220   Columbus, Ohio 43217
513-861-2497   614-662-5931

PROFESSIONAL   A challenging position in sales or public relations
OBJECTIVE   with a medium-sized corporation. Geographical
                 preference for the Midwest.

EDUCATION   University of Cincinnati, Cincinnati, Ohio.
1984-88   Candidate for B.A. degree in June, 1988. Major in
                 Communication with minor in Business (Marketing).
                 Overall grade point average of 3.3.

EXPERIENCE   Sales. Lazarus Department Store. Full-time
1987-88   summer and Christmas vacation; part-time during
                 school year. Experience in clothing, appliances,
                 and jewelry.

1988   Internship WLW-TV. Received 3 cr. hrs. for working
                 10 hours per week Spring quarter. Worked with
                 sales force selling commercial time.

ACTIVITIES   Forensics. Represented the University of Cincinnati
                 at five individual events tournaments over a two-
                 year period. Won first place in extemporaneous
                 speaking at Ohio Forensic Championships in 1987.

                 President, Women in Communication, an organi-
                 zation for women who aspire toward careers
                 in communication.

INTERESTS   Sports (tennis and racquetball); travel

REFERENCES   On request

Figure G.1 Sample résumé

Special skills

Professional or academic activities

Societies

Foreign language proficiency

Source of financing

Experience:

*Employment in field in which you are seeking a job

*Self-employment

*Part-time employment—summer or school year

*Military service

*Volunteer work

(For each of these indicate company name, location, time period, responsibilities, and accomplishments.)

Activities:

*Employment-related activities

Other activities

Hobbies

References:

Names and addresses

Preparation for the Interview

It is a good idea to give yourself a practice interview session. Try to anticipate some of the questions you will be asked and think carefully about your answers. You need not write out or say answers aloud; before the actual interview, however, you should have anticipated key questions, and you should have thought about such subjects as your salary expectations, your possible contributions to the company, and your special skills.

The Interview

You are likely to make a favorable impression in your interview if you follow these guidelines.

    1. *Do your homework.* Know about the company's services, products, ownership, and financial health. Knowing about a company shows your interest in that company and will usually impress the interviewer.

2. *Be prompt.* The interview is the company's only clue to your work behavior. If you are late for such an important event, the interviewer may well conclude that you are likely to be late for work. Give yourself plenty of time in travel to cover any possible traffic problems.

3. *Be alert and look at the interviewer.* Remember that your non-verbal communication tells a lot about you. Company representatives are likely to consider eye contact and posture as clues to your self-confidence.

4. *Give yourself time to think.* If the interviewer asks you a question that you had not anticipated, give yourself time to think before you answer. It is better to pause and think than to give a hasty answer that may cost you the job. If you do not understand the question, paraphrase it before you attempt to answer.

5. *Ask questions about the type of work you will be doing.* The interview is your chance to find out if you would enjoy working for this company. You might ask the interviewer to describe a typical work day for the person who will get the job. If the interview is conducted at the company offices, you might ask to see where you would be working.

6. *Do not engage in long discussions on salary.* On your résumé you have probably indicated a range of salary expectations. If the company representative tries to pin you down, ask, "What do you normally pay someone with my experience and education for this level position?" Such a question allows you to get an idea of what the salary will be without committing yourself to a figure first.

7. *Do not harp on benefits.* Detailed questions about benefits are more appropriate after the company has made you an offer.

As a further guide for your behavior, you will want to make sure that you don't do anything that will label you as "an undesirable applicant." Briefly, the undesirable applicant:

1. Is caught lying

2. Shows lack of interest

3. Is belligerent, rude, or impolite

4. Lacks sincerity

5. Is evasive

6. Is concerned only about salary

7. Is unable to concentrate

8. Is indecisive

9. Is late

10. Is unable to express self clearly

11. Wants to start in an executive position

12. Oversells case[4]

PRACTICE in Employment Interviewing

By Yourself

Prepare a cover letter and a résumé for a position such as you might apply for after graduation.

In Pairs

Select a partner in class and interview each other for a particular job for which the résumé was prepared. Try to follow the guidelines suggested for employment interviewing discussed in this section.

Summary

You are most likely to be interviewed when you are looking for a job.

When you are interviewing prospective applicants for a job, you will need to structure your interview carefully to elicit maximal information about the candidate. Before the interview starts, make sure that you are familiar with the data contained in the applicant's application form, résumé, letters of recommendation, and test scores if available. Be careful how you present yourself, do not waste time, avoid loaded questions, do not ask questions that violate fair employment practice legislation, and give the applicant an opportunity to ask questions. At the end of the interview explain to the applicant what will happen next in the process.

When you are being interviewed for a job, you should learn about the company and prepare an appropriate cover letter and résumé. For the interview itself you should be prompt, be alert and look directly at the interviewer, give yourself time to think before answering difficult questions, and ask intelligent questions about the company and the job.

Notes

1. B. Sheatsley, "Closed Questions Are Sometimes More Valid Than Open End," *Public Opinion Quarterly* 12 (1948): 12.

2. For further information on résumés and cover letters you may want to read one of the many current books available, such as Burdette E. Bostwich, *Resume Writing*, 3rd ed. (New York: Wiley, 1985).

3. "As You Were Saying—The Cover Letter and Résumé," *Personnel Journal* 48 (September 1969): 732–733. This article summarizes information provided by Harold D. Janes, Professor of Management, University of Alabama. It is also supported by suggestions from up-to-date books and manuals of résumé writing.

4. Selected from Charles S. Goetzinger, "An Analysis of Irritating Factors in Initial Employment Interviews of Male College Graduates," unpublished Ph.D. dissertation, Purdue University, 1954. Reported in Charles J. Stewart and William B. Cash, *Interviewing: Principles and Practices*, 3rd ed. (Dubuque, Iowa: Wm. C. Brown, 1982), p. 189.

Module H

Communication

in Work

Relationships

Objectives

After you have read this module, you should be able
to define and/or explain:

Supervisor-subordinate
relationships

The vertical dyadic linkage
model

Co-worker relationships

Relationships with customers
and clients

Boundary spanning

Adults spend approximately half their waking hours at work. Most of these individuals work in specific jobs or roles within a larger organization. Thus, many of the relationships that adults maintain occur within this organizational context. This module discusses three types of relationships that are common to work contexts and explores the role of communication in these relationships.

Supervisor-Subordinate Relationships

Of all relationships at work the *supervisor-subordinate relationship* is undoubtedly the one that has been most exhaustively studied. In these relationships one person, the boss or supervisor, has authority and responsibility for the work performance of the other person, the subordinate.

Supervisors are responsible for seeing that the people who report to them perform their job duties. Three tasks that are of central concern to supervisors are (1) teaching their subordinates how to perform tasks effectively and efficiently, (2) giving feedback to subordinates to indicate whether or not they are performing their jobs well, and (3) motivating subordinates to try to achieve more.

In order to accomplish these tasks effectively, supervisors must be competent communicators.[1] Instructing subordinates requires not only that the supervisor be knowledgeable about the tasks subordinates must perform but also that the supervisor be able to transmit this knowledge to the subordinate. In effectively providing feedback to subordinates managers must know both how to praise and how to criticize. And if managers are to be successful at motivating their subordinates, they must become aware through conversation of subordinates' needs. With this information they can then use influence skills to communicate their willingness to meet employees' needs if performance goals are reached.

Of course, everyone in an organization—from the chief executive officer (CEO) to the operating-level employee—has the experience of being a subordinate in the supervisor-subordinate relationship. The company's CEO is subordinate to the board of directors, the vice president of marketing is subordinate to the CEO, the branch manager is subordinate to the vice president of marketing, and so on down the hierarchy of authority.

Individuals in subordinate roles must also communicate skillfully because their bosses are likely to be only human and prone to mistakes. Thus, subordinates ensure that their conversations with their bosses are effective by knowing how to listen, question, paraphrase, ask for feedback, and assert themselves. When both persons in a supervisor-subordinate relationship recognize the importance of communication and jointly assume responsibility for sharing meaning, then communication breakdowns are less likely to occur.

As with any other relationship, the one between a supervisor and a subordinate develops over a period of time. Yet not all individuals who have the same supervisor establish the same type or level of relationship with that person. Why do the relationships between a given supervisor and his or her subordinates vary? Is it a matter of interpersonal attraction, luck, or something else? One explanation was proposed by George Graen and his associates.[2]

Vertical Dyadic Linkages Model

Graen's model is called the vertical dyadic linkages model. The word *dyadic* acknowledges that a relationship exists between two people. The *vertical* label is used because the two people are at different levels of the organization's hierarchy. The word *linkage* in the model's title reminds us that the supervisor-subordinate relationship joins or links levels in the hierarchy in order to reach the organization's goal.

The model is based on the assumption that in organizations supervisors are given responsibility for more work to do than can be accomplished by their work unit if everyone simply performs the duties that their formal job descriptions call for. Therefore, supervisors begin to look for subordinates who are willing to perform beyond the normal role requirement and to take on special assignments to help the boss out. Over a period of time, as these individuals become more and more valuable to the boss, they begin to establish a greater power base from which to negotiate with the boss. Obviously, individuals who are performing more than their assigned role tasks would not continue to do so if rewards were not in line with their contributions to the work unit.

In order to maintain a "fair exchange" with these individuals, the supervisor must begin to negotiate special rewards, thus initiating an *exchange relationship* that differs from the formal role relationship. These rewards can take many forms: financial bonuses, choice task assignments, better office space, access to information not usually shared with their peers, a closer interpersonal relationship with the boss. Individuals who have attained this close working relationship with their boss often describe the experience as a *mentoring relationship*, indicating that what they have gained has helped them to develop skills and expertise beyond the learning that would normally take place on the job. These skills will help them to advance in the organization or in their individual careers.

Outcomes of the Model. What, then, becomes of individuals who are performing their role assignments well but who are not doing anything extra to help the boss out? According to the Graen model these individuals maintain role-centered relationships with their bosses. They may receive good work evaluations, adequate raises, and fair treatment, but they will rarely be promoted or become close to their bosses.

Thus, if you observe your boss with his or her subordinates over a period of time, you will notice that certain subordinates seem closer to the boss while other, equally competent people appear to be relating to the boss only on a formal business level. Those subordinates who are close to their supervisors form what can be called an "in-group," composed of those individuals the boss has learned can be trusted to go beyond what is expected and help in areas not formally prescribed to be part of their job. Those subordinates who are not close to the boss can be thought of as forming an "out-group," composed of those individuals who may or may not perform their jobs competently but who, regardless of their performance, are usually not asked to perform extra assignments because in the past they have either been unwilling to do so or, when asked, have failed to perform.

Linking Pin Effect. Now imagine the total organizational effect of this process. You can be "in" or "out" with your boss, who may be "in" or "out" with his or her boss, who may be "in" or "out" with his or her boss, and so on. When you consider this *linking pin effect*, you can begin to appreciate how individual perceptions of the same organization can differ.

Let's suppose that Jim, a computer programmer working in one programming group, has developed an effective exchange relationship with his boss, Janet. Katherine, another programmer in a different group, has also developed an effective exchange relationship with her boss, Bill, who reports to the same boss that Janet does. Whereas Bill has established an in-group relationship with this boss, however, Janet never volunteers her group for extra-tough assignments and thus has only a role relationship with this boss. If this boss has an opening for another group leader and both Jim and Katherine are recommended by their bosses, the linking pin effect suggests that the promotion is most likely to go to Katherine, because her boss, Bill, has a closer relationship with the boss who will make the decision. Similarly, if the boss is faced with making budget cuts, it is less likely that he will cut the budget of Bill's group because this group, through Bill, is perceived as being more productive or helpful.

If the vertical dyadic linkages model accurately describes supervisory relationships, then an important question you may be asking is: How can an effective working relationship be established with your boss?

Improving Your Position in the Organization

In order to establish an effective supervisor-subordinate relationship, you must first assess what skills and expertise you possess that may be of value in helping your boss accomplish the work that falls outside of the formal role prescriptions of your job. These skills may be those that are in short supply in your work unit or those that your boss lacks. For example, Marion notices that her boss really seems to labor over what are to her, simple reports. Because she knows that this task is one that takes her boss an inordinate amount of time, she volunteers to write the report for a project with which she is familiar even though it isn't part of her normal duties. Her boss takes note of the speed and ease with which she completes that report, and soon he is relying on her to edit and advise him on writing more complex reports and memos.

If you think you have no special skills or expertise, then develop some. For example, if your company is considering a new computer application that your boss is unfamiliar with, you might do some research, take a course at the local college, or volunteer for the company training program in order to become a valuable asset.

Beyond simply being aware of what you can bring to an exchange relationship, you must be willing to communicate your willingness to perform extra assignments. Supervisors often feel embarrassed about asking for help, and so a request for assistance many times is hidden in a vague statement like "I'm just swamped with work and now Personnel says they have to have these affirmative action forms filled out and returned by Monday." This statement is a subtle cry for help. Some employees might respond, "Yeah, Personnel is so unreasonable. Well, I've got to get back to my desk." But the individual seeking to establish a close relationship with the boss might respond with a feelings paraphrase: "Gee, Barb, I get the feeling you don't really think you'll have time to do it. Anything I can do to help?"

Because the essential bond in a close supervisor-subordinate relationship is mutual trust, not only must you be willing to take on additional assignments, but they must be performed well and on time. To do this often means negotiating with your boss to be removed from more mundane assignments. Thus, if the individual in the previous example is also overburdened with work, volunteering to take on an additional task can only result in some type of performance failure. Either the individual's own work will suffer, the affirmative action report will be poorly done, or the individual will experience great stress.

You may be thinking that these recommendations sound like a prescription for "buttering up" the boss. To a certain extent they are. But the reality of relationships between supervisors and subordinates is that power in the relationship is unequally distributed. The boss has more power than most of the subordinates. By increasing the boss's dependence, however, a subordinate can develop a more evenly balanced relationship. People needn't like their bosses or their subordinates in a social sense to have mutually satisfying work relationships. They simply must understand that at work, more than in other contexts, *reciprocity* is the essential outcome. If a boss and subordinate become friends, then they have begun a different relationship. Although it may influence their working relationship and may in fact be a benefit of an effective working relationship, other mutually acceptable exchanges must continue to take place if the working relationship is to remain close.

Communication is the process through which supervisor-subordinate relationships are established and maintained. Thus, although the majority of examples in this book have focused on personal applications of communication skills, communication competence is critical in work-based relationships as well. By skillful use of listening, perception checking, describing, questioning, and paraphrasing, you can control the manner in which your vertical dyadic relationships develop. Without careful and attentive use of these skills you are likely to have a distant and ineffective working relationship with your boss and, in time, with your subordinates.

PRACTICE in Role Playing

By Yourself

Think of your last job. How would you characterize your relationship with your boss? Did that boss seem to depend on certain individuals more than others? If so, what effect did it have on the work group?

In Groups

Working in groups of three, two people should role-play a supervisor-subordinate feedback session. Decide who is to be the supervisor and who the subordinate. Develop and enact first a praise session and then a criticism session. The third person should observe the use or abuse of the essential communication skills. Switch roles until all three people have had an opportunity to serve in each role.

Co-Worker Relationships

Your *co-workers* are the other members of your work group, team, or department who are at the same job level as you are. It has been shown that co-workers, among other things, influence individual performance levels and individual job satisfaction.[3] Because people need people, the threat of social isolation is a very powerful influencing strategy.

Organizational members form relationships with their co-workers not only to satisfy social needs but also to obtain information about the organization. Organizational activities are so complex that people can rarely rely on their own senses and experiences to obtain a complete or accurate picture of what is happening in the organization. Co-workers thus are a major source of organizational information.[4] When co-workers have the same general perceptions of and experiences in the organization, they are unlikely to disagree with one another. Disagreement is something that most individuals, especially in a work situation, wish to avoid. Many times, therefore, real differences that exist in the ways co-workers view the organization are glossed over. This pressure to conform reduces the interpersonal discomfort caused by conflict and is especially strong during times of high environmental uncertainty (such as when layoffs are threatened, when a new boss has suddenly taken over, or when a new co-worker enters an established work group).

The Importance of Communication Skills

Like other relationships, your relationships with your co-workers are developed through your communication experiences with them. But just as you will probably not choose your boss, you will also not be in charge of selecting those with whom you work. Thus, as in supervisor-subordi-

At least five days a week, the people you spend the most time with will be your co-workers. How you get along with them can play a large part in your success and satisfaction with your job. Businesses may foster a sense of teamwork among co-workers, but they may also promote competition. Treating your peers as your equals is one strategy that will encourage harmony at work.

nate relationships, how well you get along with your co-workers depends on your communication competence. If, for example, you choose to be insensitive to the needs and feelings of your co-workers by not listening attentively, then you are likely to find that these relationships are not satisfying.

People sometimes perceive themselves as competing with co-workers for raises and promotions. Thus, it is not uncommon to find business situations in which co-workers behave as adversaries. In these settings communication generally will be ineffective at best and permanently damaging to relationships at worst. Yet competition between co-workers can be effectively managed and communication facilitated simply by remembering and enacting the Golden Rule: "Do unto others as you would have them do unto you." Many bright and ambitious people have had their careers short-circuited because they were insensitive to their co-workers feelings and needs. By contrast, most successful business people attribute part of their success to their effective working relationships with their co-workers.

Good co-worker relationships can greatly benefit the organization as well as the individuals involved.[5] If the work group has set high internal standards for work and these standards have been communicated to and accepted by most group members, the pressure to maintain uniform thoughts and behaviors will keep that work group productive. Individual co-workers can share a wealth of job-related information that will help new members develop the skills they need to be productive in the organization. The organization's grapevine has been shown to relate surprisingly accurate information and thus is often a more thorough and efficient means of information transmittal than the formal communication channels. Individuals who have close relationships with co-workers generally like their jobs and thus are less likely to leave the organization. Because it is expensive to train new employees, most organizations prefer to keep turnover rates low. Finally, enjoyable co-worker relationships greatly enhance the satisfaction derived from the time spent at work.

PRACTICE in Analyzing Work Relationships

By Yourself

1. Consider your last job. How would you characterize the group you worked with? Were they close-knit? What means of communication were used to help socialize you?

2. Have you ever quit a job or felt like quitting simply because of the other individuals you had to work with? Try to describe what made you feel that way.

Relationships with Customers and Clients

Every organization contains individuals who occupy roles whose central task is to deal with people outside the organization. These *boundary-spanning roles* require their occupants to form work-related relationships with individuals who are not members of the organization. Examples of typical boundary-spanning roles are sales representatives, delivery persons, buyers, purchasing agents, dispatchers, real estate agents, public relations personnel, marketing research interviewers, and nurses. By having to relate to individuals who are not members of their organization about business matters, people who occupy such boundary-spanning roles must deal with several unique problems.

The Use of Technical Jargon

In most cases individuals working for the same organization have been socialized to use common job-related language. This technical jargon may be idiosyncratic to a particular organization and thus create decoding difficulties for people who are not part of that organization. People who must deal with government employees, for example, often find it impossible to understand the alphabet soup of agency abbreviations that are commonplace symbols within the bureaucracy. Imagine the recently hired government clerk who tries to help an inexperienced company representative complete several government forms by saying, "All you have to do is get your CEO to assign ASOP the compilation of the K-10 to the V.P. of R&D. This form should be attached to your FTC-LOB forms and mailed to us annually." Although such a sentence makes perfect sense to the government clerk, it probably lost the company rep at the first string of letters.

The fact that individuals in boundary-spanning roles may not speak the same language can be a source of relational difficulty. Because your organization's terminology is second nature to you, you may be unaware of its effect on others. Sensitive boundary spanners, therefore, need to ensure that jargon is explained to customers in order to communicate effectively.

The Formation of Adversary Relationships

Individuals in boundary-spanning roles for different organizations are often placed in adversarial relationships. For instance, purchasing agents for firms are charged with the responsibility of getting the best deal on the supplies needed by their companies. The sales representatives with whom the purchasing agents must deal are charged by their companies with trying to make financially advantageous sales for their companies. When agents and sales representatives meet, each is primarily concerned with securing the deal that is in the best interests of the company they represent, regardless of the outcome for the other company.

Long-term boundary-spanning relationships often exist on thin strands of trust that develop between two individuals. When such trust has been established, disrupting a boundary-spanning relationship by replacing either party can have serious consequences for the firm. For example, a well-established sales representative who is highly regarded by clients leaves the firm for which he was working and goes to work in the same territory for a competing company. As you might expect, he is able to "deliver" over half of his clients to the new firm simply because of the trust that he has developed with the boundary spanners in those companies.

The Lack of Control

Boundary-spanning roles are also fraught with tension because individuals usually have little control over the company policies they must follow. For example, the extent to which customer service representatives for a company can accept returned merchandise is not entirely up to them. Most retail stores have policies established high in the company hierarchy that guide and direct what such individuals can say or do.

"The customer is always right" isn't always true, but successful salespeople consider their customers' point of view and emphasize mutual interests. The relationship between professionals and their clients is a particularly delicate balance of trust, influence, and negotiation. A realtor and his customer, for example, may have an adversarial relationship—each wants the best deal possible, but what's best for one is not necessarily the best for the other.

Similarly, sales representatives can promise delivery to their clients on a certain date, but they are dependent on other members of the organization to actually deliver the goods on time. In both of these cases the boundary spanner had little control of the situation. Yet if the outcomes are not satisfactory to the clients, it is this individual whom they will hold responsible.

Boundary spanners can, however, maintain good communication climates with their customers if they recognize the importance of explaining not only the policy but the reason for it to the customer. Many discount stores have a no-return policy. In addition to in-store signs, this policy can be communicated to each customer by the cashier at the time of purchase with a simple explanation, "We cannot accept returns and keep our prices this low, so be sure to check the merchandise before you leave." Such a policy will probably reduce the number of customer complaints. Similarly, if a sales representative explains to a client that the company policy is to ship 90 percent of all orders in three days but that he cannot guarantee that this order might not take longer, then even if the merchandise arrives late one time, the good working relationship between the sales representative and that client is not likely to be permanently damaged.

The Failure to Recognize Dependence

A final problem frequently found in boundary-spanning relationships is the failure of boundary spanners to recognize their dependence on the other individual. Because most boundary-spanning roles involve some type of customer-client relationship, failure on the part of the boundary spanner to acknowledge the importance of the client's needs often causes problems. More than one "high fashion" store or expensive restaurant has failed in business because the sales clerks or servers conveyed an attitude of superiority in their communication styles when dealing with customers. A friend recently related a story that dramatically illustrates this point. After playing tennis, she stopped to shop in a very exclusive and expensive store. She asked a salesclerk to show her some merchandise. The salesclerk, noting that she was dressed in an old sweat suit, wrinkled her nose and said loudly, "I don't really think you could afford these. Perhaps you should look at . . ." and named a different store. Our friend, who has a preferred credit line at the store, was of course very hurt by what she felt was a particularly rude comment based on confusion of fact and inference. Such behavior is likely to cost a store many excellent customers.

By contrast, most people can cite at least one example of a salesperson's behavior that is so extraordinary that a person will shop from that salesperson only. For instance, a woman might buy her cosmetics from only one salesclerk at one department store when she finds that this clerk goes out of her way to explain how to use the products, to recommend colors, and to send cards to the customer when special offers are available. This special attention and extra communication effort on the part of the salesclerk are likely to ensure the loyalty of that customer.

Boundary-spanning relationships exist because members of organizations must relate to outsiders in order to conduct business. Individuals occupying boundary-spanning roles are responsible for developing good relationships with the publics they serve, even though they are often asked to take adversarial positions and may have little control over organizational policies and deadlines. Thus, even though the customer or client may not always be right, it is imperative for the boundary spanner to communicate effectively to that client or customer the organization's needs and concerns.

PRACTICE in Analyzing Boundary-Spanning Effectiveness

By Yourself

1. Make a list of the individual boundary spanners you encounter in a typical week. Note the ones with whom you have a continuing relationship. What would happen if these persons no longer served those roles? Would you continue to do business with that organization or would you consider using another organization?

2. Think of one satisfying and one unsatisfying episode you have had with a boundary spanner. Write a short essay in which you compare and contrast the communication processes in each encounter.

Summary

Adults spend approximately half their waking hours at work. Thus, many of the relationships that adults maintain occur within the organizational context.

Of all the relationships at work, the supervisor-subordinate relationship has been most studied. Nearly everyone in an organization is involved in a relationship of this type. The vertical dyadic linkages model helps explain how these relationships evolve over time.

A second type of relationship at work is with co-workers. Organizational members form relationships with co-workers to satisfy social and informational needs. Co-worker relationships are powerful forces in determining individual work standards and levels of satisfaction.

Some people in organizations occupy boundary-spanning roles in which they must form relationships with people outside the organization. Differences in organizational policies can create potential problems for these relationships. Many effective relationships of this type are based on individual trust that develops over time.

Notes

1. W. C. Redding, *Communication Within the Organization: An Interpretive Review of Theory and Research* (New York: Industrial Communication Council, 1972).

2. George Graen, "Role Making Processes Within Complex Organizations," in M. D. Dunette, ed., *Handbook of Industrial and Organizational Psychology* (Chicago: Rand McNally, 1976), Chapter 28.

3. Fredrick M. Jablin, "Task/Work Relationships: A Life-Span Perspective," in Mark L. Knapp and Gerald R. Miller, *Handbook of Interpersonal Communication* (Beverly Hills, Calif.: Sage, 1985), p. 637.

4. D. C. Feldman, "The Multiple Socialization of Organization Members," *Academy of Management Review* 6 (1981): 309–318.

5. Ibid.

Appendix A

Glossary

Of Basic Communication

Skills

Skill	Definition	Use	Procedure	Example
Appropriateness (pp. 81–82)	Using language that adapts to specific person or persons and the context of the conversation.	To increase interaction effectiveness.	1. Assess whether word or phrase used is less appropriate than it should be. 2. Pause to mentally brainstorm alternatives. 3. Select more appropriate word.	When talking to a minister, Jamie thinks, "I just feel so bummed out," but says, "I just feel so depressed lately."
Asking for criticism (feedback) (pp. 173–176)	Asking others for their reaction to you or your behavior.	To get information that will help you understand yourself and your effect on others.	1. Ask to avoid surprises. 2. Think of criticism as in your best interest. 3. Outline kind you are seeking. 4. Ask only when you want an honest response. 5. Avoid verbal/nonverbal contradictions. 6. Give reinforcement to those who take requests seriously. 7. Paraphrase what you hear.	Mary asks, "Tim, when I talk with the boss, do I sound defensive?" Tim replies, "I think so—your voice gets sharp and you really look nervous." "Thanks for verifying that for me, Tim."
Assertiveness (pp. 254–259)	Standing up for what you believe in, but doing so in interpersonally effective ways.	To show clearly what you think or feel.	1. Identify what you are thinking or feeling. 2. Analyze the cause of those feelings. 3. Choose the appropriate skills necessary to communicate feelings. 4. Communicate these to the appropriate person.	Believing you have been overcharged: "I have never been charged for a refill on iced tea before —has there been a change in policy?"
Constructive criticism (feedback) (pp. 228–231)	Evaluation of behavior given to help a person identify or correct a fault.	To help people see themselves as others see them.	1. Make sure person is interested in hearing criticism. 2. Describe person's behavior accurately. 3. Precede negative with positive if possible. 4. Be specific.	Carol says, "Bob, I've noticed something about your behavior with Jenny. Would you like to hear it?" After Bob assures her that he would, she continues. "Well, the last few times we've all been together,

Skill	Definition	Use	Procedure	Example
			5. Consider recent behavior. **6.** Consider behavior that can be changed. **7.** Include guidelines for improvement.	whenever Jenny starts to relate an experience, you interrupt her and finish telling the story."
Crediting others (p. 171)	Verbally identifying the source of ideas you are using.	To give credit to others in order to confirm them, avoid possible hard feelings, and clarify source.	Include the names of sources of ideas.	"We've got to make some changes in our course offerings. Laura suggested that we offer a course in attitude change, and I agree."
Crediting self—owning feelings (pp. 171–172)	Making "I" statement to identify yourself as the source of an idea or feeling.	To help listener understand that thought or feeling is yours.	When an idea, opinion, or feeling is yours, say so.	Instead of saying, "Maury's is the best restaurant in town," say, "I believe Maury's is the best restaurant in town."
Dating generalizations (pp. 85–86)	Including a specific time referent that indicates when a fact was true.	To avoid the pitfalls of language that allow you to speak of a dynamic world in static terms.	**1.** Before you make a statement, consider when observation was true. **2.** If not based on present information, include when it was true.	When Jake says, "How good a hitter is Steve?" Mark replies by dating his evaluation: "When I worked with him two years ago, he couldn't hit the curve."
Describing behavior (p. 229)	Accurately recounting specific observable actions of another without labeling the behavior as good or bad, right or wrong.	To create a supportive climate, to give helpful criticism, and to help support descriptions of feelings and perception checks.	**1.** Become aware of what you see or hear. **2.** Report only what you observed. **3.** Refrain from judging the merit of the observation.	Instead of saying, "She is such a snob," say, "She has walked by us three times now without speaking."

Skill	Definition	Use	Procedure	Example
Describing feelings (pp. 163–170)	Putting emotional state into words.	For self-disclosure; to teach people how to treat you.	1. Get in touch with the feelings you are having. 2. Identify them specifically as, for example, hate, anger, joy. 3. Indicate what has triggered the feeling. 4. Credit feelings as yours.	"I'm depressed and discouraged because I didn't get the job," or "I'm feeling very warm and loving toward you right now because of the way you stood up for me when I was being put down by Jan."
Empathizing (pp. 192–195)	Being able to detect and identify the immediate affective state of another. Responding in an appropriate manner.	To create or to promote a supportive climate.	1. Consider both verbal and nonverbal messages. 2. Adopt an attitude of caring. 3. Try to recall or imagine what you would feel like under those same circumstances. 4. Speculate on the emotional state of the person. 5. Respond with words that indicate your sensitivity to those feelings.	When Jerry says, "I really feel embarrassed about wearing braces in college," Mary empathizes and replies, "Yeah, I can understand that—I remember the things I had to put up with when I wore braces."
Equality (pp. 147–148)	Seeing others as worthwhile as oneself.	To create or promote a supportive climate.	1. Consider what you are about to say. 2. Consider whether it contains words or phrases that indicate or imply that you are in some way superior to the receiver. 3. If so, recast the sentence to alter the tone.	Instead of saying, "As you gain maturity, you'll learn to cope with these situations," say, "That was a difficult one. But handling difficult ones helps you gain the experience—and we all need experience to help us with special cases."
Eye contact (pp. 98–100)	Looking directly at people while you are talking with them.	To strengthen the sense of interaction.	1. Consciously look to the face of another while you are talking. 2. If your eyes drift away, try to bring them back.	[Not applicable]
Indexing generalizations (pp. 86–88)	Mentally or verbally accounting for individual differences.	To avoid "allness" in speaking.	1. Before you make a statement, consider	"He's a politician and I don't trust him,

Skill	Definition	Use	Procedure	Example
			whether it pertains to a specific object, person, or place. **2.** If you use a generalization, inform listener that it is not necessarily accurate.	although he may be different from most politicians I know."
Interpreting (pp. 225–227)	Attempting to point out an alternative or hidden meaning to an event.	To help a person see the possible meanings of words, actions, and events.	1. Consider your motives for interpreting. 2. Phrase an alternative to the person's interpretation—one that is intended to help the person see that other interpretations are possible. 3. When appropriate, preface the interpretation with a supportive statement.	Pam says, "Sue must really be angry with me Yesterday she walked right by me at the market and didn't even say 'Hi.'" Paula replies, "Maybe she's not angry at all—maybe she just didn't see you."
Listening (pp. 181–235)	Making sense out of what you hear.	To receive oral communication.	1. Attend. 2. Understand. 3. Interpret. 4. Evaluate. 5. Remember. 6. Respond.	[Not applicable]
Negotiating (pp. 277–278)	Managing conflict through tradeoffs.	To manage conflict when people will not change their positions.	1. Determine whether activities in conflict cannot both be accomplished. 2. Are negotiable elements of fairly equal importance? 3. Suggest a compromise position or suggest	"You've got to get to the store, and I've got to get this paper done. I'll drive you to the store tonight and help you with the shopping if you'll help me by typing my paper tomorrow morning."

Skill	Definition	Purpose	Procedure	Example
				that if one person's idea is followed now, the others will be followed next.
Paraphrasing (pp. 216–221)	Putting into words your understanding of the meaning you get from another's statement.	To increase listening efficiency; to avoid message confusion; to discover speaker's motivation.	1. Listen carefully. 2. Determine what the message means to *you*. 3. Restate the message using your own words to show the meaning you received from the message.	Nancy says, "At two minutes to five, the boss gives me three letters that have to be in the mail that evening!" Jan replies, "If I understand you correctly, you were really resentful that the boss would dump important work on you right before closing time."
Perception checking (pp. 58–61)	A verbal statement that reflects your understanding of the meaning of another person's nonverbal cues.	To clarify the meaning of nonverbal behavior.	1. Watch the behavior of another. 2. Describe the behavior to yourself or aloud. 3. Ask yourself: What does that behavior mean to me? 4. Put your interpretation of the nonverbal behavior into words to verify your perception.	As Dale frowns while reading Paul's first draft of a memo, Paul says, "From the way you're frowning, I take it that you're not too pleased with the way I phrased the memo."
Praise (pp. 227–228)	Give people a verbal reward for what they have said or done.	To help people see themselves positively.	1. Make sure the context allows for praise. 2. Describe the behavior. 3. Focus on one behavior. 4. Be specific. 5. Identify the positive feeling you experience.	"Marge, that was an excellent writing job on the Miller story. Your descriptions are especially vivid."
Precision (pp. 79–81)	Choosing words that are recognized by others in our culture as symbolizing those thoughts and feelings.	To increase the probability of the receiver's decoding message accurately.	1. Assess whether word or phrase used is less precise than it should be. 2. Pause to mentally brainstorm alternatives. 3. Select more precise word.	"Bill, would you go get my watch off of the [thinks hutch, mentally corrects] buffet?"

Skill	Definition	Use	Procedure	Example
Problem-solving method (pp. 318–323)	An organized procedure for solving problems.	To settle conflicts cooperatively; to help individuals and groups solve problems.	1. Identify the problem. 2. Analyze the nature of the problem. 3. Suggest possible solutions. 4. Select the solution that best meets the needs. 5. Implement the solution.	[See detailed example on pp. 321–322.]
Provisional statement (pp. 145–146)	Wordings that suggest ideas are correct but may not be.	Allows you to express your opinion but recognizes that others may have different ideas; helps create or maintain a positive communication climate.	1. Consider what you are about to say. 2. Determine whether it contains a wording that shows an attitude of finality, positiveness, or allness. 3. If it does, formulate a message using skills of dating, indexing, or "I" statements.	Instead of saying, "That was the wrong way to sell the consumer on the product," say, "I don't think that was the best way to sell the consumer the product."
Questioning (pp. 212–215)	A sentence phrased to get additional information.	To help get a more complete picture before making other comments; to help a shy person open up; to clarify meaning.	1. Determine motives for questioning. 2. Determine what kind of information you need to know. 3. Phrase question(s) to achieve the goal. 4. Use appropriate nonverbal clues.	When Mary says, "Well, it would be better if she weren't so sedentary," Carl replies, "I'm not sure I understand what you mean by *sedentary*—would you explain?"

Skill	Use	Procedure	Example
Self-disclosure (pp. 157–161)	Sharing biographical data, personal ideas, and feelings that are unknown to another person.	Necessary to the initiation and development of a relationship.	1. Begin with information you want others to disclose. 2. Determine risk. 3. Move gradually to deeper levels. 4. Restrict intimate disclosures to long-term relationships. 5. Continue disclosure only if it is reciprocated. 6. Remember that people's attitudes about disclosure vary.	May tells her current boyfriend, "I've been engaged three times before."
Specific, concrete words (p. 81)	Using words that indicate a single item within a category or a single representation of an abstract concept or value.	To help listener picture thoughts analogous to speaker's.	1. Assess whether word or phrase used is less specific than it should be. 2. Pause to mentally brainstorm alternatives. 3. Select more specific word.	Instead of saying, "Bring the stuff for the audit," say, "Bring the records and receipts from the last year for the audit."
Supporting (pp. 221–225)	Saying something that soothes, reduces tension, or pacifies.	To help people feel better about themselves or what they have said or done.	1. Actively listen to the message. 2. Try to empathize with the person's feelings. 3. Phrase a reply that is in harmony with these feelings. 4. Indicate your willingness to be of help if possible.	In response to Tony's statement, "I'm really frosted that I didn't get the promotion," Carl replies, "I can understand your disappointment, you've really worked hard for it."

Appendix B

Glossary
Of Communication
Problems

Problem	Definition	Cost	Suggestions
Aggression (p. 270)	Attempting to force another to accept your ideas through physical or psychological threats or actions.	Conflicts are created or escalated.	1. Resist the urge to threaten. 2. Describe your feelings.
Competitive attitude (pp. 274–275)	Viewing conflict as a win-lose situation.	Creates or escalates conflict. Heightens competitive feelings in others.	1. Approach situation cooperatively. 2. Demonstrate your desire to resolve perceived conflict in a mutually beneficial way.
Defensiveness (p. 144)	A negative feeling and/or behavior that results when a person feels threatened.	Interferes with open communication.	1. Be descriptive rather than evaluative. 2. Be problem solving rather than control-oriented. 3. Be spontaneous rather than strategic. 4. Be empathic rather than neutral. 5. Be equal rather than superior. 6. Be tentative rather than dogmatic.
Evaluative response (pp. 143–144)	Statements that judge a person's ideas, feelings, or behaviors.	Creates defensiveness.	Be descriptive rather than evaluative.
External noise (p. 13)	External factors clogging the channels of communication.	Overrides or interferes with message reception.	1. Listener can eliminate the noise or turn up powers of concentration. 2. Speaker can compensate for the noise.
Hidden agenda (pp. 144–145)	A reason or motive for behavior that is undisclosed to others.	May destroy trust between individuals; causes defensiveness; is manipulative.	1. Speaker should disclose motives. 2. Listener should describe behavior and check perceptions.

Problem	Definition	Cost	Suggestions
Inappropriate response (pp. 231–234)	Response that does not meet the expectation of the other person or that disconfirms the other person.	Causes defensiveness.	Substitute paraphrasing, questioning, interpreting, or supporting.
Incongruous response (p. 233)	Message whose verbal cues conflict with nonverbal cues.	Causes defensiveness.	1. Speaker should be honest and describe true feelings. 2. Listener should check perceptions.
Information overload (pp. 177–178)	Receiving more information than you can process at that time, or sending more information than the other person can process.	Loss of at least part of the message. Possible frustration.	1. Listener should use selective perception and, if possible, paraphrase. 2. Speaker should limit details, group ideas, and emphasize key points.
Internal noise (p. 13)	When thoughts and feelings of the listener interfere with meaning.	Overrides or interferes with message reception.	Turn up power of concentration.
Interrupting response (pp. 233–234)	Breaking in before the speaker has finished.	Creates climate of superiority.	Allow person to finish sentence or complete thought.
Irrelevant response (p. 232)	Response that bears no relation to what has been said.	Tends to disconfirm, to make people question their own value.	Listen to what people have to say; at least acknowledge that you heard.
Semantic noise (p. 13)	Decoding with a different meaning from what speaker intends.	Distortion of meaning.	1. As speaker, determine meanings, encode with care, analyze receivers to determine whether they are likely to understand language you have selected. 2. As listener, listen actively and paraphrase if possible.

Term	Definition	Effect	Suggestions
Serial communication (pp. 176–177)	An intervening stage of communication; one passes through several receivers before getting to destination.	Message distortion. Usually, the greater the number of transfer stations, the greater the distortion.	1. Create face-to-face settings whenever possible. 2. If message must be sent serial fashion, each listener should paraphrase carefully.
Surrender (p. 269)	Giving in to another for sole purpose of avoiding conflict.	Can become martyr; can infuriate others.	1. Describe your feelings. 2. Credit your feelings.
Tangential response (pp. 232–233)	Statement that changes the subject without appropriate response.	Implies that speaker's statements are not important enough to deal with.	Consider what people were saying; then, before you change the subject, deal with the implications of their statements.
Vocal interference (pp. 106–108)	Speaking with such fillers as "you know," "um," and "well, uh."	Tends to antagonize others; increases noise; hurts message reception.	1. Become aware of usage. 2. Practice to see how long you can go without an interference. 3. In conversation note usage.
Withdrawal (pp. 267–269)	Removing oneself physically or psychologically from setting.	Conflicts are not resolved, only put off.	Resist urge to withdraw; describe feelings.

Appendix C

Analyzing Interpersonal Communication

Analyzing communication means determining what you did right and what you did wrong—or at least what you might have done differently. The old saying "Hindsight has perfect vision" suggests that analyzing past conversation is futile because it cannot change what happened. Yet by analyzing past conversations to determine what you did right and what you did wrong—or at least what you might have done differently—you will develop communication competence and behavioral flexibility. As you think about your past interpersonal communication, we suggest you ask yourself the following questions:

1. How well did my (our) use of available skills contribute to accomplishing the purpose?

2. What other or additional skills might I have used in this situation?

3. What skills worked well? Why?

In addition to using skills well you should also be aware of your behavioral flexibility. *Behavioral flexibility* means being able to choose the skills that are likely to be most effective in a particular situation. Thus, competent communication must be behaviorally flexible.

There are times, for instance, when a supportive statement, a paraphrase, or a question might be used in response to some message. One of them, however, may work better than another under the circumstances. Some people are very familiar and comfortable with one or two skills and try to use them at all times. Although this strategy may meet with modest success, the diversity of people and situations with which most adults deal suggests that such behavioral rigidity will result in ineffectiveness in the long run. Most of your conversations require spur-of-the-moment decisions about what to say, and although you are not always going to make the best decision, as you add additional skills to your repertoire, you will find yourself becoming better able to share meanings with others.

Of all the forms of communication, interpersonal communication is the most difficult to analyze and evaluate. Why? Because the greatest amount of your interpersonal communication is in informal settings with no "audience." Moreover, the flow is quick, people switch roles from speaker to listener rapidly, a response may be as short as one or two words, and some of the meaning is sent and verified by nonverbal means.

Nevertheless, to assume that interpersonal communication is beyond analysis is false. You can improve your communication by analyzing what you are doing and how you are doing it, but you need some objective system of analysis. To provide a working base for evaluation, let's take a look at criteria for communication effectiveness and see how these fit together into a method for interpersonal analysis.

The key to an analysis is determining effectiveness. Because communication involves sharing meaning in a relationship, effectiveness depends on communication of meaning. If each partner in a conversation understands or "hears" what the other is saying, then communication has taken place. Of course, the analysis of effectiveness, or outcome, is complicated by the importance of the communication, the length of time involved, and the complexity of the message. A one-hour encounter with your friend on an important issue over which you are at odds requires a considerably higher level of communication skill than a three-minute encounter with an acquaintance about getting together for lunch. Likewise, the analysis of each encounter would require differing degrees of skill.

Let's consider two questions on which the analysis will be based:

1. *What was the apparent purpose of the encounter?* Was it for enjoyment? Fulfilling social expectations? Building a relationship? Negotiating with others? Exchanging information? Problem solving? Influencing?

2. *How were the elements of communication handled?* Did the people contribute to or detract from the effectiveness? Did the verbal or nonverbal messages contribute to or detract from the communication? Was a climate created that helped the communication to occur?

Before looking at a communication analysis outline, we need to consider who should analyze your interpersonal communication. Because there is seldom an observer present during your conversations, you may have to make the analysis yourself after the fact. Such an analysis is difficult, but it can be done. After an encounter you have feelings about whether it was satisfactory or not, and it is useful to take the time to "replay" it to determine whether your communication was effective and why. Of course, you should be an even more effective critic of encounters you are able to observe.

The first example is a descriptive-analytical, after-the-fact outline (see Figure C.1). With this outline you can analyze why communication was or was not successful.

The second outline enables you to evaluate the means (see Figure C.2). This outline calls for you to replay the conversation, noting the presence or absence of various skills.

PRACTICE in Analyzing Communication Encounters

By Yourself

Using either analysis form (Figure C.1 or C.2), analyze one of your communication encounters. Select one that occurred during the past day or two so that the dialogue is fresh in your mind.

In Pairs

Prepare a four- to six-minute role-play, in which you demonstrate competency. Each person should first determine the nature of the relationship. During the role-play use a paraphrase, a perception check, and a description of feelings. Select a topic on which you are inclined to take opposite sides—your goal is to explain your position. You may or may not reach any agreement. Dialogue should be spontaneous. Although you may want to have practice sessions, do not try to write out scripts or memorize parts.

1. Participants:

2. Apparent purpose of the encounter:

3. Outcome:

4. Describe the entire encounter. Use dialogue wherever possible.

5. List and discuss the reasons for the success or failure of the communication.

Figure C.1 Communication analysis: descriptive

1. Participants:

2. Apparent purpose of the encounter:

3. Outcome—what was the result:

4. Indicate those skills that were used positively to affect

    a. Climate

    b. Communication of ideas and feelings

    c. Response

5. List and discuss the reasons for the success or failure of the communication.

Figure C.2 Communication analysis: skills

Index

Acknowledgments

Photos courtesy of: Suzanne Arms Wimberly/Jeroboam (p. 1); Bob Daemmrich/ImageWorks (p. 8); Richard Kalver/Magnum (p. 11); Richard Pasley/Stock, Boston (p. 23); Suzanne Arms Wimberly/ Jeroboam (p. 44); Kent Reno/Jeroboam (p. 46); Frank Siteman/Jeroboam (p. 52); Gabor Demjen/ Stock, Boston (p. 72); Evan Johnson/Jeroboam (p. 80); Marc Ribaud/Magnum (p. 83); Costa Manos/ Magnum (p. 99); Alex Webb/Magnum (p. 104); George S. Zimbel/Monkmeyer (p. 110); Ken Graves/ Jeroboam (p. 115); Arlene Collins/Monkmeyer (p. 121); Owen Franken/Stock, Boston (p. 127); Robert Burroughs/Jeroboam (p. 131); Phyllis Graber Jensen/Stock, Boston (p. 147); Budd Gray/Jeroboam (p. 159); Davidson/ImageWorks (p. 163); Steve & Mary Skjold/ImageWorks (p. 165); Mark Antman/ ImageWorks (p. 174); Christopher Morrow/Stock, Boston (p. 185); Elizabeth Crews (p. 189); Frank D. Smith/Jeroboam (p. 197); Susan Meisalas/Magnum (p. 213); Mark Antman/ImageWorks (p. 216); Cary Wolinsky/Stock, Boston (p. 220); Arlene Collins/Monkmeyer (p. 226); Howard Dratch/ImageWorks (p. 246); Alan Carey/ImageWorks (p. 255); Laimute Druskis/Jeroboam (p. 268); Sheila Sheridan/ Monkmeyer (p. 271); Frank Siteman/Jeroboam (p. 277); Alan Cary/ImageWorks (p. 283); Michal Heron/Woodfin Camp (p. 291); Evan Johnson/Jeroboam (p. 301); Frank Siteman/Jeroboam (p. 308); Mark Antman/ImageWorks (p. 320); Alan Carey/ImageWorks (p. 337); Mark Antman/ImageWorks (p. 376); Gans/ImageWorks (p. 380)